D1121724

Budgetary Politics

Lance T. LeLoup
University of Missouri-St. Louis

KING'S COURT COMMUNICATIONS, INC.
BRUNSWICK, OHIO

**King's Court Communications, Inc.
Brunswick, Ohio 44212**

Library of Congress
Catalogue Card Number 80-51148

ISBN: 0-89139-025-1

Budgetary Politics

Lance T. LeLoup
University of Missouri-St. Louis

KING'S COURT COMMUNICATIONS, INC.
BRUNSWICK, OHIO

**King's Court Communications, Inc.
Brunswick, Ohio 44212**

Library of Congress
Catalogue Card Number 80-51148

ISBN: 0-89139-025-1

To Theodore E. LeLoup

Preface

The Budget of the United States in the 1980s increasingly is found in the center of a political storm. Inflation, federal spending, taxation, balancing the budget, and economic leadership are the most prominent domestic issues of the times. Yet the issues continue to be shrouded in uncertainty, confused by rhetoric, subjected to politically expedient analyses. More than ever before we need a penetrating, objective view of budgeting and political economy.

A second edition is a rare privilege that allows one to build on strengths, remedy weaknesses, and incorporate new material. The opportunity is much appreciated by this author. Since the first edition was published, we have had a new president, Proposition 13 in California, the tax revolt, proposals for constitutional amendments to balance the budget and limit expenditures, the Humphrey-Hawkins Act, a scandal involving the OMB Director, five years experience with the congressional budget process, and a return to double digit inflation. At the same time, we still have familiar agency strategies, OMB budget cutting and juggling, congressional authorization and appropriation, execution and audit: the regular cycle of budgeting that is little changed.

The basic objectives of *Budgetary Politics* remain similar to those of the first edition. This book is intended to provide a comprehensive and objective explanation of the national budget process and the policies it produces. Second, it attempts to develop a conceptual framework that enables readers to understand the phenomenon of budgeting in the future as well as in the past. Finally, its goal is to focus on the politics of budgeting, the interesting and occasionally exciting dramas of taxing and spending.

Many persons provided invaluable assistance in the preparation of the first and second editions, including the many unnamed participants I have interviewed since 1975. I would like to offer special thanks to Patrick Hynes, Steve Shull, Eugene Meehan, Bill Moreland, Randall Ripley, Ken Slavens, Steve Ryals, Bill Morrow, Tom Uhlman, Mary Roberts, Don Phares, Mickey Sego, L.J. Foley, Bill Hungate, Jerry Meunier, Martha Lane, Steve Wade, and to my students who used the first edition and provided many valuable ideas for the second edition. I appreciate the thoughts of those readers who wrote to me about the first edition, and many of their suggestions are incorporated in this volume. I am most grateful to Mary Hines and Trish Hibler for their secretarial help, to Valda Tuetken for her editorial and administrative assistance, and to Jean LeLoup for her patient proofreading and incomparable moral support.

Lance T. Leloup
St. Louis, March 1980

Table of Contents

Budgetary
Politics

Budgeting

Chapter I

*Three hundred million here, two billion there, and
pretty soon, you're talking about real money.*
—Senator Everett Dirksen

T wo hundred years ago, Alexander Hamilton called
money the vital principle of politics.[1] If money is the
lifeblood of government, the national budget is its
circulatory system, allocating resources to agencies,
programs, and a variety of federal activities. The Budget
of the United States passed the $500 billion mark in 1979
and pushes towards the $1 trillion mark. But budgeting is
not just big money, it is the very essence of American
politics. There are many examples. In 1952, candidate
Dwight Eisenhower criticized the excessive spending of
his Democratic predecessors and promised to balance the
budget. When President Lyndon Johnson requested a tax

surcharge in 1967, congressional leaders insisted that he limit expenditures as the price for its passage. In 1976, congressional Democrats substantially increased the requests of President Gerald Ford, complaining that he was trying to cut spending while millions of citizens were unemployed. In 1979, the Conference of Mayors passed a resolution supporting a balanced budget from the Carter Administration as long as no funds for the cities were eliminated. The budget can be technical and complex: endless columns of figures and tiresome minutiae, wrapped in econometric and bureaucratic jargon. But the politics are basic: who wins, who loses, who pays, who benefits?

A budget tells much about a nation: its health, wealth, problems, and priorities. It reveals the size of the public sector compared with the private sector and the degree of government control of the economy. It reveals the proportion of national resources devoted to defense and to human resources. It reveals a set of social choices developed over a period of many years. It reveals national policies on food stamps, nuclear power plants, space probes, and tax loopholes. The budget document itself, however, does not reveal the battles and bargains that establish social choices; that is the task of this book.

Purposes and Objectives

The budget is an accounting of revenues and expenditures. Depending on the stage of the process, a budget may be a planning document, a set of proposals, a guide to actual operations, or a historical record of what was collected and spent. The national budget serves various purposes simultaneously, and over the years budgeting has evolved to encompass new and different purposes. Prior to 1920, there was no national budget. Agencies submitted requests directly to Congress, and funding was approved by various committees and subcommittees. By the beginning of the Twentieth

Century, government already had outgrown this
primitive system. Although the federal establishment
was tiny by today's standards, the lack of centralized
control resulted in confusion and inefficiency. In 1921,
Congress passed the Budget and Accounting Act
establishing a national budget. The President was
responsible for gathering agency requests and submitting
a single national budget. At this time, the main purpose of
the budget was *control;* the 1921 act created the Bureau of
the Budget (BOB) to assist the President in taking an
overview of the budget and controlling federal
expenditures.[2]

In the 1930s, President Franklin D. Roosevelt's "New
Deal" radically expanded the size and scope of American
government. Mirroring these changes, the budget became
increasingly complex and detailed with the addition of
new agencies and programs. In 1939, the BOB was moved
from the Treasury Department to the newly created
Executive Office of the President. The federal budget was
now oriented to *management* as well as control. The
reorganization and creation of the institutionalized
presidency was designed to improve management of the
executive branch, and the budget became an important
component of this effort.

In the 1960s, the complexity of government again
increased as Washington embarked into new areas of
public policy: health, education, welfare, space
exploration, and regulation. Technological changes
helped usher in the era of systems analysis to meet the
more sophisticated policy problems. In 1965, President
Johnson ordered the implementation of Planning
Programming Budgeting (PPB), and the purposes of
budgeting expanded to include *planning.* Although PPB
was discontinued in 1971, the planning orientation
continues in the 1980s in various systems and
approaches. The BOB was renamed the Office of
Management and Budget (OMB) in 1970, with an
orientation to both management and planning.

While encompassing control, management, and
planning purposes, the major conflict inherent in the

national budget decisions is among *fiscal, allocative,* and *political* objectives. Since the 1930s, the budget has served as the main instrument of national fiscal policy as Congress and the President attempt to insure economic growth, stable prices, and full employment. This was mandated by the Employment Act of 1946, and the full employment goal was reemphasized by the Humphrey-Hawkins Act, passed in 1978. Decision makers must attempt to establish totals for revenues, expenditures, and the deficit or surplus that will stabilize swings in the private sector of the economy. How much should be spent? Should taxes be lowered or raised? Should the budget be in balance or in deficit to stimulate the economy? The answers to these questions are partially determined by the fiscal objectives of the budget.

At the same time, the budget disburses scarce resources to various activities and programs. Because demands for resources far outstrip their availability, budgeting attempts to achieve allocative objectives. The classic question under conditions of scarcity is "guns versus butter": how much should be spent on national defense as opposed to social welfare programs? The budget establishes national priorities and helps answer the question "Who gets what?" Is cancer research more important than defense? Is foreign aid a more pressing need than national health insurance?

In addition to the allocative and fiscal objectives of budget decisions, officials pursue political objectives. Pressures to balance the budget are often as much for political reasons as for economic reasons. Budget totals are not only financial statements, they are also political symbols. Some Presidents and congressional leaders seek a balanced budget as a symbol of their fiscal restraint and prudent management; others seek a budget with bold new expenditures as a symbol of their leadership in solving the nation's problems.

Conflict is inherent in budgeting because the participants have different objectives and do not always agree on the objectives. There is a tension in the process because these various objectives must be pursued concurrently. At the same time that it is desirable to economize and hold down budget totals, more money may be needed for health, or energy, or national defense. The budget process consists of concurrent policy streams: economic advisers recommend totals that will have the desired effect on the economy, while agencies and departments request significant increases in funding to expand their activities. And, of course, the President wants to submit a budget that is "good" politically. With the passage of the Budget and Impoundment Control Act in 1974, Congress faces a similar tension in their budget decisions. The standing committees propose spending more money for new activities, while the Budget Committees attempt to set and enforce totals that will achieve fiscal goals.

Leaders often discover conflicting budget objectives and how difficult it is to keep campaign promises after taking office. Eisenhower found in 1953 that it would be impossible to balance the budget in his first year as he had promised. He also discovered, when the recession of 1958 resulted in a large deficit the next year, that economic constraints can affect decisions. Gerald Ford pledged fiscally conservative budgets when he took office in 1974, but the severe recession of 1973-1975 left him facing the largest deficits in history over the next few years. Ford wanted to trim spending for domestic programs but increase funding for the Pentagon, an objective basically incompatible with his overall fiscal goal of reducing spending. President Carter discovered the incompatibility of attempting to balance the budget and initiating new programs in national health insurance, energy, and environmental protection. The budget serves many purposes, and is a vehicle to achieve various objectives. Conflict is endemic to the budget process because all these masters must be served at the same time.

Decisions

There are literally millions of actions taken in a year that can be classified as budget decisions. They range

from broad decisions on how much to spend in a given
year to very specific decisions on where and when an
agency official will spend money. Budget decisions can be
categorized by their level of specificity and their duration
over time. The budget process is most obviously an annual
process, and proceeds with regularity every year. But
many decisions are multiyear, committing funds for
future years.

Priority Decisions

The most general level of budget decisions concerns
broad national priorities and establishes the budget
totals. Decisions include total expenditures, estimates of
total revenues, and the resulting deficit or surplus. Special
tax provisions, such as surcharges or rebates, may be
proposed to achieve a desired balance in the totals. These
choices determine the fiscal objectives of the budget.
Priority decisions also establish subtotals for general
budget functions, such as defense, health, education, and
energy. These choices reflect the allocative objectives of
the budget. Participants at this level are faced with
choices between goals that are at cross-purposes, and
must make the overall decisions that shape the
parameters of the budget. Priority decisions are
predominantly annual in duration, and are revised or
reaffirmed in the next year's budget. But decision makers
do not start from scratch in establishing budget priorities;
they inherit a set of commitments and a federal
establishment that has evolved over many years. Priority
decisions are the most visible and most publicized of the
decisions on the budget, and are of particular concern to
the President and Congress.

Program Decisions

Program decisions constitute a middle level of
budgeting and cover a wide range of actions on agency
requests, authorizations and appropriations, taxes,
federal projects, and entitlement programs. The duration
of impact of the decisions may be annual, multiyear, or
indefinite. Annual program decisions include agency

decisions on how much to request for the coming year,
OMB decisions on what requests to allow in the
President's budget, and congressional decisions on what
to fund and what new programs to approve. Multiyear
decisions commit the federal government to collect taxes
(or exempt taxation) or spend funds for periods of longer
than one year. The construction of water projects,
buildings, or weapons systems may take many years to
complete, obligating the government to make outlays in
future years. Other programs, like grants to state and
local governments, may be approved for a fixed period of
time such as four years. Entitlement programs guarantee
the payment of funds to all individuals who qualify for
them. They are permanent in the sense that they require
outlays until the legislation is repealed or modified. These
mandatory expenditures are classified as
"uncontrollable," but as Chapter 3 will show, are subject
to some modification and control, even in the short run.

Operation Decisions

Decisions on actual operations are the most specific
budget decisions. They encompass the daily and monthly
allocation of funds for specific purposes. Agencies retain
considerable discretion in terms of expending their funds
and timing their expenditures. They may attempt to carry
over balances, forward-fund certain items, or hold back on
spending. Operation decisions are continual, and may be
made at any time during the year. Operation decisions
include choosing contractors and subcontractors, hiring
personnel, purchasing automobiles and other supplies,
choosing the location of facilities and installations. Also
included are decisions on the transfer of funds,
reprogramming, and timing of expenditures. This level of
budgeting is primarily under the purview of agencies, but
the President and Congress occasionally get into the act.
Congress is particularly interested in agency decisions on
the location of projects and buildings and other decisions
requiring capital outlays. Most commonly, operation
decisions are the routine actions taken to implement the
budget.

Participants and Processes

The budgetary process in the U.S. is characterized by fragmentation. From start to finish, many groups, individuals, and institutions have a hand in determining outcomes. The main participants include agencies, departments, and the Office of Management and Budget (OMB); the President and his advisers; Budget Committees, Appropriations Committees, and authorizing committees; the Congressional Budget Office (CBO), and the General Accounting Office (GAO). The process is fragmented in the sense that there are multiple decision stages — many steps in the process where actions are taken and access is available.

The Budget Cycle

Despite the diversity of participants, decisions, and duration of actions, budgeting encompasses a very regular cycle of activity. Recognizing both multiyear decisions and periodic actions, the budget process itself is primarily an annual exercise that follows a strict timetable. Unlike budgeting in less-developed countries, the budgetary process in the U.S. is characterized by stability and predictability.[3] It shares with most other governmental units a common sequence of executive formulation — legislative approval — execution. Figure 1-1 shows the national budget cycle in summary form as it occurs in these three general stages. It also indicates the participants that dominate action at a particular stage.

The federal government operates on a fiscal year (FY) running from October 1 to September 30. The accounting period begins three months before the start of the calendar year (for example, FY 1981 began on October 1, 1980). The entire budget cycle takes over three years from start to finish. Agencies submit requests 12 to 18 months before the start of the fiscal year, the President submits the budget nine months before, Congress must approve the budget by October 1, agencies have 12 months during the fiscal year to spend the money, and the GAO

Figure 1-1 The National Budget Cycle

	Executive Formulation	Legislative Approval	Execution
STAGES	Requests → Central review and submittal →	Authorization, appropriation, and budget resolution →	Obligation and outlay → Audit
MAIN PARTICI-PANTS	(Agencies) (President and OMB)	(Congress: Budget, authorizing, and appropriations committees)	(Agencies and OMB) (GAO)
TIMING	12-18 months (agencies), 9 months (President) before the start of the fiscal year	Jan. to Sept. 30 (9 months before and up to the start of the fiscal year)	Oct. 1 to Sept. 30 (the 12 months of the fiscal year) / Oct. 1- (up to 12 months after the fiscal year)

completes its selective audits up to a year after the end of the fiscal year. At any given point in time, at least three budgets are in the various stages of formulation, approval, and execution.

Executive Formulation and Submittal The Budget of the United States is submitted to the Congress every January by the President. During the preceding nine months, the budget is compiled by the Office of Management and Budget, in consultation with the agencies and the President. Agencies and departments put together a set of proposals, including their program goals and financial needs, and present these estimates to the OMB. At the same time, the President directs the OMB to stress certain programs and priorities and indicates his main concerns. The OMB arrives at a set of final figures in December attempting to balance agency desires with the President's program.

Congressional Authorization, Appropriation, and Budget Resolution There are three distinct steps in congressional consideration and approval of the budget. Before money can be approved, a program must be authorized. Legislation must be passed establishing the program and setting a maximum amount that may be spent on this program. This is the responsibility of a set of standing committees in the House and Senate, each covering its own area of substantive policy. Most authorizations are for periods of longer than one year; therefore, only agencies whose programs require annual authorizations have to go through this process each year. The space program, foreign aid, and atomic energy are examples of programs requiring annual authorizations.

The second step is the appropriations process. Once a program is authorized, money may be appropriated, which creates budget authority and allows federal funds to be drawn from the Treasury and spent. This is the responsibility of the House and Senate Appropriations Committees. The President's budget is broken down into approximately a dozen separate bills which are then sent to subcommittees. The subcommittees make their recommendations to the full committee, which, in turn, makes recommendations to the full House or Senate.

Differences between the two versions are resolved in conference committee.

The third step, actually occurring *before* and *after* the authorization-appropriations process, involves congressional approval of budget resolutions. The process was begun in 1975 as an attempt by Congress to gain greater control over the budget. The First Concurrent Resolution on the Budget, passed in May, sets targets for total revenues, expenditures, and subtotals by function. The second resolution, passed by October 1, sets binding totals. The House and Senate Budget Committees are responsible for the budget resolutions and make recommendations to the Congress. After the second resolution is passed and before the fiscal year begins, the totals from the appropriations bills must be reconciled with the totals in the resolution.

Budget Execution and Audit After the budget has been approved by Congress, funds are apportioned by the OMB. Agencies revise their operating budgets for the year based on the outcome in Congress. Agencies incur obligations by drawing money from the Treasury. This results in actual outlays (also called expenditures). If the situation has changed since their budget was approved, they may request supplemental appropriations, request to transfer funds between accounts, or reprogram funds within an account. The final stage is audit. After the fiscal year has been completed, the GAO performs selective audits on departments, agencies, and programs to insure that money is spent in accordance with the law. The GAO reports its findings to Congress, the OMB, and the particular agencies being audited.

Chapters 4 through 9 examine the various participants and the timetable of budgeting in detail. Appendices I-III present more precise summary charts of the budget cycle.

Roles

Participants in the national budget process have different perspectives, depending on their duties, sequence in the cycle, and self-interest.[4] One of the key variables in distinguishing budget roles is whether a participant has responsibility for the whole budget or only a part. The tension between fiscal and allocative objectives of the budget is related to the struggle between the whole and the parts. Three dominant budget roles can be identified.

Advocate. This role is one of advocating greater spending, promoting expansion or programs, activities, and funding. Agencies tend to be advocates, or spenders, to promote their own interests and continued survival. They make their requests in isolation from other participants and are only responsible for part of the budget. The authorizing committees in Congress also display the advocates' role, but only in relation to Congress itself. They are concerned with protecting "pet" programs and securing tangible benefits for their constituents. When considering agency requests for new programs or reauthorization, however, they tend to adopt the role of guardian.

Guardian The role of guardian is that of a "saver," protecting the taxpayer from unnecessary spending. The OMB adopts the role of guardian in cutting the agency requests. The House and Senate Appropriations Committees also adopt the guardian role in cutting requests in the President's budget. Like advocates, guardians also tend to take their actions in relative isolation from decisions on the whole. This is the case for the Appropriations Committees and OMB budget examiners, but upper-echelon officials in OMB must link the separate parts of the budget together and adopt the role of overseer.

Overseer The overseer is a balancer. Overseers must balance fiscal objectives with needs and demands for increases or decreases in the components of the budget; they must take an overview of the budget and are responsible for decisions on the whole. The President and his top advisers adopt the overseer role in considering the fiscal, allocative, and political objectives of the budget. Before 1975, no group in Congress took an overview of the budget. With the implementation of budget reform, the House and Senate Budget Committees play the role of overseer in the legislative branch. They face the same dilemmas as the President in attempting to restrain totals, balancing defense with domestic needs, and attempting to provide adequate funding for federal programs.

The three roles are generalized simplifications of more complex behavior. The actual behavior of the participants reveals considerable variation; combinations of the three roles and hybrid roles are in evidence. For example, some agencies are strong advocates, while others are less assertive. Congressional committees may adopt different roles depending on whether they are dealing with the executive branch or with their colleagues in Congress.

Explaining Budget Outcomes

Budgeting encompasses a range of decisions, participants, and concurrent policy processes. What determines the outcomes of budgeting? What theories can explain the decisions that are made?

Incremental Budgeting

The most popular explanation is incrementalism, a theory of the budgetary process proposing that policy makers give only limited consideration to small parts of the budget and arrive at decisions by making marginal adjustments in last year's budget.[5] Incrementalism explains budgetary decision making on the basis of fragmentation, complexity, specialization, sequential decision making, and the roles adopted by the participants. According to the incremental theory, agencies play the role of "spender," while Congress plays the role of "saver," attempting to limit the demand for scarce resources. Participants reduce uncertainty in playing these roles by developing stable relationships with other participants. According to the incremental explanation, by acting in their own selfinterest, participants make decisions through a process of bargaining and negotiation. Participants seek to maximize their bargaining position. Agencies, for

example, attempt to cultivate clientele groups to support
their programs.

The process is called incremental because the budget as
a whole is not considered. Instead, participants make
marginal changes on an already existing base. In this
way, incremental budgeting is nonprogrammatic,
focusing on dollars rather than goals and objectives.
Hypothetically, agencies arrive at their requests by
taking a slight increase in last year's budget in making
this year's requests. Congress decides on what to
appropriate by making slight cuts in the agencies'
requests. Ultimately, budgeting is described as
incremental because changes in agency appropriations
from one year to the next are usually less than 10 percent
— and are highly predictable.[6]

Not only does incrementalism describe how the process
operates, but, according to its advocates, incremental
budgeting is how budgets should be made. In addition to
an explanation of budgeting, incrementalism is a
normative theory as well.[7] From the incremental
perspective, any attempt to make budgeting
comprehensive and coordinated would be doomed to
failure because of the diverse, pluralistic nature of our
society.[8] Despite the fact that incrementalism does not
consider the entire budget, avoids programmatic
considerations, and never takes a view of the larger public
interest, its proponents argue that it is both rational and
coordinated. According to this view, comprehensive
budgeting would necessitate coercion, would increase
conflict, and would require basic changes in the nature of
American politics.

Rational Comprehensive Budgeting

In juxtaposition to incrementalism is the view that the
national budget should be considered as a whole and
should serve as a plan of action for the government.[9]
Proponents argue that there should be explicit
consideration of goals and a comparison of alternative
means, with conscious choices made of the best
alternatives.[10] Such a method of budgetary decision

making would serve to coordinate policy activities of the federal government. In this view, the federal budget should be a centralized policy-planning mechanism; budget allocations should lead to positive actions to achieve social goals.

The incremental and rational approaches have very basic disagreements, incremental theorists claiming that the rational model is naive and impossible. Several reforms have been implemented at the federal level to move towards the rational model. These include Planning-Programming Budgeting (PPB), Management by Objective (MBO), and Zero Base Budgeting (ZBB).

"Bottom-up" Versus "Top-down" Budgeting

The rational-comprehensive theory of budgeting has always been more an ideal to be achieved than an accurate description of how budgets are actually made. Incrementalism is useful in demonstrating the shortcomings of the rational-comprehensive approach, and in stressing the part that political bargaining and mutual accommodation play in the process. But incrementalism does not provide an adequate explanation of national budgeting.[11] If budgeting is incremental because this year's budget looks like last year's budget, then the theory is true by definition. Because most of the decisions are multiyear, because of so-called uncontrollable spending and other constraints, continuity from year to year is assured. Despite this continuity, individual figures within the budget often change more than 10 percent.

Concentrating only on advocates and guardians, incrementalism neglects the role of overseer and the mixed roles adopted by participants in certain circumstances. Incrementalism explains budgeting only as a "bottom-up" process, the summing of individual decisions. This ignores budgeting from the top down: priority decisions made by the President and Congress in balancing the fiscal, allocative, and political objectives of the budget totals. Rational-comprehensive theories of

Figure 1-2   Simultaneous Budget Processes

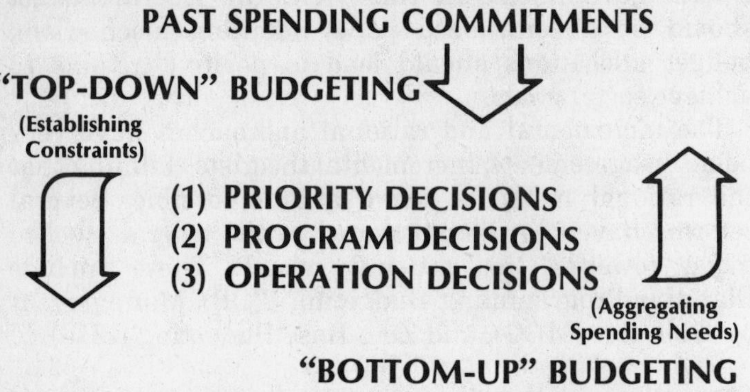

PAST SPENDING COMMITMENTS

"TOP-DOWN" BUDGETING
(Establishing
Constraints)

(1) PRIORITY DECISIONS
(2) PROGRAM DECISIONS
(3) OPERATION DECISIONS
(Aggregating
Spending Needs)

"BOTTOM-UP" BUDGETING

budgeting, on the other hand, overemphasize "top-down" budgeting, minimizing the importance of political bargaining and mutual accommodation among participants.

No simple theory can adequately explain national budgeting. Outcomes are determined by a set of complex processes working both from the bottom up and from the top down. Using the concepts of levels of budget decisions, the relationships can be compared. Priority decisions, choices on totals made by the President and by the Congress through budget resolutions, attempt to shape the budget from the top down. They establish constraints on the lower-level decisions. Decisions on programs establish constraints on actual agency operations in the same fashion. At the same time, the President and Congress are themselves limited in establishing totals. They are committed to past spending decisions and to agency requests for the coming year. Building the budget from the bottom is a process of aggregating component parts into a whole. Through these processes, priority decisions are affected by lower-level decisions and the combined spending pressures.

Figure 1-2 presents a summary of these interactions. Bound by past spending and taxing commitments, the national budget is formulated each year both from the top down and from the bottom up. At any given time, the aggregate spending needs and desires are greater than the totals that the President or Congress feels are prudent. In most cases, they are concerned with restraining budget expansion. In the formulation stage, the OMB helps the President by defining the degree of flexibility he has in establishing totals. Given the economic assumptions for the next two years, previous commitments, and his political objectives, the President attempts to establish parameters for the rest of the executive branch. In most years, the President could recommend totals about 5 percent above or below current policy (the amount necessary to maintain programs at the same level as last year). In the 1960s, Presidents promoted budget expansion and new priorities. In the 1970s, Presidents attempted to restrain budget expansion and establish totals as low as feasibly possible. In the midst of a serious recession, President Ford in 1976 wanted to reduce expenditures. He instructed his budget director to hold expenditures to $395 billion, some $20-30 billion below current policy.[12] At the same time, Ford wanted to increase spending for national defense, making cutbacks necessary in the domestic portion. Action in shaping the budget from the top down is only partly effective. Given agency requests far above $400 billion, it meant that the OMB had to inflict painful cuts on many agencies. And despite Ford's attempts, the FY 1977 budget had a sizable deficit; his flexibility at the top was inadequate to balance the budget.

In years when the economy is healthier, less emphasis may be placed on cuts. Certain new programs may be infused with millions of dollars. A President committed to reducing unemployment could expand spending beyond current policy levels and recommend a tax cut at the same time. At the priority level, totals often take on a political significance that is more symbolic than substantive. In 1963, President Johnson personally made cuts in the budget to make sure outlays would remain below the symbolic $100 billion level. In 1976, Ford did the same thing to keep outlays below $400 billion. In 1978, in contrast, Carter ignored the symbolic implications of the first half-trillion budget and submitted requests slightly greater than $500 billion.

With the addition of the Budget Committees and the budget resolutions, Congress now engages in some degree of "top-down" budgeting. The Budget Committees attempt as the President does to establish totals that accommodate fiscal, allocative, and political objectives. They, too, are constrained by the economy, past spending commitments, and the pressures from "bottom-up" budgeting. The standing committees create pressure for expanded spending programs, and their estimates are usually accommodated in the budget resolutions. Congress may disagree with the priorities of the President and may approve totals above or below his requests. President Ford, the first President in office after budget reform in Congress, found the Democratic majorities voting for greater spending in an effort to reduce unemployment, despite his opposition.

Budgeting is the art of the possible, and the inherent imprecision of estimates reduces the effectiveness of "top-down" budgeting. The President must begin to formulate totals almost a year and a half before the beginning of the fiscal year. The economic situation can change drastically in this period. Although the time lag is less for congressional decisions, the imprecision is still apparent. Between September of 1978 and May of 1979, inflation was greater than predicted and Congress had to revise its totals in the middle of FY 1979. Imprecision is also caused by erroneous estimates of entitlement outlays, and underspending by agencies. Both the President and Congress have an opportunity to revise their actions as they go along. The President revises his January requests in April and again in July, and may request supplemental appropriations. Congress may pass a third or even a fourth budget resolution during the fiscal year if it is deemed necessary.

Theories of the national budgetary process must include both horizontal (Figure 1-1) and vertical (Figure 1-2) relationships. The cycle of budgeting, from formulation to legislative approval to execution, involves political bargaining within changing parameters. These parameters are established by balancing general decisions on totals with specific decisions on programs and operations. No one participant dominates the budget process or is able to impose his will on all others. Instead, budget outcomes are the result of a series of conflicts, deals, negotiations, and agreements in a continuing series of decisions.

The Arena of Budgeting

In any nation or governmental unit, decisions on taxing and spending fit into a broad social and historical context. Budgeting is just one of many manifestations of social change and human development within a particular era. Over a period of decades, one can see meaningful changes that are often obscured in the year-to-year figures.

The budgets of developed nations have expanded over time primarily in response to conditions of war and political shifts expanding the legitimate functions of government. Of course, national wealth and economic growth make budget growth more possible in certain periods and in certain nations. The expansion of the U.S. budget to meet additional social responsibilities occurred most dramatically in the 1930s. Social Security, unemployment compensation, and a variety of welfare programs were begun. Another major expansion began in the 1960s, with new ventures in medical care and education, and additional resources allocated to poverty and welfare programs. Prior to the 1970s, the vast proportion of national debt was accumulated during World War II, and to a lesser extent, the Korean War. Until the Vietnam War, there was a national consensus that military expenditures to win the wars were inevitable and justified. While there were questions of waste and inefficiency such as those raised by the Truman Committee during World War II, basic objectives were never questioned. Vietnam raised more troubling problems for the country and the government. As support for the war eroded, the costs of the war became increasingly controversial, and the defense budget itself became an issue.

Development and change in the nation's budget has been the result of social, political, and economic trends. Changes in the U.S. budget in the 1930s illustrate the interrelation of these factors. An economic crisis — the Depression — triggered social and political changes. A new Democratic majority emerged, changing the basic scope of government. Public attitudes changed regarding the role of government in protecting the general health and welfare of citizens. In the immediate postwar period, a reaction to the budget expansion caused by the New Deal and the war was in evidence. Elections changed the party in control of Congress and government economy became a major issue.

Budgetary politics in the 1980s is a result of the social, political, and economic trends of the previous years. After Vietnam and Watergate, public cynicism and mistrust were rampant. "Big" government was no longer trusted in the 1970s, and budget deficits were blamed for the national economic problems. Numerous symptoms of these changes were in evidence. The tax revolt and Proposition 13 in California in 1978, which mandated a property-tax rollback, were signs of malaise. The movement to call a constitutional convention to draft an amendment requiring a balanced budget indicated that the normal pressure for fiscal restraint had gone beyond customary bounds. The climate of fiscal conservatism in Congress was a manifestation of the mood of the country.

Economic issues are basic to American politics, related to both political and social change. The impact of historically high levels of inflation in the 1970s has resulted in changes in public attitudes and behavior. The economy, still dominated by private business, is only partially under the "control" of the government. But government is given the responsibility to deal with the problems — and the blame when the problems go unsolved.

International events can have far-reaching effects on the nation and ultimately the budget. The Arab oil embargo in 1973 created an energy crisis and altered the

Figure 1-3 The Budgetary Arena

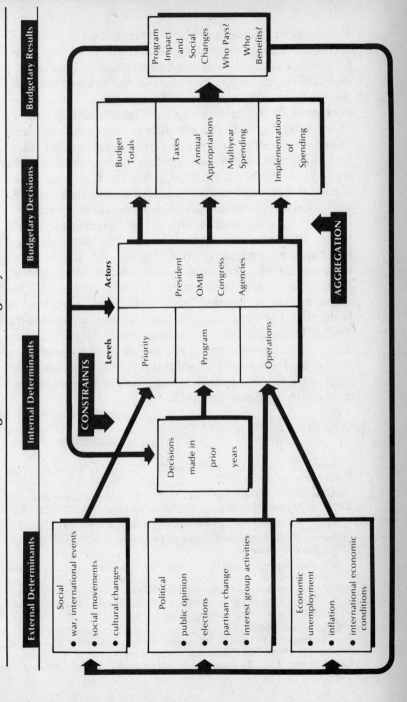

stability of U.S. energy policy. It created an inflationary
spiral that complicated the international economic scene
for several years. The Islamic revolution in Iran in 1979
and additional OPEC increases in the price of crude oil
caused a similar reaction. The budgetary impact was
evidenced in the creation of the Department of Energy
and the rapid growth in its budget and other expenditures
going to energy research and development. The
launching of the Russian Sputnik had precipitated the
same kind of reaction in 1957, when the U.S. created the
National Aeronautics and Space Administration (NASA)
and poured billions into the American space venture.

Figure 1-3 summarizes some of the major elements that
make up the arena of budgeting. The decisions and
processes of budgeting are affected by a variety of
external forces. The final consideration of budgetary
politics is results: who pays and who benefits? This
chapter has presented the analytical skeleton of
budgeting; the remaining chapters attempt to provide the
flesh of budgetary politics. Because there are always more
demands and needs than there are resources to meet those
needs, and because the solution to one problem may
aggravate another problem, budgeting remains a critical
dimension of American politics.

FOOTNOTES

[1]Alexander Hamilton, "Federalist No. 30," in *The Federalist* (New
York: Modern Library, 1937).

[2]Allen Schick, "The Road to PPB: The Stages of Budget Reform,"
Public Administration Review 26 (December 1966): pp. 243-258.

[3]Aaron Wildavsky, *Budgeting* (Boston: Little, Brown, 1975), p. 12.

[4]Aaron Wildavsky, *The Politics of the Budgetary Process* (Boston:
Little, Brown, 1964), pp. 24-26.

[5]Major works describing the theory of incremental budgeting include
Charles Lindblom, "The Science of Muddling Through," *Public
Administration Review* 19 (Spring 1959): 79; Richard Fenno, *The Power
of the Purse* (Boston: Little, Brown, 1966); Wildavsky, *Budgeting ;* and
Wildavsky, *Budgetary Process.*

[6]Otto Davis, Michael Dempster, and Aaron Wildavsky, "A Theory of
the Budgetary Process," *American Political Science Review* 60
(September 1966): 529, "Towards a Predictive Theory of Government
Expenditure: U.S. Domestic Appropriations," *British Journal of*

Political Science 4. (October 1974): 419-452, and "On the Process of Budgeting II: An Empirical Study of Congressional Appropriations," in *Studies in Budgeting,* ed. Byrne (Amsterdam: North Holland Publishers, 1971).

[7]Allen Schick, "Systems Politics and Systems Budgeting," *Public Administration Review* 29 (March/April 1969): pp. 137-151.

[8]Wildavsky, *Budgetary Process,* p. 131.

[9]This general view has a long tradition in reform literature and guided most early assessments of budgeting. As incrementalism rationalized existing procedures, more recent reformers have focused on specific approaches like PPB to make budgeting more rational. Chapter 12 examines some of these reforms.

[10]V.O. Key, "The Lack of a Budgetary Theory," *American Political Science Review* 34 (December 1940): 1137-1144; Arthur Smithies, *The Budgetary Process in the United States* (New York, McGraw-Hill, 1955); Jesse Burkhead, *Government Budgeting* (New York: Wiley, 1956); Schick, "PPB"; Charles Schultz, *The Politics and Economics of Public Spending* (Washington, D.C.: Brookings Institution, 1968); and PPB literature, for example. See also Fremont J. Lyden and Ernest G. Miller, *Planning Programming Budgeting* (Chicago, Markham, 1972); and David Novick, ed., *Program Budgeting* (Cambridge: Harvard University Press, 1965).

[11]Lance T. LeLoup, "The Myth of Incrementalism: Analytical Choices in Budgetary Theory," *Polity,* Vol. X, no. 4 (Summer 1978): pp. 488-509.

[12]Current policy as defined by the Congressional Budget Office, *Budget Options for Fiscal Year 1977,* March 15, 1976; Current services as defined by the Office of Management and Budget, *Current Services Estimates for Fiscal Year 1977,* November 10, 1975. See chapter 7 for a discussion of differences in these estimates.

Economics
Versus
Politics

We are all Keynesians now.
                    —*Time,* 1965
We have entered a non-Keynesian world, a world of
                    inflation.
                    —Arthur F. Burns, 1975

When the stock market crashed in 1929, budgetary
policy in the U.S. was firmly grounded in the belief that
the budget should be balanced annually. Following the
Great Depression of the 1930s, government undertook a
new and active role in promoting economic stability. The
federal budget remains a most important instrument for
the achievement of economic objectives, but economic
decisions are made in a highly politicized context. Fiscal
goals must be balanced with political pressures and
demands.

The severity of the Great Depression pushed President Franklin D. Roosevelt and his advisers to look for new economic solutions. Attention was focused on the ideas of Britain's John Maynard Keynes, probably the foremost economist of the Twentieth Century.[1] His theories were instrumental in developing an activist role for government in capitalist economies. At the same time that Keynesian economics was revolutionizing budgetary policy, Roosevelt was revolutionizing the presidency. His administration was the beginning of the modern presidency and represented an activist departure from the past. The two historical trends of Keynesian economics and presidential government merged in the 1930s and 1940s and were institutionalized in 1946 with the passage of the landmark Employment Act.[2] This law made it the responsibility of the federal government, under presidential leadership, to pursue economic policies leading to the dual goals of full employment and stable prices. No longer was the government to be a passive bystander in the economy.

National Economic Policy

The U.S. economy is mixed; the private sector includes consumption and investment, the public sector consists of government spending. Before 1930 the level of economic activity was determined primarily by the private sector. Expansion and contraction of investment and consumption over the years led to the business cycle. Periods of economic boom (inflation and high employment caused by overexpansion) were followed by periods of recession or depression (deflation and unemployment caused by reductions in private spending). Economists identify two basic government tools available to intervene in the economy: monetary policy, the regulation of the supply and the cost of money (interest rates), and fiscal policy, the level of taxing and spending of the national government.

The total amount of spending by consumers, business, and government determines the amount of output, the level of employment, and the level of prices. These three concepts provide an indication of the "health" of the economy. Prices and employment are measured in a variety of ways. The most familiar are the rate of inflation in a given year (Consumer Price Index or CPI) and the unemployment rate (the percentage of persons in the labor force actually seeking a job who are not employed). Total output and growth are most frequently indicated by the Gross National Product (GNP), which represents the dollar value of goods and services produced in the United States. The inflation rate, the unemployment rate, and the GNP are the basic indicators of economic activity and conditions.

Discretionary Fiscal Policy

Keynes proposed that by manipulating government spending and revenues, the public sector could stimulate or depress economic activity. This is sometimes referred to as compensatory fiscal policy, since the public sector compensates for inadequacies or extremes in the private sector.[3] At the discretion of budgetary decision makers, the budget could be designed to slow the economy or promote more rapid economic growth. The conventional Keynesian view suggested three alternatives for fiscal policy:

(1) **Balanced Budget** If the economy is already stable — minimal inflation, full employment,[4] experiencing sufficient growth in GNP to absorb new additions to the labor force and increasing productivity — the government should leave the economy alone, i.e., balance the budget. The budget should provide for expenditures approximately equal to revenues.

(2) **Deficit Budget** If the economy is experiencing recession or depression — deflation (falling prices), high unemployment, and a declining GNP — the government should stimulate the economy, i.e., have a deficit budget. The government should spend more than it collects. This can be accomplished by lowering taxes, increasing

spending, or both. It entails government borrowing and the accumulation of a national debt. Expansionary fiscal policy is designed to compensate for inadequate spending by consumers and business and to negate downward swings in the business cycle.

(3) **Surplus Budget** If the economy is experiencing a "boom" period of rapid expansion — high inflation, low unemployment, and rapid growth in GNP — the government should seek to "cool off" the economy, i.e., have a surplus budget. The government should take in more money than it spends. This can be accomplished by the opposite fiscal actions: raising taxes, lowering spending, or both. A budget surplus can be used to pay off debt accumulated in prior years. Such a contracting fiscal policy is designed to compensate for excess demand and spending in the private sector and to slow sudden upward swings in the business cycle.

Both inflation and unemployment are detrimental to the quality of life. Persons vainly seeking jobs are frustrated and discouraged, may even turn to criminal activities, or are left to the care of the government. High unemployment cuts significantly into the revenues taken in by taxes; if people are out of work they are not paying income taxes. Similarly, inflation affects the lower- and middle-income groups most severely by reducing the value of a dollar and their real purchasing power. Inflation in energy, food, and other essentials creates a hardship particularly for those on limited or fixed incomes. The undesirable consequences of both inflation and unemployment make economic stability a fundamental goal of any government.

Monetary Policy

The second major tool of government in affecting the economy is monetary policy: decisions on the supply of money and interest rates. Monetary policy is largely determined by the Federal Reserve Board and the member banks. The powerful chairman of the Federal Reserve is appointed by the President for seven years but is not subject to removal as are most presidential appointees,

although Congress may impeach him. The Federal
Reserve Board determines interest rates and credit flows
that affect spending in the private sector on housing,
consumer purchases, and business capital investment. If
the Federal Reserve wants to restrict economic expansion,
they may reduce the supply of money and increase the
interest rates. Conversely, they can stimulate the
economy by expanding the money supply (reducing
interest rates), ultimately making all kinds of business
and consumer loans cheaper and more available.

Monetary policy can reinforce fiscal policy moves, but it
can also negate the effects by moving in a contrary
direction. The only mechanism for coordination of
monetary and fiscal policy is informal agreement between
decision makers. Such agreements are often missing, as
the following exchange between former Federal Reserve
Board Chairman Arthur Burns and the Senate Budget
Committee demonstrates.[5]

> SENATOR MUSKIE: (D-Maine) We call for more monetary
> stimulus than you want to provide. You call for less fiscal
> stimulus than Congress is likely to provide. Now, what
> happens if we cannot agree?
>
> DR. BURNS: (Federal Reserve Chairman) Well, Senator, we
> have a government based on a system of checks and balances.
> Clearly we must communicate with one another, and that is, as
> you so clearly indicated, what we are about today.
>
> SENATOR CHILES: (D-Florida) Can we give some kind of
> picture to the American people that the Federal Reserve and
> the Congress and the President are working in the same
> direction or have some kind of general plan? If Congress is
> going off in one direction with fiscal policies and the Reserve is
> going in another direction in monetary policy, certainly you
> are going to be working at cross-purposes.
>
> DR. BURNS: We, at the Federal Reserve, are not working at
> cross-purposes with the Congress. The Congress has passed
> certain legislation. With a view to what? With a view to
> bringing about certain improvements in our economy, with a
> view to lifting the country out of recession. We at the Federal
> Reserve are trying to do precisely the same thing.
>
> SENATOR MUSKIE: The fact that our purposes are the same
> doesn't mean that the policies are coordinated. As I see it,
> uncoordinated policy has led to higher and higher interest
> rates than they would like, and this results from two decades of
> disagreement in which the Federal Reserve always favored

less stimulus than the Congress and the Administration. The
temptation, since you won't provide the additional stimulus, is
for us to provide more. So that even though the purposes are the
same, the effects are effects that presumably neither side
wants.

This historic divergence has frequently resulted in
fiscal and monetary policy pulling the economy in
opposite directions. Presidents as well as Congress have
been frustrated with the "independence" of monetary
policy. Even before he was inaugurated, President Carter
and Chairman Burns disagreed publicly about the proper
role of monetary policy. Several weeks after Carter's
election Burns indicated that, in spite of the downturn in
the recovery, the supply of money would only be allowed
to expand slowly and interest rates would not be lowered.
While Carter was able to replace Burns with G. William
Miller, he could not replace the rest of the Federal Reserve
Board until their individual terms expired. Our system of
checks and balances is one of dispersed power, but the
fragmentation may lead to confusion and ineffective
actions.

Other Economic Policies

Although fiscal and monetary policy are the most
salient of tools in the government's economic arsenal,
other actions are available. Wages and prices may be
subjected to guidelines or direct controls. Three of the past
four periods of low unemployment and low inflation were
marked by some form of guidelines or controls, sometimes
called "incomes policies." President Kennedy established
wage-price guidelines in the early 1960s in an attempt to
control inflation. His famous confrontation with the big
steel producers arose in response to steel price increases
greater than those set by the guidelines. President Nixon
imposed direct wage-price controls in 1971. They proved
effective in holding down inflation in the short run, but
their removal further aggravated the inflationary
pressures in 1973. President Carter announced wage and
price guidelines of 7 percent in an attempt to prevent
double-digit inflation from returning, but the results of the
voluntary program were disappointing.

In addition to incomes policies, other government policies can be used to affect unemployment, inflation, and the economy. Targeted employment policies, public service and training jobs, and other manpower programs can be used to reduce unemployment without using fiscal policy. Changes in trade restrictions and international trade agreements can affect the balance of payments and the strength of the dollar on international exchanges. Many other policies affect the economy. In the 1980s, energy policy in particular has an impact on the domestic economy. As inflation and unemployment become more difficult to deal with using traditional fiscal and monetary remedies, other government policies may be increasingly necessary to achieve economic objectives. Nonetheless, choosing the fiscal objectives of the budget remains one of the crucial dimensions of budgetary politics.

Fiscal Realities in the 1980s

Implicit in the traditional Keynesian economic theory is the notion of a trade-off between unemployment and inflation, i.e., that one is lowered by increasing the other. The experience of the 1970s has shown the limited nature of this trade-off and the limits to the traditional Keynesian approach. The history of economics in the 1970s illustrates that it is possible to have both high inflation and high unemployment at the same time, a phenomenon sometimes called "stagflation."[6] Inflation, in particular, is vulnerable to external pressures and is not simply a function of excess demand relative to the productive capacity of the economy. Reductions in supply, as in the case of oil, and increased world demand, as in the case of food, triggered a massive round of price increases that moved rapidly through all sectors of the economy. Two devaluations of the U.S. dollar in 1973 resulted in a 24 percent rise in the price of imported foreign goods.[7]

In the early 1970s, the Mideast oil cartel quadrupled prices, contributing heavily to worldwide inflation. The U.S. became shockingly aware of its economic dependence on foreign sources of oil. An additional factor responsible for the burst of inflation in this period was the

Figure 2-1 Unemployment and Inflation

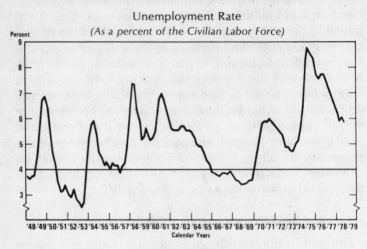

Unemployment Rate
(As a percent of the Civilian Labor Force)

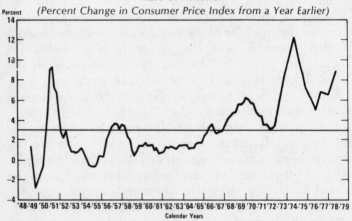

Rate of Inflation
(Percent Change in Consumer Price Index from a Year Earlier)

Reported in Congressional Budget Office, *The Fiscal Policy Response to Inflation*, January 1979, p. 57.
Source: U.S. Department of Labor, Bureau of Labor Statistics.

worldwide food shortage brought on by drought and poor harvests. Because of the time lag involved in increasing the supply of food, domestic prices rose to record high levels. Increases in food and energy prices accounted for 62 percent of the increase in the Consumer Price Index in 1973.[8]

The U.S. economy began a period of recovery in 1975 that continued through the rest of the decade. A fairly steady rate of economic growth helped to reduce unemployment from over 8 percent to around 6 percent by 1979. The continuing dilemma was inflation. Despite a slowing in the rate of growth in 1979, inflation once again reached double-digit magnitude. Figure 2-1 shows the rates of unemployment and inflation over the past three decades. Through the 1960s the sum of the unemployment and inflation rates was in the range of 6 to 8 percent. By 1974-1975, the sum was a staggering 20 percent. Although both receded from the 1974-1975 highs, they continued at a combined rate of 12 to 15 percent. This made the economic choices of budgeting all the more difficult as the trade-off between inflation and growth appeared to diminish in the short run.

The phenomenon of stagflation has suggested limitations to traditional fiscal policy in guiding the economy. Several other modifications to Keynesian economics should be noted. The first is that prices only move in one direction — upward. Deflation no longer seems to be a possibility; prices are relatively inflexible in a downward direction. While selected commodities and products may decline in price, the Consumer Price Index has not registered an overall annual decline in almost three decades.[9] Post-war recessions (excluding the 1973-1975 recession) have been characterized not by deflation but by a declining rate of inflation. Inflation is a one-way street; the concern of policy makers is with slowing the pace, since it does not appear feasible for the overall price level to decline.

The policy of a surplus budget in times of prosperity has been called the "forgotten part" of Keynesian theory. Political realities make this a rather distasteful alternative for decision makers. In the short run, it involves either cutting spending or raising taxes. Agencies are reluctant to cut back operations, and congressmen are not anxious to see their "pet programs" reduced or eliminated. Raising taxes has always been an anathema to politicians (in spite of its frequent occurrence) and is generally unpopular with voters. For these reasons, a surplus budget, even in the most prosperous times, is a rarity. For every surplus dollar of revenue, there are literally dozens of actual and potential demands for it. The result is that the realistic alternatives are a deficit or a balanced budget, not a budget with a surplus that would have any significant impact on debt reduction.

The Size of the Public Sector

At the priority level of budgeting, choices must be made on fiscal impact — should the economy be stimulated, restricted, or left alone? Decisions on spending, revenues, and deficit have a political side as well: is government too big? Not only are there conflicts over the relative evils of inflation versus unemployment, but there are concurrent policy conflicts over the size of the public sector and the national debt. Debate over budget totals focuses not only on economic issues but on highly emotional political issues of "big government" and deficit spending.

How big is the federal budget? What seems to be a rather straightforward question can actually be answered in a number of ways, each providing a different impression.

Current Dollars The budget expressed in current dollars is the most common indicator of size; it is the amount of spending stated in dollars at the existing level of prices. In current dollars, the budget has grown dramatically; in 1794 the budget was around $7 million. In 1980 the budget was approximately $530 billion, or some 76,000 times greater. The growth of federal revenues, expenditures, and deficits (or surpluses) in the Twentieth Century, particularly in recent years, is shown in Table 2-1. Current dollar spending in recent years has

TABLE 2-1　Budget Receipts and Expenditures

(in millions of dollars)

Year	Expenditures	Receipts	Surplus + or deficit (-)
1905	567	544	-23
1915	746	683	-63
1925	2,924	3,641	-717
1935	6,497	3,706	-2,791
1945	92,690	45,216	-47,474
1955	68,509	65,469	-3,041
1960	92,223	92,492	+269
1961	97,795	94,389	-3,406
1962	106,813	99,676	-7,137
1963	111,311	106,560	-4,751
1964	118,584	112,662	-5,922
1965	118,430	116,833	-1,596
1966	134,652	130,856	-3,796
1967	158,254	149,552	-8,702
1968	178,833	153,671	-25,161
1969	184,548	187,784	+3,236
1970	196,588	193,743	-2,845
1971	211,425	188,392	-23,033
1972	231,876	208,649	-23,227
1973	246,526	232,225	-14,301
1974	268,392	264,932	-3,460
1975	324,000	281,000	-43,000
1976	366,439	300,005	-66,434
TQ*	94,729	81,773	-12,956
1977	402,725	357,762	-44,963
1978	450,836	401,997	-48,839
1979 (est.)	493,368	455,989	-37,379
1980†	532,000	502,000	-30,000
1981†	604,000	574,000	-30,000
1982†	655,000	661,000	+6,000
1983†	706,000	149,000	+43,000
1984†	755,000	849,000	+94,000

†Congressional Budget Office projections, Five Year Budget Projections Fiscal Years 1980-84.
*Transition Quarter

Source: *Budget of the United States Government, Fiscal Year 1980,* p. 579.

risen faster than it did previously. Federal spending
increased $100 billion, or 35 percent, in the two years
between 1974 and 1976. It had taken the budget 170 years
to rise to a total of $100 billion in 1961, only 10 years to
double to $200 billion in 1971, and only six years to double
again to a level of $400 billion in 1977. The budget will
double again, to a level of $800 billion, by 1984. In these
figures one finds the ammunition of those who warn of the
spectre of big government and decry the growth of federal
spending.

Constant Dollars   Much of the growth in the budget
is a result of inflation. The dollar is worth a tiny fraction of
its value in 1800 and buys only half of what it did 10 years
ago. Expressing the budget in constant dollars allows one
to examine real growth, controlling for the effects of
inflation. Any year can be used as a base — 1926, 1956, or
1976. In 1972 constant dollars, federal spending in 1982 is
equivalent to $300 billion, not the $614 billion of current
dollars. Figure 2-2 compares the growth of spending in the
past 20 years in constant and current dollars. High
inflation in the 1970s has accounted for a large proportion
of growth in current budget dollars.

In addition, the population of the United States has
increased substantially throughout its history. On a per
capita basis, spending has increased at a slower rate than
even constant dollar growth would indicate.

Spending as a Proportion of GNP   While the
budget has grown, so has the U.S. economy. Perhaps the
most accurate indicator of budget size is as a proportion of
the Gross National Product. Critics of big government
and the growth of the budget suggest that the public
sector is gobbling up the private sector, that we are on the
path to government takeover of the private economy.
Examination of the relative share of federal spending to
all goods and services reveals the fallacy of this assertion.
While spending as a percentage of GNP has risen, it has
remained relatively close to the 20 percent level. Federal
spending constituted 17 percent of the GNP in 1956 and
rose to 22.6 percent in 1976. By 1977 this proportion was
lowered to 22 percent, and down again to 21.5 percent by
1979. The public sector also includes state and local

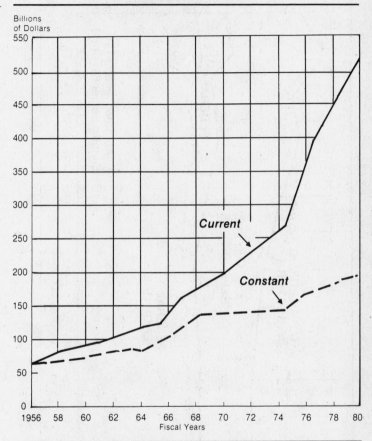

Figure 2-2   Federal Outlays in Current and
Constant Dollars, 1956-76

Source: Congressional Budget Office, *Budget Options for Fiscal Year 1977*, March 15, 1976, with additional years.

spending. Spending at this level of government has shown a steady increase over the past twenty years. Combined federal, state, and local spending in the U.S. now constitutes approximately one-third of the GNP. It is ironic that most of the antagonism to government spending has been focused at the national level when it is state and local spending that has experienced the greatest relative growth.

Figure 2-3 Public Spending Trends, 1949-78
(*Expenditure as a Percentage of Gross National Product*)

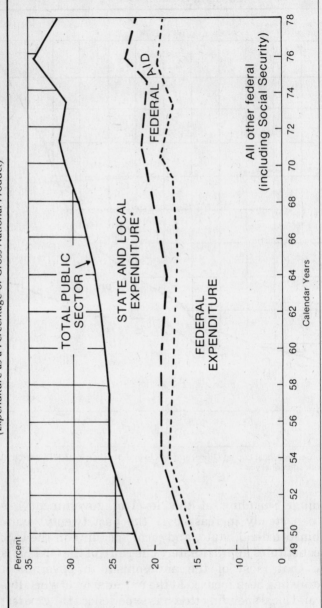

Percent

TOTAL PUBLIC SECTOR

STATE AND LOCAL EXPENDITURE*

FEDERAL AID

FEDERAL EXPENDITURE

All other federal (including Social Security)

Calendar Years

*From own funds.

Source: Advisory Commission on Intergovernmental Relations, May 1979.

Figure 2-3 shows public spending as a percentage of GNP since 1949, broken down into federal expenditures, state and local expenditures, and federal aid to state and local governments. In response to the opponents of increased federal spending and the generally more conservative sentiment of the country, the public sector actually began to decline after 1976, and this trend has continued in the 1980s. The private sector is alive and well in the U.S. As a proportion of GNP, government spending in the U.S. is lower than in Canada, France, Germany, the United Kingdom, Italy, Sweden, Norway, the Netherlands, and many other Western democracies.

Spending as a Proportion of Potential GNP The fourth indicator of budget size goes one step further in assessing the size of the budget relative to the productive capacity of the nation. Potential GNP is sometimes called full employment GNP; it is the maximum amount of goods and services that could be produced with the existing labor force if everyone were employed, excluding frictional unemployment.[10] This indicator, according to some economists, best reflects the economic impact of the budget. Because actual GNP fell considerably behind potential GNP in the 1973-1976 period, the budget as a proportion of potential GNP fell to approximately 19 percent in 1977.

The size of the federal budget can be measured in numerous ways; politicians and journalists have the habit of using the indicator that best serves their political purposes. Spending conservatives look at current dollars and condemn the unchecked growth of the federal budget. Spending liberals point to the budget as a proportion of full employment GNP to support claims that the budget is shrinking. Spending as a percentage of GNP is probably the most valid indicator of the relative size of the private versus the public sector, and spending as a proportion of potential GNP is the best indicator of the fiscal impact of the budget, but each measure of budget size can be useful if its limitations are understood.

Debt, Deficits, and
Balanced Budgets

The National Debt

The economic impact of the budget depends not only on
the amount spent, but the amount of revenues and
resulting deficit or surplus. Table 2-1 showed the sizable
deficits that have piled up in recent years leading to a total
public debt estimated to be over $800 billion by 1980. Is
this a crime of national bankruptcy, or is it sound fiscal
policy designed to stimulate a sluggish economy?
Compare the following assessments of the record $74
billion deficit approved by Congress for fiscal year 1976:

REPRESENTATIVE DELBERT LATTA: (R-Ohio) The federal
borrowing needed to support a deficit of that magnitude would
push interest rates up and crowd out private borrowing needed
to operate businesses, keep industry humming, and create jobs.
Such spending would set off another round of aggravated
inflation which in turn would inevitably bring on recession. It
is not a pleasant prospect.[11]

REPRESENTATIVE JOHN ASHBROOK: (R-Ohio) Let me point out to
the budget-busters in the 94th Congress that for the past
several years we have chalked up the biggest budget deficits in
our history as a nation. Let me also point out that for 16 of the
last 18 years the United States has engaged in deficit spending.
If deficit spending is truly the answer to a healthy economy
then the United States should now be feeling the glow of our
healthiest economy ever. This, of course, is not the case. The
'spend, spend, and spend some more' policies of the liberal
politicians have instead led to an economic nightmare.
Inflation and recession are the products of the liberal
economics.[12]

GEORGE MEANY (President, AFL-CIO):   The problem is not the
budget deficit. My, God, AT&T can borrow $600 million just
like that, one single corporation. Why can't we borrow? We owe
it to ourselves. Why can't we borrow from ourselves — every
American? If you said to the people you can't buy anything
unless you got cash in hand [sic], well then forget it. But to say
that the greatest corporation on this continent, the
government of the United States, is afraid of a $90 billion
deficit is to have the Congress of the United States hypnotized
by these people over in the White House measuring everything
on the basis of dollars. I am here asking you to measure the
deficit on the basis of people rather than dollars. And as far as

going in debt, if you say we can't afford a $90 billion debt, well then you have no confidence in America.[13]

ROBERT T. PARRY (Vice-President, Security Pacific National Bank): The historical record during the post-war period does not support the idea that large federal budget deficits lead to high interest rates and a crowding out of other borrowers. In fact, interest rates have typically declined in periods of large deficits and increased during periods of budget surpluses or small deficits. Not surprisingly, large federal deficits occur primarily in response to weak economic activity, and the financial impact of greater government demands for funds typically has been muted by a sharp reduction in the demands of other borrowers. A $70 to $80 billion deficit could be financed without significant distortions in the economy.[14]

The national debt has been an emotional issue ever since the government first dared spend more than they collected. Debt consists of obligations or liabilities of the U.S. government.[15] Perhaps the most familiar form of government borrowing is U.S. Savings Bonds, held by many citizens and financial institutions. Government borrowing takes the form of both public issues (like Savings Bonds) and special issues (held by federal agencies and trust funds).[16] Some issues are marketable, i.e., traded on the security markets like stocks; others are nonmarketable like Savings Bonds. About 80 percent of the total national debt is held by the public, with federal agencies holding most of the remainder.

Where did the national debt come from? Historically, it arose to finance military spending for wars. Because revenues and expenditures can only be estimated, government borrowing constitutes a buffer to adjust the imbalance between them. Since the 1930s, deficit spending has been used, in the Keynesian tradition, to stimulate the economy. This has been its most controversial application. In spite of general acceptance of the validity of discretionary fiscal policy, spending more than one takes in raises the hackles of many citizens and politicians.

How large is the public debt? As in gauging the size of the budget, there are various means of answering the question. Figure 2-4 shows that the public debt as a proportion of GNP has declined dramatically in the past 30 years, from over 80 percent in 1950 to approximately

Figure 2-4   Federal Debt* as a Percent of GNP

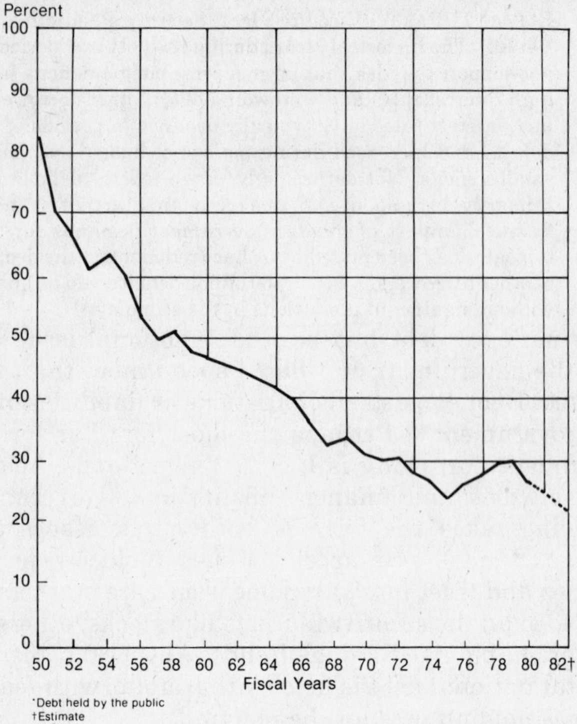

Source: *Special Analyses of The Budget of The U.S., FY 1980,* p. 108.

27.5 percent in 1980. While the debt has grown in terms of
current dollars, it has shrunk relative to the growth of the
economy. What about the cost of borrowing all that
money? In fiscal year 1980, interest on the national debt is
estimated at $56 billion, about 9 percent of the total
spending.[17] But where are the interest payments going?
They are going back into the U.S. economy: to the citizens,
institutions, and agencies that hold the debt. Does the
national debt impose burdens on future generations?
Most economists conclude that it does not.[18] Deficit
spending does not reduce the goods and services available
in future years, and the restoration of full employment
would actually make future generations better off.

The major fear expressed by bankers and economists over a large deficit is that government borrowing would create a credit crunch and crowd private investors out of the market.[19] The question becomes one of relative size; in an economic recession, private borrowing for investment is depressed. It is difficult to determine the point at which public borrowing begins to impinge on private borrowing. It is also a question of duration; extremely large deficits over a period of years may begin to cause more severe problems in the lending markets. Critics also suggest that public hostility to large deficits causes psychological effects that may negate the stimulative impact.[20] To some extent these fears are valid; there remains a widespread fear among many citizens that deficit spending and growing debt are lending to national bankruptcy. Finally, one of the main concerns has been the inflationary impact of deficit spending relating to the question of a trade-off between unemployment and inflation in choosing economic priorities. Government spending is only part of inflationary pressure on the economy. In the 1975-1976 period with historically large deficits, the inflation rate dropped considerably from the 1973-1974 period.

Attempts to Restrain the Budget

During the middle and late 1970s, the federal government ran sizable deficits as a result of the recession and continued high levels of unemployment. Inflation continued to be a problem, and much of the blame was placed on government fiscal policies. Inflation also pushed middle-income groups into higher tax brackets, and despite some tax breaks, the tax burden was increasingly borne by the middle class. All these factors created a climate of public cynicism and disillusionment with government programs and spending. By the late 1970s, public opinion polls revealed a pervasive mood of fiscal conservatism and support for restraint in spending. Although journalists have written about tax revolts as long as taxes have been collected, the tax revolt in 1978 appeared to be real. Proposition 13 was passed in California, rolling back property taxes and limiting future increases. Although the situation in heavily taxed California was very different from that in other states and the national government, the movement picked up steam after its impressive first victory. By November of 1978, a dozen states had some kind of tax- or expenditure-limitation proposal on the ballot. The 1978 midterm elections were dominated by the theme of fiscal conservatism and a balanced budget. Polls showed that about 80 percent of the public favored a balanced budget; Republicans and Democrats alike campaigned on the issue. Leading Republicans flew around the country, campaigning for Republican candidates, in a chartered aircraft dubbed the "Tax Clipper." Despite Republican efforts to monopolize the issue of fiscal restraint, many Democrats were sounding just as conservative.

By 1978, another movement began to attract national attention. Led by the conservative National Taxpayers Union, a number of states adopted resolutions calling for a constitutional convention to draft an amendment to require the federal government to balance the budget. Such proposals had been around for generations, but by 1979, 28 states had approved resolutions, only a few short of the needed three-fourths of the states. Proponents argued that this was the only way to end deficit spending, that other pressures had been inadequate. Opponents argued that not only was a constitutional convention risky, but that a constitutional amendment was too drastic an action. As several national figures, such as California's Governor Jerry Brown, became involved with the issue, the proposal began to receive more careful scrutiny and the momentum slowed drastically. The popularity of the proposal, even as its possibilities were waning, sent a message to Congress. A variety of proposals emerged in the House and Senate to curtail revenues, expenditures, and deficit spending.

Table 2-2 summarizes some of the various proposals for fiscal restraint that were suggested. They range from using current processes and indirect statutory controls (columns A and B) to more stringent and radical statutory and constitutional limitations (columns C and D). The

Table 2-2 A Classification of Various Proposals for Introducing Greater Fiscal Restraint at the Federal Level

Type of Restraint (Fiscal Policies)	Character of Restraint (Political Implementation Strategies)			
	Ad Hoc Adjustments (Current Policy)	Indirect Statutory Controls (Strengthened Political Accountability)	Direct Statutory Controls	Direct Constitutional Controls Subject to Extraordinary Majority Rule
Income Tax Controls	**A1** Ad hoc moderate tax reductions.	**B1** Indexation to prevent unlegislated tax rate increase due to inflation.[1]	**C1** Statutory income tax limits tied to specified percentages of a national income measure (Kemp-Roth and Jarvis tax proposals).	**D1** Income tax collections tied to specified percentages of a national income measure, unless restriction lifted with *extraordinary majority* approval in both houses.
Expenditure Controls	**A2** Slowdown in expenditure growth — no major new initiatives, most existing programs funded at current service levels. Some program reductions.	**B2** "Sunset" legislation that requires Congress to evaluate systematically the effectiveness of existing programs.[1]	**C2** Statutory spending limits tied to specified percentages of a national income measure (Kemp-Roth expenditure proposal).	**D2** Expenditures tied to specified percentages of a national income measure, unless restriction lifted with *extraordinary majority* approval in both houses (National Tax Limitations Committee proposal).
Balanced Budget Controls	**A3** A gradual reduction in budget deficits.	**B3** If President and Budget Committees submit unbalanced budgets, they must also submit balanced budget alternatives (Long amendment).[2]	**C3** Statutory mandate for balanced budget (Dole proposal).	**D3** Deficits prohibited unless approved by *extraordinary majority* vote in both houses (Most common of the Constitutional proposals).[3]

Note: Moving from left to right, the restraints become more restrictive or more difficult to alter, or both.   [2]Public Law 96-5 — beginning with the fiscal year 1981, Congress must consider a balanced budget resolution.
[1]ACIR recommendation.   Certain proposals for amending the Constitution are even more restrictive — S.J. Res. 18 (Senator Thurmond) also contains a provision for repayment of the national debt; S.J. Res. 16 (Senator Wallop) requires that revenues after the third year exceed expenditures by at least 5% for the next 20 years.
Source: ACIR staff analysis.

most extreme proposals would tie expenditures to a certain percentage of GNP (D2), and constitutionally require a balanced budget (D3). The Kemp-Roth proposal provided for major reductions in income taxes over a three-year period and the limitation of future tax collections to percentage of national income (C1).

The impact of the tax revolt and the mood of fiscal conservatism were manifested in other ways on Capitol Hill. So-called meat-ax amendments — across-the-board cuts of 2 to 5 percent — were offered to both budget resolutions and appropriations bills. The Budget Committees found new support for their efforts to hold down spending. At the start of the 96th Congress in 1979, the House Budget Committee was the most requested committee assignment, reflecting member interest in fiscal affairs and budgetary restraint.

Everyone agrees that balanced budgets are desirable, and there hardly breathes a politician who would not express support for spending no more than is collected. But much of the tirade against federal fiscal policies is emotional rhetoric designed to play on public fears and misunderstanding. Deficit spending is not the only cause of inflation and a balanced budget alone cannot cure it. Deficits are economically justified on some occasions because there are multiple objectives to be achieved through fiscal policy. There are reasonable arguments against deficit spending and debates over targeting policies to address inflation, unemployment, or growth. However, proposals to require a balanced budget would render the government impotent to affect the course of the economy by taking away its ability to compensate for deficiencies or excesses in the private sector, heading us back to the Nineteenth Century. Many of the proposals are antidemocratic: in requiring two-thirds majorities, they would allow a minority to dictate policy. Public pessimism about politicians is understandable, perhaps, but the reductions in the public sector and deficit spending in the early 1980s indicate that the regular political processes are responsive to the public. When a single objective, such as a balanced budget, is placed above all

others, budgetary policy will lack the broad perspective
that is necessary for the long-term interests of the nation.

The Fiscal Dilemma

National policy makers face a difficult task in
determining fiscal policy. The budget is but one tool to
affect the economy, and they must consider its relation to
other actions. Economic advice is not unambiguous; the
experience of the 1970s has raised questions about the
effectiveness of economic actions. The budget not only
affects the economy, but the economy also directly affects
the budget.

Automatic Stabilizers

Important components of the budget are fiscal
stabilizers — automatic tax and spending changes
written into law that cushion upward and downward
shifts in the economy. Stabilizers are part of the
uncontrollable budget items that will be discussed more
thoroughly in the next chapter. On the expenditure side,
transfer payments to individuals such as welfare, food
stamps, and unemployment compensation rise when the
GNP falls and more people are out of work. On the revenue
side of the budget, the progressive income tax has the
same effect. As the GNP falls and fewer people are
working, persons move downward into lower taxable-
income categories and pay less tax. Conversely, if GNP
rises, with more people working at higher levels of income,
cash-transfer payments will tend to be reduced, while
persons move into higher tax brackets and pay more tax.

The fiscal year 1976 budget with its record deficit is a
good example of how the economy affects the budget. The
deficit in 1976 resulted from the recession, not vice versa.
For each percentage rise in unemployment (which is
roughly equivalent to a 3 percent decline in GNP), the
deficit increases by approximately $17 billion.[21] This is a

result of less tax revenue taken in and increased
payments for unemployment compensation, welfare
payments, and other transfers. If unemployment in fiscal
year 1976 had been at 4 percent instead of 8 percent, the
federal budget would have been balanced. Most of this
deficit fell on the revenue side; the recession cost the
Treasury around $60 billion in lost receipts. The major
expenditure jump was in unemployment compensation;
costs increased from $5.8 billion in 1974 to over $20 billion
in 1976. A part of this increase, however, was the result of
extending the duration of benefits.

The complex interrelationship between the budget and
the economy makes it necessary to discriminate between
automatic stabilization and discretionary fiscal policy in
assessing economic priorities. Here the concept of full-
employment GNP becomes important; it allows one to
remove the budget changes caused by shifts in economic
activity and to focus solely on discretionary fiscal policy.
In the 1976 budget, the deficit was largely a function of the
recession, not of planned stimulative fiscal policy. This
decision was a compromise between competing coalitions
of those who wanted a smaller deficit and less spending to
lower inflation versus those who wanted more spending
and a bigger deficit to lower unemployment.

The Efficacy of Fiscal Policy

In the 1960s, it was generally believed that fiscal policy
was an effective means for shaping the national economy,
counteracting cyclical and external forces. The tax cut of
1964, implemented by the Democrats, was seen as
monumentally successful, leading to a period of economic
growth and stability. By 1968, the economy appeared to be
overheated, and inflation was worsening. Again, a fiscal
remedy in the form of a tax surcharge was agreed to be the
proper action. In the 1970s, there was a shift of attitudes
towards fiscal policy, a pessimism about its capability.
Pervasive inflation, the recession of 1973-1975, and
stagflation have led to skepticism. Figure 2-5 shows that
what the Joint Economic Committee called the "great
recession" was the most severe since World War II. The

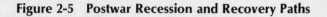

Figure 2-5   Postwar Recession and Recovery Paths

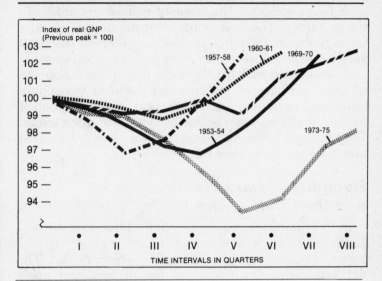

Reported in: *The 1976 Joint Economic Report,* p. 6.
Source: Department of Commerce.

1973-1975 recession not only cut real GNP more severely, it bottomed out later and failed to recover fully in over two years. Unemployment had reached a postwar record of 8.9 percent in April of 1975, and was as high as 30-40 percent for some groups.[22]

Despite the skepticism about fiscal policy, a study by the Congressional Research Service (CRS) suggests that traditional fiscal policy still has some effectiveness as a countercyclical force.[23] Using econometric models developed independently by Data Resources Incorporated and Wharton Econometric Forecasting Associates, the CRS study assessed the impact of governmental economic policies in the 1960s and 1970s. The study concluded that fiscal policies do work, although their long-run impact is not necessarily the same as their short-run impact. They found that it was important to implement corrective policies quickly, and that fiscal actions have their major impact within three years of their implementation.

The study also noted some limitations and problems with fiscal actions.[24] Government policies are unable to make more than a slow improvement in the unemployment/inflation tradeoff — there is no easy solution to stagflation. Monetary policies, when they are not coordinated with fiscal policies may offset the impact of both. Because of the time lag between developing economic assumptions and the actual implementation of policy, decision makers have increased uncertainty. Despite these problems, fiscal policy actions can be used effectively over the long run.

Humphrey-Hawkins and the Goals of the 1980s

In 1978, the Congress passed the Full Employment and Balanced Growth Act, more commonly known by the name of its sponsors, the Humphrey-Hawkins Act. The act establishes an ambitious list of economic goals including full employment, balanced growth, increased productivity, a balanced budget, improvement in the balance of trade, and price stability. Specific targets for unemployment and inflation were included in the act: 3 percent unemployment and 3 percent inflation by 1983.[25] Although such targets are not impossible by historical standards, they are very improbable for 1983. The act does not specify how the goals are to be achieved and tends to ignore the incompatibility of the goals. The act does acknowledge the limitations of achieving the goals using only aggregate monetary and fiscal policy and suggests the desirability of alternate policies to be used in conjunction with the two basic approaches.

The Congressional Budget Office has analyzed the prospects for achieving the goals of Humphrey-Hawkins and found them quite slim.[26] Changes in the labor force such as the rising proportion of women and young persons make the 3 percent goal more difficult than it was two decades ago. Institutional changes, such as increases in unemployment compensation and the minimum wage, have tended to increase unemployment. The inflation target may also be unrealistic given the degree of indexing (linking benefit and wage increases to the Consumer Price Index) now present in the economy. The continued vulnerability of the economy to external shocks such as OPEC oil price increases makes the inflation problem more difficult to deal with.

A study by George Perry of the Brookings Institution demonstrates that inflation has developed a momentum of its own that will take many years to reduce.[27] Stagflation can occur because even when there is a slackening in aggregate demand, inflationary inertia has a continued impact on wage increases. Although this phenomenon was present in the 1960s, the higher rates of inflation in the 1970s tend to perpetuate a given rate of inflation for more years than was the case in the past. Perry's study also shows that despite the prevalence of the view that budget deficits create inflation, they have played a relatively minor role in causing the chronic inflation of recent years.[28]

Both the Perry study and the CBO analysis indicate that the trade-off between unemployment and inflation still exists. Policy makers may lower one by raising the other, but such actions have exceptionally high costs and take many years to achieve. If the target of 3 percent unemployment is to be reached using high-growth fiscal policy, inflation rises sharply. Conversely, to achieve a reduction in inflation to 3 percent, high levels of unemployment must be maintained for a number of years. Figure 2-6 shows two alternative paths for unemployment and inflation. The high-growth path could reduce unemployment, and the low-growth path could reduce inflation, but fiscal policy alone cannot achieve the goals of Humphrey-Hawkins simultaneously.

If the economy is to reach stability in the 1980s like that of the 1960s, additional government policies must be pursued. The CBO suggests that supply-enhancing and incomes policies are likely candidates for this role. Policies could include reductions in unemployment benefits and the minimum wage, incentives to increase productivity, monitoring bottlenecks in the supply of capital and labor, limits on energy price increases, and

Figure 2-6 Solving Inflation or Unemployment

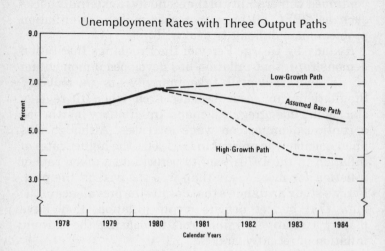

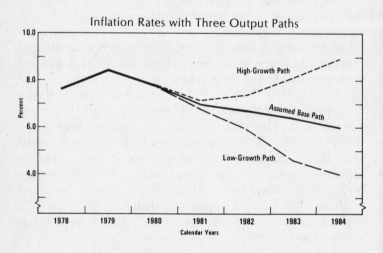

Source: Congressional Budget Office, *The Fiscal Response to Inflation*, January 1979, p. 63.

reduction of trade barriers. Incomes policies would mean some kind of controls on wages to slow the wage-price spiral. The difficulty of these alternate economic actions is that some of them are inconsistent with the goals of Humphrey-Hawkins and other federal legislation, and their coordination with fiscal policy remains questionable.

The economic climate of the 1980s poses a dilemma for fiscal policy makers. Choices are difficult and complex. Economic decisions are inexorably linked with political considerations. Despite these difficulties, as the President and Congress engage in the process of annual budgeting, the fiscal objectives and actions remain one of the most salient concerns. If decision makers are able to avoid highly restrictive statutory or constitutional limitations, they will have a better chance to make choices that serve the best interests of the nation politically as well as economically.

FOOTNOTES

[1]Keynes' most important work was *The General Theory of Employment, Interest, and Money,* published in 1935. As early as 1933 and 1934, however, Keynes wrote to and met with Roosevelt. See John Kenneth Galbraith, "Came the Revolution," *New York Times,* May 16, 1965; and Lewis H. Kimmel, *Federal Budget and Fiscal Policy, 1789-1958* (Washington, D.C.: Brookings Institution, 1959).

[2]An account of the legislative history of this act is found in Steven K. Bailey, *Congress Makes a Law* (New York: Columbia University Press, 1950).

[3]Kimmel, pp. 195-204.

[4]Unemployment has conventionally been defined in terms of those actively seeking a job; "frictional" unemployment of around 3-4 percent is expected because of people moving and changing jobs. Full employment is the situation where only frictional unemployment exists. Government economists now suggest redefining full employment as an unemployment rate of 5 percent instead of 4 percent.

[5]Committee on the Budget, U.S. Senate, *Hearings, Second Concurrent Resolution on the Budget, FY 1976,* vol. 1, September 25, 1975, 94th Congress, 1st session, pp. 131-180.

[6]Congressional Budget Office, *The Fiscal Response to Inflation,* January 1979, p. 67.

[7]Barry H. Blechman, Edward M. Gramlich, and Robert M. Hartman, *Setting National Priorities: The 1976 Budget* (Washington, D.C.: Brookings Institution, 1975), p. 25.

[8]Committee on the Budget, U.S. Senate, "Controlling Inflation,"

Hearings, First Concurrent Resolution on the Budget, FY 1977, vol. 4, February 26, 1976, p. 10.

[9]Blechman, Gramlich, and Hartman, p. 26.

[10]Congressional Budget Office, *Five Year Budget Projections Fiscal Years 1977-1981,* January 26, 1976, pp. 8-11.

[11]*Congressional Record,* U.S. House of Representatives, April 30, 1976.

[12]*Congressional Record,* U.S. House of Representatives, November 17, 1975.

[13]Committee on the Budget, U.S. Senate, *Hearings, Second Concurrent Resolution on the Budget, FY 1976,* September 24, 1975.

[14]Committee on the Budget, U.S. House of Representatives, *How 13 Bankers View the Deficit,* 94th Congress, 1st session, March 1975.

[15]Office of Management and Budget, *Special Analyses, Budget of the U.S. Government Fiscal Year 1977,* pp. 45-63.

[16]David J. Ott and Attiat F. Ott, *Federal Budget Policy* (Washington, D.C.: Brookings Institution, 1965), pp. 95-103.

[17]Committee on the Budget, U.S. House of Representatives, *Chairman's Recommendations for the First Concurrent Resolution on the FY 1977 Budget,* 94th Congress, 2nd session, March 23, 1976, p. 8.

[18]Ott and Ott, pp. 95-103.

[19]Committee on the Budget, U.S. Senate, "Crowding Out in 1975 and 1976," *Effects of Fiscal and Monetary Policies on Capital Formation and Economic Growth,* September 11, 1975.

[20]Ott and Ott, p. 105.

[21]Joint Economic Committee, U.S. Congress, *The 1976 Joint Economic Report,* 94th Congress, 2nd session, pp. 11-12.

[22]*Ibid.,* p. 78.

[23]Congressional Research Service, *Economic Stabilization Policies: The Historical Record 1962-1976,* 95th Congress, 2nd session, November 1978.

[24]*Ibid.,* p. 9.

[25]Congressional Budget Office, *Fiscal Policy Response to Inflation,* 1979, p. 55.

[26]*Ibid.,* p. 56.

[27]George L. Perry, "Slowing the Wage-Price Spiral: The Macroeconomic View," in *Curing Chronic Inflation,* eds. George L. Perry and Arthur M. Okum (Washington, D.C.: Brookings Institution, 1978), pp. 23-65.

[28]*Ibid.,* p. 44.

Revenues,

Expenditures,

and Control †

3

The Defense budget is the most controllable in a
technical sense; it is the least controllable in a
political sense.
—A member of the U.S. House

For all the stability of the budgetary process, some
major shifts in patterns of revenues and expenditures
have taken place in the last decade. National priorities
include not only economic decisions but also decisions on
the relative share of the budget to be allocated to defense,
health, natural resources, income maintenance, and the
multitude of other programs in which government is
involved. While the President's budget has traditionally
indicated a general set of policy priorities, not until 1975
did Congress develop procedures to consider the budget as
a whole. At the same time that Congress has increased its

ability to express budget priorities, many argue that the budget is increasingly out of control. Only through clarification of the confusion surrounding "controllability" can one begin to define both long- and short-term discretion in budgeting.

Budget Composition and Trends

Spending

The classical economic illustration of scarcity is the

Table 3-1   Budget Outlays by Function
(in millions of dollars)

	1978 Actual	1979 Estimate	1980 Estimate
Budget outlays by function:			
National defense	105,186	114,503	125,830
International affairs	5,922	7,312	8,213
General science, space, and technology	4,742	5,226	5,457
Energy	5,861	8,630	7,878
Natural resources and environment	10,925	11,207	11,456
Agriculture	7,731	6,224	4,269
Commerce and housing credit	3,325	2,968	3,390
Transportation	15,444	17,449	17,609
Community and regional development	11,000	9,063	7,281
Education, training, employment, and social services	26,463	30,656	30,210
Health	43,676	49,136	53,379
Income security	146,212	158,867	179,120
(Social Security)	(92,242)	(102,323)	(115,237)
(Other)	(53,970)	(56,544)	(63,883)
Veterans' benefits and services	18,974	20,329	20,461
Administration of justice	3,802	4,351	4,388
General government	3,777	4,413	4,412
General purpose fiscal assistance	9,601	8,936	8,814
Interest	43,966	52,766	57,022
Allowances	—	—	1,398
Undistributed offsetting receipts	−15,772	−18,670	−19,021
Total budget outlays	450,836	493,368	531,566
Budget surplus or deficit (−)	−48,839	−37,379	−29,013

Source: *Budget of the U.S. Government, F/Y 1980*, p. 523.

social choice of "guns" versus "butter." Debate over budget priorities in the U.S. often centers on the relative shares to national defense and social programs. How does the U.S. government spend its money — on guns or butter? Table 3-1 shows outlays by function in the years 1978-1980. Income security is the largest outlay category in the budget, accounting for $179 billion in 1980. Most of this, $115 billion, consists of Social Security payments. Defense is the second largest budget function with outlays of $126 billion in 1980, an increase of $20 billion in two years. The other major expenditure categories are health ($53 billion) and interest ($57 billion). During the 1970s, major increases in spending occurred. Spending for health and income security underwent some of the largest jumps. Defense, while increasing every year, exhibited much slower growth and, in real terms, remained constant until the end of the decade. Certain areas, like energy, increased hundreds of times over from 1970 to 1980. Other areas, like foreign assistance, underwent very little or no increase, declining in real terms.

Figure 3-1 shows the trends in the composition of the federal budget since 1958, projected through 1984. In the past 25 years, spending for national defense has declined significantly as a proportion of the budget. Defense spending totaled around $25 billion in 1951 and grew to over $100 billion in 1977. In 1951, it constituted 48 percent of the budget; by 1977, this proportion fell to 25 percent. The composition of federal expenditures has shifted significantly as a result of the rapid growth in income maintenance programs. Another function that has increased its share of the budget is grants to state and local governments. Figure 3-1 also indicates a general decline in the relative share of other federal operations.

There has been a shift in priorities over the past quarter-century from military spending to human resource programs. Social programs grew in the mid-1960s as a result of the "Great Society" programs (medicare, medicaid, social services, federal aid to education, and manpower programs). In the 1970s, spending growth came in the form of income security program increases (Social Security benefits, supplemental security income,

Figure 3-1   The Composition of Federal Spending

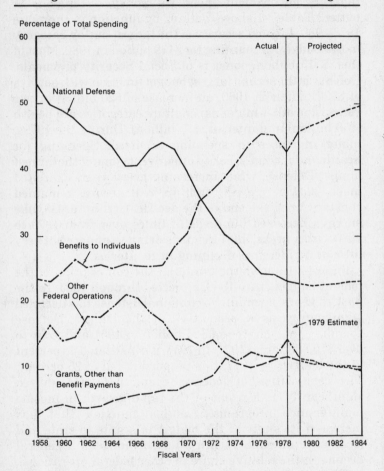

Percentage of Total Spending

Actual   Projected

National Defense

Benefits to Individuals

Other
Federal Operations

1979 Estimate

Grants, Other than
Benefit Payments

Fiscal Years

Source: Congressional Budget Office, *Five Year Budget Projections and Alternative Budget Strategies for FY 1980-1984,* January 1979, p. 20

food stamps, public assistance) and grants to state and local governments (special and general revenue sharing). These budget expenditures are different from other federal spending; they represent transfer payments rather than direct government purchases of goods and services. This trend has been characterized as "the transformation of the federal government into largely a 'check-writing' organization."[1] There are several important implications of this trend in spending. First, with the increasing size of income maintenance payments, the federal government is becoming more involved with income redistribution. Income maintenance programs, along with the tax system, make income redistribution a major policy component of the budget. Second, the growth of income maintenance programs has substantially increased the amount of the budget classified as uncontrollable and not allocated through the annual appropriations process.[2] Third, it has raised serious objections in some quarters concerning the adequacy of U.S. military preparedness, leading to efforts to promote a larger defense budget.

Spending by Agency

The budget can be represented in various degrees of detail. In its simplest form, the budget can be expressed in terms of totals and subtotals by function. Substantially greater detail is contained in the 1,500-page *Appendix to the Budget,* which lists spending by each individual appropriation account. Even this massive document does not convey the full detail of each agency's budget and actually combines many activities into each account.[3]

The executive branch of the federal government is organized by departments and agencies, not by function. It is important to remember that program decisions and appropriations are made on the basis of agencies. Functional totals provide decision makers with a useful summary of federal activities for making priority choices and assessing what the current priorities are. The difference in these measures of spending can cause confusion; "crosswalking" is the process of translating

64   BUDGETARY POLITICS

Table 3-2   Budget Authority and Outlays by Agency
(in millions of dollars)

Department or other unit	Budget authority			Outlays		
	1978 actual	1979*	1980*	1978 actual	1979*	1980*
Legislative branch	1,071	1,213	1,273	1,049	1,209	1,305
The Judiciary	458	539	625	435	526	619
Executive Office of the President	78	83	91	75	88	89
Funds appropriated to the President	7,528	11,372	10,345	4,450	5,090	5,133
Agriculture	16,535	23,660	20,544	20,368	20,205	18,404
Commerce	2,308	2,533	3,217	5,239	4,331	3,261
Defense — Military	115,322	125,209	135,041	103,042	111,900	122,700
Defense — Civil	2,797	2,669	3,059	2,553	2,644	2,724
Energy	10,695	9,716	7,447	6,286	8,946	8,893
Health, Education, and Welfare	162,192	184,002	205,170	162,856	180,714	199,428
Housing and Urban Development	38,000	31,112	33,295	7,589	8,962	10,634
Interior	4,590	4,683	4,438	3,821	4,015	3,764
Justice	2,370	2,510	2,398	2,397	2,586	2,505
Labor	20,028	28,911	27,534	22,896	22,854	24,484
State	1,483	1,674	1,712	1,252	1,399	1,677
Transportation	13,478	17,272	17,813	13,452	15,363	15,793
Treasury	56,771	65,570	70,051	56,355	65,462	69,890
Environmental Protection Agency	5,498	5,410	5,087	4,071	4,194	4,753
General Services Administration	151	313	308	83	158	131
National Aeronautics and Space Administration	4,060	4,562	4,723	3,980	4,401	4,593
Veterans' Administration	19,010	20,486	20,992	18,962	20,315	20,450
Other independent agencies	32,851	34,728	56,959	25,396	26,675	27,961
Allowances	—	100	2,426	—	—	1,398
Undistributed offsetting receipts: Employer share, employee retirement	-4,983	-5,388	-5,482	-4,983	-5,388	-5,482
Interest received by trust funds	-8,530	-9,782	-10,940	-8,530	-9,782	-10,940
Rents and royalties on the Outer Continental Shelf lands	-2,259	-3,500	-2,600	-2,259	-3,500	-2,600
Total Budget authority and outlays	501,500	559,658	615,526	450,836	493,368	531,566

*Estimate.
Source: *Budget of the United States Government FY 1980*, p. 524.

functional totals into agency or committee jurisdictions and vice versa.

The United States had approximately 1.9 million civilian employees in 1980.[4] They are employed by 12 Cabinet departments and the agencies under them as well as by the independent agencies, government corporations, boards, bureaus, and commissions. Table 3-2 shows budget outlays and authority broken down by department, major independent offices, and the legislative, executive, and judicial branches. Most agencies administer programs in many functional areas. The natural resources function, for example, groups together programs administered by the Departments of Agriculture, Defense, Commerce, Interior, State, Energy, and Transportation, and agencies including the Environmental Protection Agency, Federal Power Commission, Federal Energy Administration, Nuclear Regulatory Commission, and even the Susquehanna River Basin Commission.[5] The array of agencies composing other budget functions is comparable, with the possible exception of Defense. The composition of the budget can be represented either by function or by agency. Most commonly, priority decisions are made in terms of functions, with program and operation decisions in terms of agencies.

Revenues

Taxes not only raise the money to be allocated to the various programs and federal policy functions but they also may affect the distribution of income and can provide incentives or discouragement for citizen behavior. Special provisions in the tax laws (or loopholes) provide indirect payments, tax expenditures, to certain subgroups of the population eligible to take advantage of them.

Table 3-3 shows the source of federal tax revenues for the period 1978-1980. Like expenditures, receipts have increased rapidly in recent years, but the increases have not been uniform across all types of taxes. Figure 3-2 shows the shifts that have occurred in federal receipts since 1958. The main source of revenue is personal income

Table 3-3   Budget Receipts
(in millions of dollars)

Description	1978 actual	1979 estimate	1980 estimate
Budget receipts by source:			
Individual income taxes	180,988	203,602	227,322
Corporation income taxes	59,952	70,307	70,987
Social insurance taxes and contributions	123,410	141,789	161,453
Excise taxes	18,376	18,395	18,455
Estate and gift taxes	5,285	5,686	6,011
Customs duties	6,573	7,517	8,447
Miscellaneous receipts	7,413	8,693	9,878
Total budget receipts	401,997	455,989	502,553

Source: *Budget of the United States Government FY 1980*, p. 523.

taxes. In spite of three tax cuts between 1967 and 1979, collections have increased by over $140 billion. Personal income taxes make up about 45 percent of revenues, but that share is projected to increase in the coming years. In 1967, corporate income taxes and social insurance taxes raised nearly equal amounts of revenue. Since that year, collections from social insurance taxes have increased by $130 billion, while money collected from corporate income taxes has increased by only $37 billion. Figure 3-2 shows the divergence in the trend lines beginning in 1967, and the rapid increase in social insurance taxes as a component of federal revenues. Table 3-3 indicates that federal revenues are collected primarily from three sources. Excise taxes, estate and gift taxes, customs duties, and other miscellaneous taxes provide only a small portion of total revenues.

The sources of federal revenues and trends in their composition have a number of important policy implications. As GNP rises and persons move into higher tax brackets, one would expect the proportion of taxes derived from the personal income tax to increase rather than remain stable or decrease. This was not the case

Figure 3-2 The Composition of Federal Revenues

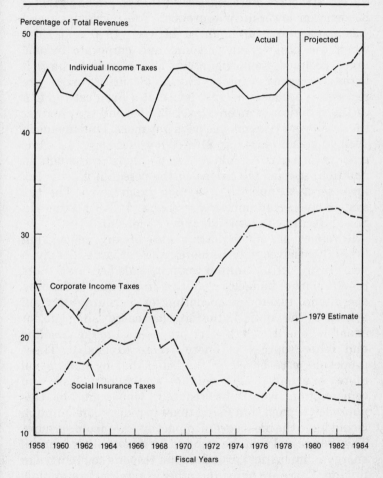

Percentage of Total Revenues

Individual Income Taxes

Actual

Projected

Corporate Income Taxes

1979 Estimate

Social Insurance Taxes

Fiscal Years

because of tax cuts in 1962, 1964, 1969, 1971, and 1975. The
relative increase of social insurance taxes (from 12
percent in 1955 to 31 percent in 1979) has tended to make
the tax structure more regressive, that is, placing greater
burdens on lower-income groups.[6] The regressive trend
was particularly pronounced between 1970 and 1975,
when the progressive personal and corporate income
taxes declined proportionately, and regressive payroll
taxes increased rapidly. Social Security taxes are
regressive because they are levied at a fixed rate up to a
certain maximum income level and beyond that neither
the employer nor employee pays any more. That means in
1980 a person making $100,000 would pay the same
amount as a person making only one quarter as much. In
addition, special provisions in the personal income tax
laws serve to make it less than progressive. The tax
system has become more regressive, and 1978 increases in
Social Security taxes made it even more so.

Revenues are an important part of any budget, but
taxes themselves may be more or less at issue in a given
year. In the 1970s, annual tax proposals became a more
regular part of budgetary politics. In addition to funding
operations, taxes can encourage or discourage certain
actions by the public. In the face of an energy shortage, for
example, energy taxes were proposed to make gasoline
and other sources of energy more expensive. These
proposals were based on the belief that by making oil
more expensive, the public would buy less and
consumption would be reduced. Opponents of this
approach argued that using taxes to reduce consumption
would have the most severe impact on low-income groups.
They suggested that the demand for oil and other forms of
energy is inelastic: i.e., it does not respond to changes in
pricing. There are numerous other examples. To stimulate
the depressed construction and housing industry, a tax
credit for the purchase of newly constructed homes was
passed in 1975. Just as investment tax credits encourage
investment, home mortgage interest deductions
encourage home ownership. Some have proposed
automobile taxes based on miles-per-gallon averages to
discourage the production and sale of "gas-guzzling"

cars. As with expenditures and decisions on budget size, taxes involve many policy considerations, not simply how much money will be raised.

Federal Funds and Trust Funds

Budget receipts go into two main types of funds: federal funds and trust funds.[7] Federal funds are general monies available to be spent for any purpose. Trust funds are special monies earmarked for a specific purpose in accordance with a trust agreement or a statute. The highway trust fund (used to build the interstate highway system although recently tapped to help pay for mass transit) and the Social Security trust fund (used to pay Social Security benefits) are two of the largest. Until the 1960s, federal funds and trust funds were accounted separately; the transition to the unified budget merged the two and provided a more accurate picture of federal operations.

Budget Authority and Outlays

The congressional power of the purse is actually employed by creating budget authority.[8] As noted in Chapter 1, this is a two-stage process. Congress first enacts legislation that authorizes an agency to carry out programs and sets the limits on the amount that can be appropriated. Most authorizations are open-ended or multiyear, but some programs require annual authorization. Actual budget authority is granted through appropriations, but for a majority of uncontrollable budget items with permanent or multiyear authority, this step is automatic. Other forms of budget authority approved by Congress are contract authority and borrowing authority.

Outlays are what will actually be spent in a given year. Congress does not normally approve outlays but grants budget authority based on estimates of outlays. The President submits requests for certain levels of budget authority and estimates of outlays; Congress responds in the same fashion by approving budget authority and the budget resolutions set targets for outlays. Actual outlays

Figure 3-3 Relations of Budget Authority to Outlays
1980 Budget

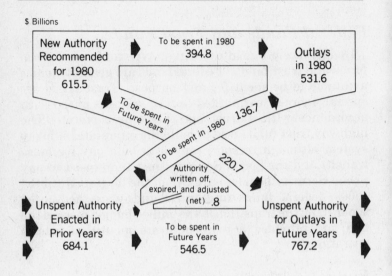

Source: *Budget of the United States Government, FY 1980*, p. 69.

are the amounts of money obligated by agencies drawing
on their approved authority in a given year.

This overlaps from year to year. As Figure 3-3 shows,
outlays in a given year are based on past budget authority
as well as current authority. Similarly, budget authority
is granted for future years as well as the current year.

Budget Controllability

Uncontrollable Spending

Spending is classified as uncontrollable if it is
mandated under current law or by a previous obligation.
It means that substantive legislation, not the President's
budget or an appropriation bill, must be changed to alter
spending.

The growth in total federal spending noted in Chapter 2 is almost completely attributable to growth in uncontrollable items. In 1967, outlays classified as controllable equaled $66.4 billion and uncontrollable outlays equaled $93.5 billion.[9] By 1977, uncontrollable outlays had grown 225 percent to $304 billion, while the controllable portion of the budget had increased only 42 percent to $94.9 billion.[10] In 1980, 75 percent of the budget was classified as uncontrollable.

The controllable/uncontrollable dichotomy is misleading to the extent that it groups dissimilar types of outlays and implies that one type may be altered by decision makers and the other may not. Uncontrollable spending can be broken down into several components.[11]

Fixed Costs These consist of charges to the federal government required by legal commitments made in prior years. Many fixed costs are in the form of permanent and indefinite appropriations, requiring the government to spend whatever necessary to meet certain expenses. The largest expenditure in this category is interest on the national debt. Public housing loans also constitute fixed costs. Such spending comes closest to a "common-sense" notion of uncontrollable. These charges are eliminated only by such extreme measures as default; in other words, there is virtually no control over fixed costs.

Multiyear Contracts and Obligations Most large-scale government projects take many years to complete and are financed over a period of many years. These include the building of dams, bridges, sewer projects, weapons systems, aircraft, and the space shuttle. Although some of these obligations are reviewed and altered periodically, this is the exception rather than the rule. The change of administrations in 1977 resulted in an uncommon recommendation by President Carter to terminate a number of partially completed water-resources projects. In most cases, the crucial budget year is the year of initiation, where recent practice has been to approve full funding of the entire project. The desire to "control" multiyear projects can result in a rather heated political clash, as in the case of the supersonic transport (SST) and of the Carter-Congress clash over water projects. Outlays can be increased by undertaking more projects; planning and execution constraints make it difficult to expand rapidly in the short run, however. Some control is possible, but generally it is quite limited.

Entitlement Programs, Payments to States and Individuals The largest category of spending officially classified as uncontrollable commits the federal government to pay certain benefits to eligible individuals if they apply. This includes Social Security, medicare, medicaid, supplemental security income, public assistance, food stamps, and federal retirement. In some cases, eligibility is determined by the federal government; in other cases, eligibility is determined by the states. Most of these programs are open-ended; expenditures increase as much as necessary to pay persons who are entitled to receive benefits.

Actions taken by Congress and the President over the past decade indicate how such outlays may be increased or decreased. Presidents Nixon and Ford attempted to cut outlays by restricting eligibility and holding the line on benefit increases. Congress increased outlays by adding cost-of-living escalators, increasing benefit levels and coverage. On the other hand, Congress has acted to control the growth in social services grants by limiting the total annual expenditure and the total each state may receive.[12]

Table 3-4 examines the amounts and distribution of uncontrollable spending in these three categories. While uncontrollable spending has increased in all three categories, the majority of the increase has occurred in payments to individuals. The last line of Table 3-4 indicates the percentage of total outlays classified as uncontrollable, now around three-fourths of the budget.

The proportion of uncontrollable outlays varies by agency and by function. Table 3-5 examines the percentage of uncontrollable outlays, by major functions. Social welfare programs in income security (99.8 percent) and in health (85.4 percent) are officially the least controllable. The majority of outlays classified as controllable are in the area of national defense. This

Table 3-4 Uncontrollable Spending 1970-1980
(in billions of dollars)

	1970	1980
Fixed Costs—		
Interest	$ 14.8	$ 46.2
Farm price supports	3.8	2.8
Other fixed costs	3.8	9.8
Subtotal	22.0	58.8
Multiyear Contracts and Obligations—		
Civilian	24.5	37.1
Defense	18.6	50.8
Subtotal	41.5	87.9
Entitlement and Open Ended Programs—		
Payments to individuals:		
Social Security	31.3	120.4
Retirement	5.6	25.7
Unemployment	3.7	13.2
Veteran's benefits	6.6	13.7
Medicare and Medicaid	9.9	46.2
Housing assistance	.5	5.1
Public assistance	4.7	26.2
Revenue sharing	—	6.9
Subtotal	62.2	257.4
Total uncontrollable*	$125.7	$404.1
Percentage of total		
outlays uncontrollable	54.0%	77.1%

*Totals reflect adjustment of offsetting receipts.
Source: *Budget of the United States Government FY 1980*, p. 560.

suggests that simply focusing on the location of controllable expenditures is an inadequate route to budgetary discretion. Political feasibility also should be considered, since there are strong pressures against making major cuts in the defense portion of the budget. The figures also suggest that different federal departments face different budget problems. The Department of Defense must try to protect its large controllable portion; the Department of Health, Education, and Welfare (HEW), on the other hand, is strapped with a budget that, for its planning purposes, is

Table 3-5   Percent of Outlays Uncontrollable
under Present Law, FY 1976

Income security	99.8
Revenue sharing and fiscal assistance	95.9
Health	85.4
Veteran's programs	78.5
Commerce and transportation	67.7
Community development	61.4
Education, manpower, and social services	53.3
Agriculture	50.0
National resources, energy, environment	46.4
International affairs	45.5
Science, space, and technology	37.0
Defense	33.9
Law enforcement	29.4
General government	0

Source: U.S., Congress, House, Committee on the Budget, *Report to Accompany the First Concurrent Resolution on the Fiscal Year 1977 Budget,* 94th Congress, 2d session, appendix C, p. 89.

effectively predetermined. The result has been that while the HEW budget has grown rapidly, the small controllable portion of its budget has actually shrunk, forcing cuts in many "controllable" health and education activities.[13]

The growth in controllable spending can be attributed partially to Congress, to the authorizing committees specifically. They successfully guaranteed growth in social welfare expenditures by writing them into substantive law. This served to protect pet programs from encroachment and possible cuts by the Appropriations Committees. While this increased the impact on budgeting of the authorizating committees, some suggest that specific spending objectives have been achieved at the cost of overall flexibility.

It would be hard to argue that the growth in uncontrollable spending has been the result of a rationally chosen plan. To a large extent it is a function of the fragmented authority of budgetary decision making, but the trend has not been completely accidental. Automatic stabilizers are purposely designed to increase outlays when unemployment rises and tax receipts decrease. The continued acceptance of automatic increases or decreases represents an implicit choice to allow the budget to be affected by predetermined factors.

Besides the economy, the actions of the states affect spending. As states commit more funds to health care, the federal government, under existing law, must match the expansion. Federal spending for social services grants is a good example of how spending control can slip away from decision makers. Martha Derthick has described how the states took advantage of loopholes in the law to expand their programs far beyond the intentions of either Congress or the executive branch.[14] Congressional action placing a ceiling on both total and individual state grants demonstrates, however, that corrective actions are possible and that "uncontrollables" can be controlled.

The growth in uncontrollable spending is the result of many factors, some conscious choices and some unforeseen or accidental developments. It should be apparent that not all spending classified as uncontrollable is equally "uncontrollable." On the other hand, neither is all spending classified as controllable equally "controllable."

Controllable Spending

Controllable spending also falls into several categories.

Salaries and Benefits The bulk of the outlays classified as controllable (60 percent) goes for salaries, wages, and fringe benefits. This includes civilian and military salaries and military benefits for housing, health care, and so on. A large proportion of the defense budget is classified as controllable because of the high proportion of outlays for salaries and benefits. Short-term changes in the civilian payroll, particularly reductions, are very difficult to facilitate. Seniority protects some of the least-needed employees; civil service rules make early retirement, severance pay, and leave accumulations as expensive as actual salaries.[15] The volunteer army has been more expensive to maintain than originally estimated, and wholesale layoffs are unthinkable either militarily or economically. While short-term spending for job programs is the most easily expanded of the controllable expenditures, there are limits on how rapidly funds can be processed and jobs created.

General Operating Expenses Agencies face rising prices for "necessities" in much the same fashion as individual households. While economies are possible, costs for heating, electricity, transportation, maintenance of grounds and buildings, and supplies keep going up. Cuts can be imposed, consumption reduced, resupply and maintenance deferred; but expenses are incurred even if operations cease, buildings are locked up, and automobiles are stored. These costs represent a sizable proportion of agency budgets and have been subject to the general price increases experienced in the rest of the economy. General operating expenses make up roughly 22 percent of controllable outlays.

Research, New Programs, and Other This final category includes a variety of expenditures, such as cancer and energy research, start-up funds for military procurement, some grants to state and local governments (in areas such as nutrition, education, and health), Amtrak, and other outlays. Research can be phased down or stopped; projects can be terminated in early stages or not initiated at all; appropriations can be cut or eliminated. Yet even in this category of outlays there are considerable limits to what can be terminated immediately. These expenditures make up approximately 18 percent of the controllable portion of the budget.

Like the rest of federal outlays the so-called controllable portion of the budget is also a set of commitments and ongoing activities, even if they are not guaranteed by law. Decision makers are limited in their ability to control the controllables as well as the uncontrollables.

Estimating Short-Term Discretion

With federal outlays further broken down into their components, it is possible to move from a dichotomy to a continuum of control, as shown in Table 3-6. First,

Table 3-6   Relative Controllability and Potential Discretion

Type of Outlay (From Least to Most Controllable)	Estimated Maximum Possible Reduction (C)	Proportion of Total Budget (P)	Potential Discretion (P×C)
Fixed Costs	0%	10%	0%
Multiyear contracts and obligations	2%	17%	0.3%
Entitlement payments	5%	46%	2.3%
Salaries and benefits	10%	16%	1.6%
General operating expenses	20%	6%	1.2%
Research, grants, new programs, other	30%	5%	1.5%
TOTAL		100%	6.0%

expenditures can be ranked from the "least controllable" to the "most controllable." Second, some rough estimates can be made of the maximum amount that each could be cut in a given year.

Recognizing that controllability refers to increases as well as decreases, most concern is about inflexibility of the budget in a downward direction. Therefore, Table 3-5 includes only estimates of the "maximum" that could be cut from current services estimates.[16] The word *maximum* is of course used tentatively. In theory, no expenditure is beyond control even in the short run, but it is ridiculous to think of defaulting on the national debt, stopping all long-term projects, or terminating Social Security. It is crucial to remember that these estimates consider the bounds of political feasibility as well as the nature of the outlay. Some evidence from other studies tends to support these figures. For example, a study by the Brookings Institution concluded that of the $105 billion classified as controllable in the FY 1976 budget, only $5-7 billion could actually be cut.[17]

There is virtually no potential for reduction in fixed costs. Long-term contracts and obligations also offer little potential. Only rarely are multiyear projects terminated before completion. And once funds are obligated, it is nearly impossible to avoid outlays. What good is half a

bridge? Carter's proposal to halt construction of water
projects nonetheless suggestive of a small margin of
control. Entitlement programs offer more potential for
cuts. The proposed actions of recent Presidents with
regard to Social Security, food stamps, medicaid, and
federal pay are instructive. In submitting his FY 1976 and
FY 1977 budgets, Ford proposed increases in Social
Security taxes and a restriction on benefit increases. He
proposed withholding automatic increases in civilian and
military pay. Proposals for food stamps included a
reduction in benefits and restrictions on eligibility. Ford's
proposed changes in medicaid programs were designed to
increase recipient costs for the same level of benefits.

Savings in salaries and benefits probably could not
exceed 10 percent without radically disrupting federal
operations. Likewise, seemingly modest economies of 20
percent in operating expenses would be difficult to
achieve. Even among the most controllable expenditures,
it is unlikely that more than 30 percent could be
immediately cut.

It is easier to expand than to cut, but short-term
expansion is restricted not only by political and economic
constraints but by time requirements for major program
development and implementation. In the past, rapid
expansion has often resulted in a wasteful, inefficient use
of funds. Unusual circumstances, such as severe national
calamity (nuclear accident, major earthquake), a war, or
severe domestic unrest and violence could require
expansion beyond "normal" boundaries. In the vast
majority of years, fears of inflation from overstimulation
of the economy and political pressures to hold down
spending tend to keep budget increases within certain
limits.

A crucial point demonstrated in Table 3-6 is that
projections of potential discretion depend not only on
estimates of relative controllability but on the *relative
share of the budget.* While it has been estimated (perhaps
conservatively) that 5 percent or less of the outlays
classified as uncontrollable could be cut, this still provides
decision makers with *as much potential discretion* as in
all of the so-called controllable expenditures (the

percentages in the last column of the table are the products of estimates of maximum cuts and their shares of the budget). While general operating expenses and research, grants, and new programs may be cut proportionately more, they constitute only slightly more than 10 percent of all outlays.

The controllable/uncontrollable dichotomy does not provide a realistic view of budgetary discretion. In reality, the budget is locked in far more than the "75 percent uncontrollable" indicates. The proportion of the budget beyond the reach of annual manipulation is closer to 90-95 percent.

The Adequacy of Control

Is the budget out of control? Is short-term flexibility adequate? Conclusions about the adequacy or inadequacy of discretion depends upon the time frame. Major reallocation is undesirable over the period of a single year. Stability in planning and program development, in implementation, and in the delivery of services and benefits is essential for effective public policy. Alteration of annual expenditures above or below the 5 percent range is likely to have negative economic consequences.

As the federal budget has passed the half-trillion-dollar mark, a range of ± 5 percent translates into at least $50 billion. An increase or decrease in total outlays of $25 billion from current service levels provides adequate discretion. New programs may be initiated, old ones abandoned; new spending commitments may be written into substantive laws, old ones modified; budget growth may be retarded or fostered. In terms of the actual dollar figures for budget functions, agency appropriations, and programs, $50 billion provides significant flexibility. In most years it would probably be more than enough.

Annual budgeting is increasingly concerned with fiscal stabilization, emergencies, and situations that demand rapid action. Manipulation of budget totals for fiscal policy does not depend solely on expenditures. Because relative stability in expenditures is desirable in the short run, manipulation of tax receipts through rebates,

ion may be used to
affect the degree of fiscal stimulation. Although
historically tax legislation has been slow in passing
Congress, the new budget process may create additional
pressures on the House Ways and Means Committee and
the Senate Finance Committee to act.

Concern with controllability and budget inflexibility
may be as much a function of our "annual" mentality
about budgeting as anything else. At any given point in
time, there exists a rough consensus concerning the
proper scope of federal activities. We should not expect or
advocate major reallocation in the short run.
Controversial political decisions to embark on major new
activities, such as comprehensive welfare reform or
national health insurance, are not annual decisions. They
are policy choices that must be approached in terms of
their long-term implications. The amount of short-term
discretion available to decision makers is adequate to deal
with even a rapidly changing environment. Long-term
policy choices provide the opportunity to change national
priorities and to make major reallocations within the
budget.

FOOTNOTES

†Portions of this Chapter previously appeared in "Discretion in
National Budgeting-Controlling the Controllables," *Policy Analysis,*
Vol. 4, No. 4, pp. 455-475, copyright 1978, Regents of the University of
California.

¹Barry H. Blechman, Edward M. Gramlich, and Robert M. Hartman,
Setting National Priorities: The 1976 Budget (Washington, D.C.:
Brookings Institution, 1975), p. 8.

²*Ibid.,* p. 9.

³As the executive branch becomes more complex, less detailed
information on line-item expenditures and appropriation accounts is
made available to Congress and the public. The fiscal year *1977
Appendix to the Budget* was several hundred pages shorter than the
1976 Appendix. This was accomplished by reducing the number of
categories, making them more inclusive.

⁴Office of Management and Budget, *Budget of the United States
Government Fiscal Year 1980,* p. 529.

⁵*Budget of the U.S. FY 1977,* pp. 332-337.

[6]See chapter 10 for a discussion of regressive, proportional, and progressive taxes.

[7]*Budget of the U.S. FY 1977*, p. 174. See also David J. Ott and Attiat F. Ott, *Federal Budget Policy* (Washington, D.C.: Brookings Institution, 1965), chapter 2.

[8]*Ibid.*, pp. 169-171.

[9]*Ibid.*, pp. 34-36.

[10]*Ibid.*, pp. 354-355.

[11]See alternative breakdowns of spending in Blechman, Gramlich, and Hartman, pp. 197-207; and Murray Weidenbaum, "Institutional Obstacles to Relocating Government Expenditures," in *Public Expenditures and Policy Analysis*, eds. Robert Haveman and Julius Margolis (Chicago: Markham, 1970), pp. 232-245.

[12]Martha Derthick, *Uncontrollable Spending for Social Services Grants* (Washington, D.C.: Brookings Institution, 1975).

[13]See John R. Gist, " 'Increment' and 'Base' in the Congressional Appropriations Process" (Paper presented at the Annual Meeting of the Midwest Political Science Association, Chicago, Ill., May 1, 1976); and Blechman, Gramlich, and Hartman, pp. 76-78.

[14]See Derthick, *Uncontrollable Spending,* chapters 5, 7.

[15]Blechman, Gramlich, and Hartman, p. 198.

[16]These estimates are obviously subject to dispute and alteration. They are based on the best available evidence — in terms of what others estimate could be cut, the actual cuts proposed by decision makers, and historical parameters of reductions. John Crecine has undertaken a study based on OMB documents of adjustments made to agency requests in both controllable and uncontrollable items. His preliminary findings suggest that cuts somewhat larger than indicated here are possible. But until concrete evidence is presented, the other factors — particularly political considerations in Congress — argue for far more restrictive estimates of what could be cut. See John Crecine et al., "The Controllability of 'Uncontrollable' Federal Expenditures: Executive Branch Decision Making" (paper presented at the Annual Meeting of the Midwest Political Science Association, Chicago, Ill., April 21, 1977).

[17]Blechman, Gramlich, and Hartman, pp. 197-207.

Agencies

We didn't pay much attention to the OMB guidelines this year. Even though they cut us back, we probably would have been worse off had we not asked for a large increase.
—An agency budget officer

Most agencies want more money to spend. Continuation of current operations usually requires a steady growth in funding while expansion of programs and activities demands major increases in appropriations. Agencies are required each year to make estimates of what they will need to spend to carry out their programs in the coming year. Between initial agency estimates and final approval of their budget stand the obstacles of the reviewing bodies: the department, the OMB (sometimes the President), and the Congress. As

advocates of greater spending, the agencies affect the
behavior of the other participants in the budgetary
process and the allocation of resources in the budget. As
distinct organizations, agencies conceive of and pursue
different strategies. Some agencies behave assertively,
actively pursuing substantial increases and expansion in
their programs. Others follow a path of moderation,
content to seek small increases and attain stability in
their activities.

Why do agencies behave differently? While large
organizations tend to share some basic behavioral
similarities, variation in agencies' internal goal structure
results in differing orientations.[1] An agency may take on
certain characteristics that reflect the dominant pattern
of attitudes of its employees and leaders.[2] Newer agencies,
staffed with younger people, tend to have a more activist
orientation; concerned with goals and missions, they are
likely to be more assertive. Older, more established
agencies tend to have a more conservative orientation;
concerned with internal stability and self-preservation,
they are likely to be less assertive.

Agencies operate in a complex environment, both
within the confines of the government and within society.
Certain social, economic, and political trends affect all
agencies. Overall budgetary reductions to combat
inflation or to economize place general constraints on
agencies. Other environmental trends may affect certain
agencies directly, some indirectly, and others not at all.
For example, the launching of Sputnik (the first artificial
satellite to orbit the earth) by the Soviet Union in 1957 had
a tremendous impact on the U.S. space program, on
federal aid to higher education, particularly in
encouraging the training of scientists and engineers, and
in the money available for scientific research. The Arab
oil boycott and the ensuing energy crisis in 1973 resulted
in sudden changes in agencies dealing with energy and
natural resources, which in turn affected agencies
concerned with the protection of the environment.

Agencies may be supported by clientele groups in
society and may try to expand and develop their friends.
Agencies also attempt to develop bases of support within

the legislative and executive branches. The President can be a most useful ally during the budgetary process. Certain coalitions in Congress may exist in support or opposition to agency programs.

Agencies attempt to devise strategies in budgetary politics that will result in satisfactory results in light of their particular objectives. While some common characteristics are present, such as the general tendency to advocate greater spending, different budgetary strategies are pursued.

Deciding What to Request

Agencies must first determine their own objectives and priorities. When requesting the same level of funding as in the previous year, an agency must make budgetary decisions on the internal distributions of funds to their various functions. Even in a year when agencies are forced to cut back, they must develop internal priorities on the location of those cuts.

How do agencies decide what to ask for? Conventional incremental theory suggests that agencies look at last year's appropriation and take a fixed percentage increase to arrive at a figure to request this year.[3] Last year's budget is considered a base in making this year's requests. However, an agency's base is composed of different parts.[4]

Uncontrollable component The large portion of the budget base for most agencies is fixed from one year to the next. While they may request legislative changes, unless Congress acts there is little to be done with this component. The Defense Department has about 60 percent of its budget classified as controllable, but even a larger portion of this is beyond short-run discretion. A department like Health, Education, and Welfare, with 95 percent of its budget classified as uncontrollable, actually makes annual request decisions over a much smaller portion of its budget than the total HEW appropriation would indicate.

Inflationary component A second portion constitutes requests necessary to keep up with inflation. Utilities such as gas, telephone, and electricity cost more for government agencies as well as for the general public, necessitating larger appropriations to maintain current services.

Discretionary component The third portion of an agency's budget is the discretionary component. Most stability in agency budgeting is a function of the uncontrollable costs and requests to maintain current operations at inflated prices. The most important source of change is in the discretionary portion. While some agencies request only a small increase or no increase in the discretionary portion, many ask for more substantial increases.

A wide range of criteria in calculating what to request is employed in decisions on the discretionary portion. Decisions reflect a variety of choices affected by the environment both inside and outside the agency. Budget officers compile data on activities, workloads, man-hours, clients served, to make estimates of changing needs in the coming year. Agency leaders assess their own goals and attempt to shape the requests accordingly. The results of planning, analysis of alternatives, and program evaluation often help shape decisions on what to request.

Agency officials are constrained by a number of external decisions. The OMB Director's Letter contains guidelines that indicate the expectations of the Office of Management and Budget. Agencies that are part of one of the Cabinet departments face an additional review stage and set of constraints. In the summer months, when estimates are being prepared, each department engages in a budget preparation process of its own. Agency budget directors meet with department officials to present their requests and justifications. For these agencies this is the only stage in the process where they present and defend their own estimates. After departmental officials make a decision on what to send to the OMB, the agencies are expected to defend the department figures, not the original requests. But departments are limited in controlling their own agencies. They wish to express their own values but must be cognizant of probable actions by the OMB and the President. Agencies may have their base of support in Congress, the OMB, or the White House; if department decisions are too far out of line with the sentiments of the subsequent actors, they may be overridden. Departments are faced with the task of balancing their own priorities with the perception of the external environment.

Because of the constraints imposed by the reviewing bodies, agencies do not simply add up the cost of all worthwhile projects and submit the total.[5] As astute political participants, agency officials have a good sense of "what will go." Some agencies respond by proposing moderate increases that would seem to have a reasonable chance of acceptance. However, many agencies are willing to ask for considerably more than they expect to get, and they usually do so without risking more severe cuts in their final budget.

Games and Strategies

Adopting the role of advocate in the budgetary process, agencies use varying degrees of assertiveness in seeking money for expansion of their own programs. Assertiveness is manifested in agencies by the clever use of games and strategies to increase their leverage, and by their willingness to request substantial increases in funding. Strategies are devised in a changing environment, and agencies are never quite sure just what impact their actions will have. Strategic planning takes place throughout the budget process, from deciding what to request, in making their case to the department and OMB, to their appropriations hearings in Congress. Consistent with their goal of getting more money, some of the following strategies may be employed from time to time by agency officials, and are all related to the basic degree of assertiveness of the agency.

Call out the Troops

Agencies not only need to develop a clientele but to mobilize their clientele to support them at budget time. This is an easier task for some agencies than for others. The Department of Agriculture and its agencies have a variety of farm organizations, such as the Grange, Four-H, and agribusiness conglomerates, to cajole, plead with, and even threaten politicians. Strong rural allies in Congress provide a backdrop of support for various subsidy, conservation, power, and water programs. Other agencies, like the Bureau of Prisons, do not have a natural clientele, or at least not one they would readily claim.[6] The Agency for International Development (AID) administers many of the foreign aid programs and lacks a vociferous domestic clientele. Although they have found allies in the White House, the unpopularity of foreign aid programs in Congress has gradually whittled away their share of the budget. Clientele groups can send letters, appear at congressional hearings, strike, and demonstrate. If they are large enough, their mere existence can help the agency. Making effective use of clientele groups is a basic agency strategy.

The Current Fashion

Agencies must be flexible and imaginative in order to succeed. This means keeping up with the latest trends in Washington, which can change as quickly as skirt lengths. In the late 1950s, science, technology, and education were the rage as Americans worried "why Ivan can read and Johnny can't." Various agencies proposed research and development programs to support scientific education and assorted new technologies, however far afield. The spirit of the space race with the Soviets permeated more than just the National Aeronautics and Space Administration. In the 1960s, social welfare and poverty programs were in fashion. Agencies involved with natural resources, labor, agriculture, commerce, and numerous other concerns were able to conceive of programs to help the poor. Before the Vietnam War soured the national mood, the spirit of social responsibility crept into agency budgets. By the late 1970s, energy was the key word. Congress could not spend money fast enough for agencies with proposals to develop alternatives to petroleum, to produce synthetic fuels, and to conserve all forms of energy.

An agency's hand is strengthened at all stages if it can tailor its proposals to fit presidential and congressional priorities. For example, President Carter supported the preservation and restoration of historic sites. The Department of the Interior was quick to classify much of the land it owned as "historic sites."[7] The same wine often looks much better in a new bottle.

The Washington Monument Ploy

Threatened with a budget cut in 1971, the National Park Service suggested it would have to close the Washington Monument to tourists.[8] This was done, of course, in the knowledge that Congress would restore whatever funds were necessary to keep the popular attraction open. The strategy is simple: threaten cuts in popular programs that are not politically feasible for the reviewing bodies to accept. Knowing that the President supports a certain program or that it is a particular favorite of a powerful committee chairman, the agency "reluctantly" can propose a cut, shielding less popular programs that might be readily cut if the agency so suggested.

Zero Base Budgeting (ZBB) has added a new dimension to the Washington Monument ploy. The system implemented by Carter in 1977 requires that agencies rank program packages by priority levels. Agencies may place the most popular programs farther down the list, hoping the OMB or Congress will act favorably on all the proposals above it. Although this strategy is not guaranteed to work, the agency can in this way try to put increased pressure on the reviewing bodies to approve more of their requests.

Capture Their Imagination

All agencies try to put their best foot forward, but some agencies are more vigorous than others in selling themselves. Some agencies emphasize their current activities and accomplishments while others talk in general terms about their history and past contributions. The most assertive agencies attempt to use anything that will legitimately promote their cause. One observer of the National Aeronautics and Space Administration recounted:

> Those guys on the Aeronautics and Space Committee love to play scientist and NASA exploits it to the hilt. Their hearings are like 'show and tell'; they bring in model rockets, sections of airplane wing, slides, movies, and other attractive gadgets. The committee members really enjoy the hearings.

Officials attempt to capture the imagination of the committee. This was obviously the case when one representative asked NASA officials if they are working on "energizing objects from one place to another, like on Star Trek."[9]

Agencies attempt to show results or explain the lack of results.[10] Some agencies stress trust and credibility, others document their stellar performance. In general, more assertive agencies are willing to use a variety of promotional devices in the presentations. Less assertive agencies often appear to pass up opportunities and sell themselves to OMB, the President, and Congress.

Obfuscate and Inundate

In sheer numbers, the agencies hold the edge over the OMB budget examiners and appropriations subcommittee members. Today's technocrats, usually experts in a highly specialized area, can mount an impressive barrage of jargon, scientific studies, and technical details. A skillful official can make a complicated subject even more complex and difficult to understand. This strategy banks on the assumption that reviewers will not cut what they do not understand. But a snow job does not always work, and congressmen can anger quickly if they feel they are getting the runaround.

Using their numerical advantages, agencies can simply inundate OMB and Congress with facts, figures, and charts. They can supply cost-benefit analyses, thousands of pages of statistics documenting their agency's activities and results. "Man-years" can be substituted for "man-hours" if it makes the outputs look more efficient. Agencies can occasionally develop indicators that show that by spending more they can actually save money.[11] Recognizing the inherent limitations of human beings to absorb multitudinous data and documentation, agencies may attempt to convince reviewers with quantity if nothing else.

Get a Foot in the Door

Programs with low start-up costs can become very expensive very quickly. Agencies attempt to begin modestly and then claim that the program is already going and should not be discontinued. An appropriations subcommittee chairman once observed, "This may be only $250 but this is the camel's nose. These things never get out of a budget. They manage to stay and grow."[12] It is easier to defend a program that is already part of the agency's current operations than it is to justify a new program. Congress has attempted to counter this tactic by requiring full funding for many projects in the first year. The Congressional Budget Office now attempts to project the total cost of new legislation to prevent exorbitant costs down the road once an agency gets its foot in the door.

The End Run

With the fragmentation of the budgetary process and the many stages of review, agencies can occasionally play one participant against another, or appeal a cut made at one stage to a higher level. An end run can take place anywhere: around the department, around the budget examiner to the top OMB officials, around OMB to the President. Most commonly, agencies dissatisfied with the handling of their requests in the executive budget will try an end run to Congress.

Those agencies are more willing to violate the "unity" of the executive budget and indicate to Congress their desire for more money than the OMB requested for them. This is a tricky position, because agencies have strict instructions not to "sell a bill of goods" on Capitol Hill. One OMB official related:

> They know they're not supposed to ask for more but it's inevitable that some of them will. We don't attend the hearings because we don't want to appear like we're looking over their shoulder. And in the past when an OMB official has been recognized in the audience, some committee members like to put him on the spot with some tough questions. So we don't go anymore. But we do read the transcript of the hearing pretty closely.

In response to a question on whether they are satisfied with their request, a skillful agency official can say "yes" and make it sound like "no." Agencies are required to answer questions honestly so that if a committee member asks them what they originally requested, they answer truthfully. This practice became increasingly prevalent in the 1970s. OMB officials suspect that such questions are often planted by the agency with a friendly committee member. Some agencies are good "team players" but others like to try an occasional end run.

But Play Fair

Despite the lapses into gamesmanship, agencies usually "play it straight" and attempt to establish confidence with the other participants in the budgetary process.[13] The games and strategies discussed above are fairly transparent and are countered by OMB and Congress, who have their own games and strategies. Agency strategies are acceptable, but within generally accepted rules of the game. Without maintaining the trust and confidence of the reviewing bodies, an agency is in for trouble.

It is essential for agencies that the OMB budget examiners have confidence in them and not be "surprised." If they lose confidence, the examiner can make life more difficult in pressing, prying, and disputing agency claims. The same is true for relations with

Congress. The Appropriations Committees cannot review all phases of the agency operations and must trust the agencies to faithfully carry out their responsibilities. A good reputation takes a long time to develop — and a short time to lose. Agencies develop a good reputation by aboveboard and honest dealings with Congress. A lie or a cover-up can be devastating. One administrator was quoted as saying, "It doesn't pay to try and put something over on them [committee members] because if you get caught you might as well pack your bags and leave Washington."[14] Good relations can be maintained by visiting congressional offices, helping committee members with constituent problems whenever possible, or inviting members to inspect agency installations and operations. Favorable relations with congressional and committee staff are also important.

Agency Assertiveness

A basic dimension of assertiveness is the willingness to request large increases in funding as opposed to more moderate increases.[15] The incremental theory suggests not only that all agencies behave similarly in calculating requests but that they pursue a strategy of moderation in asking for only small increases in their funding. According to this view, if agencies ask for too much, their credibility will decline, "with the result that the agency ends up with much less than it might have obtained with a more moderate request."[16]

Agencies are neither reckless in making requests nor oblivious to external constraints. But if an agency is assertive and asks for a substantial increase, they will tend to receive *more* than if they asked for a moderate increase.[17] "Don't come in too high" is poor advice for an agency wishing to receive more money; "come in as high as you can justify" would be better advice based on experience. Assertive agencies requesting a large increase in funding cause more problems for the reviewing bodies and are likely to suffer greater cuts in requests in dollar terms than an agency making only a modest request. But in spite of the larger cuts in their requests, the reviewing bodies do not cut them back all the way. There is no evidence that an agency has received less because they asked for a large rather than a small increase. Assertiveness is a prerequisite for substantial increases; to get more, you must ask for more.

Agency Assertiveness in the Department of Agriculture[18]

Data on the requests made by Department of Agriculture (DOA) agencies and the patterns of cuts made by the reviewing body provide an opportunity to examine several key dimensions of budgetary politics.[19]

- What are the patterns of assertiveness of moderation in initial agency requests?
- How does agency assertiveness affect the process of budget review by the department, the OMB,[20] and Congress?
- What budgetary roles are reflected in the actions of the department, OMB, and Congress?
- How does assertiveness affect the amount of money an agency finally receives?

Patterns of Assertiveness Budget requests for 36 Department of Agriculture agencies between 1946 and 1971 were used to compile Table 4-1, which breaks initial requests down into six categories.[21] Immediately obvious is the range in request patterns: in some cases, agencies did not play the role of advocate and requested a decrease (this occurred in 12 percent of the cases), while at the opposite extreme, some agencies asked for increases larger than 100 percent (this occurred in 7 percent of the cases). In two-thirds of the instances, agencies asked for more than a 10 percent increase and in almost half the cases asked for an increase of greater than 25 percent. Far from any single pattern of behavior in budgeting, DOA agencies displayed a wide variation in making their

**Table 4-1 Agency Assertiveness
Change in Initial Agency Request from
Previous Year's Appropriation**

	Requested Decrease less than 0%	0-10%	Amount of Increase Requested 10%-25%	25%-50%	50%-100%	100% and above	Total
Number of Cases	(60)	(99)	(121)	(103)	(79)	(36)	498
Percentage of Cases	12%	20%	24.3%	20.6%	15.8%	7.3%	100%

Source: Requests and Appropriations for 36 Department of Agriculture Agencies (1946-71).

initial estimate compared with what they had received the previous year. In 88 percent of the cases, agencies were advocates of greater spending.

Budget Review: Cutting Agency Requests Table 4-2 displays the pattern of cuts imposed by the Department, the OMB, and by Congress. Most apparent is the fact that the reviewing bodies usually cut agency budget requests; this is consistent with the role of guardian. It is also apparent that as agencies asked for more, they received larger cuts but showed greater increases in final appropriations. Several interesting trends emerge from Table 4-2 that provide information about budget roles and behavior.

The Department did not adopt a strict role of budget cutter. Particularly noticeable are the Department's actions to *increase* estimates for agencies that requested a decrease from the previous year. At the other extreme, the Department imposed the most severe cuts on the most assertive agencies (those agencies asking for increases greater than 100 percent). The DOA *cut* an average of over 20 percent from the requests of the most assertive cases, but *added* an average of 25 percent in the least assertive cases. For the middle group of cases where agencies requested an increase of less than 25 percent, Department

Table 4-2 Changes in Agency Requests Made by Reviewing Bodies

RELATIVE ASSERTIVENESS Change in agency request from previous budget	Number of cases	Average % change by Department	Average % change by OMB	Average % change by Congress	Budget results: Average percentage change in agency appropriation
request decrease	60	+25.5%	-6.5%	+2.4%	-21.0%
request increase	99	-2.0%	-3.0%	-0.3%	0%
0-10%	121	+1.3%	-8.0%	-0.5%	+1.3%
10-25%	103	-13.0%	-11.0%	-0.7%	+4.6%
25-50%	79	-16.5%	-14.4%	-1.3%	+17.0%
50-100%	36	-20.2%	-16.2%	-10.5%	+130.0%
greater than 100%	498	-4.0%	-9.0%	-2.0%	+11.0%
average for all agencies					

Source: Requests and Appropriations for 36 Department of Agriculture Agencies (1946-71).

changes were minimal, making few alterations in the
agency's original estimate. The pattern that emerges for
review at the Department level is a dual one; they acted as
"surrogate advocates" in the nonassertive cases and as
budget-cutting guardians in the most assertive cases. The
budget role of the Department can be characterized as
"balancing the extremes."

The pattern of OMB actions suggests the role of
guardian. For all categories of request changes, the OMB
reduced the requests. Even nonassertive requests were
reduced an average of 6.5 percent by the OMB. For more
assertive requests, the cuts were greater but, on the
average, were not as great as those made by the
Department.

Congress tended to reduce requests but made only small
cuts in most requests in the President's budget. Congress
provided a small increase in nonassertive cases, but on
the average it was insufficient to reverse the substantial
decline indicated in the last column of Table 4-2. On the
whole, Congress made relatively minor changes
compared with changes made at prior stages of the
process.

The Impact of Agency Assertiveness It was stated
earlier that to get more an agency has to ask for more. The
findings for the DOA agencies support this conclusion.
The final column in Table 4-2 shows the change in agency
funding after the cuts were made by the reviewing bodies.
While the cuts were larger for the assertive requests, the
results show greater growth. Agencies that requested an
increase of 50-100 percent ended up with an average
increase of 17 percent. Most moderate requests, those in
the 0-10 percent range, received no increases.

These findings for the Department of Agriculture are
suggestive of general budgetary roles. In conjunction
with other findings, it is clear that an assertive strategy is
necessary for agency budget growth.

Causes of Agency Assertiveness

Why do some agencies boldly ask for large increases
and others timidly propose cuts? While assertiveness may

be a function of the orientation of the agency, it must be recognized that assertive behavior in budgeting is constrained by numerous external factors. Assertiveness "pays off," but all agencies are not equally free to request large increases. Agency assertiveness is a function of several factors: the level of external support for the agency and its programs, the values, attitudes, and orientation of agency administrators, and external constraints.[22]

Public Support Agencies with public support for their programs are in a better position to be assertive than agencies without such support. This may take the form of active clientele groups or other organized interests willing to commit time and resources in demonstrating their support. It might be in the form of mass recognition and approval, such as that for the manned space program in its early years. Public support may be variable over time, such as efforts to promote mass transit during the energy crisis, or it may be stable over the long term, such as support from farmers for agriculture programs.

Presidential Support Having an advocate in the White House is invaluable for an agency that desires to expand its activities. General support may be expressed by the President in his public statements, news conferences, and legislation as well as during the budgetary process. Presidential support for an agency is strongly related to its level of assertiveness in the budgetary process.[23]

Congressional Support Agencies work hard to build supportive coalitions in Congress and maintain good relationships with their authorizing committees and appropriations subcommittees. Knowing they have backing in Congress, agencies feel more secure in asking for larger increases. In a retrenchment year, an agency may resist cutbacks threatened or imposed by the OMB on the strength of their congressional support.

Values, Attitudes, and Orientation of Administrators The level of external support is carefully considered by agency officials in preparing their budget requests, but actions based on this support will differ. Aggressive, goal-oriented agencies are most likely

to act assertively, especially if they feel secure in their
base of support. More traditional, conservative agencies,
concerned with self-preservation and stability, may act
nonassertively, even if they have strong external support.

External Constraints Despite the fact that
assertiveness usually reaps benefits for agencies, there
are numerous constraints on their actions. Economic
conditions and presidential decisions on totals may mean
a plentiful year or a tight year. These factors are formally
communicated to the agency through the OMB guidelines
for preparing their requests. Instructions are informally
communicated in a variety of ways, and agencies usually
have a pretty good idea of what is expected of them. But
agencies may stretch or even ignore formal and informal
guidelines if it is thought an extremely strong case can be
made in their favor. While the agencies are not likely to
suffer in terms of funding, such actions induce more
conflict in the process and tend to strain relationships
with the reviewing bodies. Constraints may also operate
in the opposite direction. In some cases agencies may
actually be directed to *expand* more rapidly than they
would choose to themselves. There are numerous cases of
agency budget expansion imposed by the President or
Congress.

Assertiveness: The Case of ACTION

The experience of ACTION (the agency including the
Peace Corps, VISTA, and other domestic volunteer
programs) in the preparation of their FY 1977 requests is
an enlightening example of strategic maneuvering in the
face of difficult external constraints. ACTION in reality
faced a dual problem, since its foreign operations (Peace
Corps) were included under a different appropriations bill
than its domestic operations. The early 1970s were a
period of declining appropriations for ACTION under the
Nixon Administration. Yet the agency was staffed by
young, dedicated, mission-oriented bureaucrats,
including many ex-volunteers. The Peace Corps has a
"five-year" rule; no employee can work for the agency
more than five years, to insure that they will not become
entrenched and self-preserving in orientation. Of the

ACTION agencies, the Peace Corps had the most severe budgetary problems, lacking a domestic constituency and having a difficult job in demonstrating tangible evidence of accomplishment (how do you measure international good will?). The Peace Corps frequently operated on a continuing resolution since Congress had historically been slow in passing foreign aid appropriations. They also suffered from the general antagonism towards foreign aid programs in Congress. When OMB guidelines for FY 1977 were issued in the summer of 1975, President Ford's priorities of reducing federal spending meant that ACTION stood to absorb major cuts. But that year ACTION ignored guidelines and asked for an increase of some 30 percent above the previous year.

Why did the agency administrators decide to be particularly assertive in the face of severe executive branch constraints?

They felt their programs had a stronger base of support in Congress than ever before. Volunteer programs for the elderly and retired businessmen were very popular, and congressional committees recognized this. Even the Peace Corps, for years a target of foreign aid opponent Representative Otto Passman (D-La.), perceived a much more supportive environment in Congress with a decline in Passman's vehement opposition.

ACTION felt its programs were important and effective enough to justify a substantial increase after some years of gradual decline. Because of the volunteer nature of their programs, cost efficiency was high and overhead had been kept down. The argument was used that in a period of concern for getting more benefits from federal dollars, Ford's goal of efficiency would be promoted by *increasing* their budget.

Agency officials perceived that there was little to lose in submitting a higher request. ACTION officials felt no greater budget reductions could result by acceding to the guidelines, and felt they could only help themselves. While this strategy tended to strain relationships with the OMB examiner because the request was considered so far out of line, the examiner evidenced a basic sympathy for the agency position in a year of severe cutbacks.

ACTION was willing to go to the President. When the OMB slashed their request, the director asked for and received a direct appeal to the President. ACTION was the smallest agency to appeal to Ford in 1975, and they selected the cut they felt was most unfair. The President restored the cut as they had hoped.

The general budgetary assertiveness of the agency carried through the appropriations process in 1976. The cuts imposed by the OMB were partially restored by Congress; the agency actually reversed the pattern of decline. ACTION had accurately gauged its base of support in Congress and was able through an assertive strategy to improve its budgetary position.

The Limits of Assertiveness: The Case of HEW

The budgetary situation for the huge Department of Health, Education, and Welfare presents a counterpoint to the case of relatively small ACTION. The growth of multiyear spending commitments places limitations on priority-level decisions. This trend has had a severe impact on certain agencies as well, and it can be particularly troublesome for agencies within departments whose budgets are heavily "uncontrollable," such as HEW. Between 1974 and 1976, the President proposed to limit HEW's outlay increase to $23.5 billion (from $89.8 billion to $113.4 billion). But the automatic growth in the uncontrollable portion alone of HEW's budget was estimated to be $30 billion. HEW administrators had to decide how to cut back total expenditures by $6.5 billion to meet the presidential limits. Controllable HEW programs totalled only $5.4 billion in 1974, less than the cut mandated by the President. The resulting pinch on HEW agencies with controllable programs is obvious. The only feasible solution was to hold the line on controllable programs such as the activities of the National Institutes of Health (NIH) and to propose reductions in the uncontrollables — Social Security, medicare, medicaid, etc. The only other alternative would be to reduce or eliminate some of the controllable programs. The

Brookings Institution suggests that such cases are examples of "hidden cuts in the budget."[24] While the overall totals for HEW increased by $23.5 billion, prior spending commitments forced cuts in other agency's budgets.

The constraints of prior spending decisions further complicate the problems agencies face in making budget requests and estimates and may severely limit the strategic considerations they can apply. Congress has resisted cuts in uncontrollables and in the previous case allowed the HEW budget to increase more than the President's guidelines, but it still leaves no cushion for the agencies. Between 1967 and 1976, the controllable portion of HEW's programs was reduced from $7 billion to $6.5 billion. While income maintenance payments expanded rapidly, this was partially at the expense of other health and education services.

One of the results of the changes in the composition and controllability of the budget is changes in the nature of the budget base as described earlier. Traditional explanations were founded on agencies' protecting their base and adding to it. As the base is recognized as consisting of different components, agencies are faced with a different decision-making situation. As one writer suggested, it has become necessary to mortgage the base to pay for the uncontrollables.[25]

Agencies with an exceptionally high proportion of their budget classified as uncontrollable have at least one strategy available to them. They can play the "shortfall game" — underestimate the costs of the mandatory expenditures, leaving more money available for the controllable programs.[26] Estimating entitlement outlays is an imprecise business at best, and subject to normal errors of trying to judge how many people will be eligible and will apply. Working within the general guidelines given by OMB, an administrator might assume a slightly more optimistic outlook for the economy, "lowball" estimates for a program, and shift the difference into other programs. If the actual expenditures during the fiscal year run above what was budgeted, Congress has no alternative but to make up the difference in a supplemental appropriation. Like all the budget games, this must be approached very carefully and involves some risks. But faced with extreme budget constraints, a department like HEW may attempt to employ whatever devices they can think of to increase their budget.

The process of agency request and budget review by departments, the OMB, and Congress is characterized by a variety of games, strategies, and behavioral roles. Agencies tend to be advocates but may choose assertive or moderate strategies. In balancing the extremes in their budget, departments act as both advocate and guardian in protecting their larger interests in budgetary politics. The OMB tends to mechanically reduce budget requests in assembling the executive budget to conform to presidential priorities. The growth of prior-year commitments tends to restrict short-run discretion for all participants, particularly in social welfare policy.

Agencies are strategic actors in quest of dollars to fund their programs, and the calculation of what to request is approached accordingly. After accounting for mandatory changes and increases necessary to keep up with inflation, agencies usually seek expansion in their programs. Some are assertive in pursuit of their goals while others are content to get by. Whatever strategies an agency chooses, they must be attuned to the changing political environment and adaptable to new situations if they are to continue to be successful.

FOOTNOTES

[1]See Randall B. Ripley and Grace A. Franklin, eds., *Policy-Making in the Federal Executive Branch* (New York: Free Press, 1975), for a discussion of these different variables.

[2]Anthony Downs, *Inside Bureaucracy* (Boston: Little, Brown, 1967).

[3]Otto Davis, Michael Dempster, and Aaron Wildavsky, "A Theory of the Budgetary Process," *American Political Science Review* 60 (September 1966): 529, "Towards a Predictive Theory of Government Expenditure: U.S. Domestic Appropriations," *British Journal of Political Science* 4, 4 (October 1974): 419-452, and "On the Process of Budgeting II: An Empirical Study of Congressional Appropriations," in *Studies in Budgeting,* Byrne et al., ed. (Amsterdam: North Holland Publishers, 1971).

[4]John Wanat, "The Bases of Budgetary Incrementalism," *American Political Science Review* 68 (September 1974): 1221-1228.

104   BUDGETARY POLITICS

[5]Aaron Wildavsky, *The Politics of the Budgetary Process* (Boston: Little, Brown, 1964), p. 21.

[6]*Ibid.,* p. 66.

[7]Leonard Reed, "The Budget Game and How to Win It," *Washington Monthly,* January 1979, pp. 24-33.

[8]*Ibid.,* p. 30.

[9]Committee on Appropriations, Subcommittee on HUD and Independent Offices, U.S. House of Representatives, *Hearings, National Aeronautics and Space Administration,* 94th Congress, 2nd session, February 18, 1976, p. 144.

[10]Wildavsky, chapter 3.

[11]*Ibid.,* p. 118.

[12]Quoted in Wildavsky, p. 112.

[13]*Ibid.,* p. 74-78.

[14]*Ibid.,* p. 76.

[15]It is difficult to assign a specific dividing point between assertive and moderate requests. While 10 percent has been suggested, assertiveness is relative to inflation and overall decisions on totals. Whether one considers 10 percent or 25 percent to represent assertiveness, the conclusion that a range of increases are requested still holds.

[16]Aaron Wildavsky, *Budgeting* (Boston: Little, Brown, 1975), p. 24.

[17]Lance T. LeLoup, "Agency Policy Actions: Determinants of Nonincremental Change," in Ripley and Franklin, chapter 5, and "Explaining Agency Appropriations Change, Success, and Legislative Support: A Comparative Study of Agency Budget Determination" (Ph.D. diss., Ohio State University, 1973), Ira Sharkansky, "Agency Requests, Gubernatorial Support and Budget Success in State Legislatures," *American Political Science Review* 62 (December 1968): 1222, and "Four Agencies and an Appropriations Subcommittee: A Comparative Study of Budget Strategies," *Midwest Journal of Political Science,* August 1965, pp. 254-281.

[18]The data for Department of Agriculture requests are the result of diligent research work by William Moreland. See William Moreland, "The Limits of Policy Discretion: A Non-Incremental Time-Series Analysis of Agency Appropriations" (Ph.D. diss., Ohio State University, 1973), and Lance T. LeLoup and William Moreland, "Agency Strategies and Executive Review: The Hidden Politics of Budgeting," *Public Administration Review,* Vol. X, no. 4 (May/June 1978): pp. 232-239.

[19]One of the problems with previous research on agency budgeting strategies is that initial agency requests to the department or OMB are usually not available; the OMB prohibits agencies and departments from disclosing their initial request figures. As a result, it has been necessary to assume that the figures included in the President's budget reflect agency goals and desires. But as the following analysis shows, the most significant modification of agency estimates takes place in the executive branch before a figure is sent to Congress.

[20]Although the OMB was the BOB for all but the last year of the data, to avoid confusion the agency is referred to by its present name, the Office of Management and Budget.

[21]Data for agency requests to DOA, DOA requests to OMB, requests in the President's budget, and final appropriation were collected for 36 DOA agencies that were in existence at least three years between 1946 and 1971.

[22]Sharkansky, "Four Agencies."

[23]LeLoup, "Agency Policy Actions."

[24]This discussion is based on Barry H. Blechman, Edward M. Gramlich, and Robert M. Hartman, *Setting National Priorities: The 1976 Budget* (Washington, D.C.: Brookings Institution, 1975), pp. 76-81.

[25]Allen Schick, "The Budget Bureau That Was: Thoughts on the Rise, Decline, and Future of a Presidential Agency," *Law and Contemporary Problems* 35, no. 3 (Summer 1970), reprinted in Aaron Wildavsky, *Perspectives on the Presidency* (Boston: Little, Brown, 1975), pp. 339-360.

[26]Reed, "Budget Game."

OMB

We simply carry out the wishes of the President.
—OMB official
*It is the intention of OMB to operate the Government
as it desires.*
—A member of the U.S. House*

$\mathbf{A}$ s the central budgeting organization in the
executive branch, the Office of Management and Budget
is an influential actor in its own right. In addition to the
actual preparation of the massive budget documents,
OMB examiners monitor agency budgeting on a year-
round basis, engage in planning and management
activities, and perform a central clearance function to
insure that all agency legislation is consistent with the
President's "program." The complexity and scope of the
federal government make it possible for the President to

be personally involved in only a few program and operations decisions. This inevitably leaves the OMB with a great deal of discretion in interpreting the President's priorities and in working out the details of the executive budget. This discretion is the subject of some resentment and opposition both from the agencies and from Congress. It also makes the OMB an important object of scrutiny in the study of budgetary politics.

In 1921 the Congress passed the Budget and Accounting Act, which created the Bureau of the Budget (BOB) and mandated a single annual executive budget. President Roosevelt strengthened his influence over the budget in 1939 when the Bureau of the Budget was transferred from the Treasury to the new Executive Office of the President. From 1939 to 1969 the BOB evolved to a highly influential status in national policy making.

In 1970 the Bureau of the Budget was replaced by the Office of Management and Budget under a reorganization plan proposed by President Nixon and approved by Congress. The new OMB was to emphasize executive management; a new organization, the Domestic Council, was to assume major responsibility for policy formulation.

During its existence, the Bureau of the Budget enjoyed a reputation as a highly professional agency of dedication and integrity. While OMB officials today are just as professional and dedicated as ever, they have suffered from an image problem, particularly with Congress. Much of the antagonism can be traced to events during the Nixon Administration that tarnished the image of the OMB. Regardless of some lingering suspicions and attempts to reduce their policy-making role, the OMB is recognized throughout Washington as a potent political force. This general attribution of power to the OMB is not commensurate with their relatively small size — 600 employees, diminutive by today's standards of huge bureaucracies. What does the OMB do with regard to budget, management, and policy making that makes it influential? What happened to the OMB in the 1970s to account for the problems it has encountered?

Roles and Duties

The OMB has primary responsibility for the preparation of the annual executive budget. In performing this role, they serve as a liaison between the President and the rest of the executive branch. In preparing the budget, the OMB monitors agency budgeting and reviews their estimates for future funding needs. The process of review takes place on two levels: a continual review and a periodic review. The continual monitoring process is carried out by budget examiners: OMB officials assigned to certain agencies, a group of agencies, or a specific function in some cases (civil rights activities, for example). The second level of review takes place periodically in the higher echelons of the agency when the director, division chiefs, and branch chiefs, in conjunction with the examiners, review agency proposals.

In addition to budget preparation and review, two other major functions are performed by the OMB. They are responsible for central clearance; all agency legislative proposals must be cleared through them.[1] This is to insure that every proposal is consistent with the President's priorities, and that other agencies affected have an opportunity to express their opinions on legislation before it is submitted. In practice, the legislative clearance function is shared with the White House itself, and the OMB can only imperfectly screen agency proposals. Because of the many proposals and the tiny OMB staff assigned to legislative clearance, nothing approaching a comprehensive legislative review takes place.

Finally, as the name implies, OMB is responsible for efficient management in the executive branch. While the management function was historically a concern of the BOB, the reorganization in 1970 was designed to beef up the ability of the bureau to deal with intergovernmental and interdepartmental problems. A separate management branch was established and a number of new experts were brought in. This remains a most difficult

task, and has posed a number of problems for the OMB,
both internally and externally. While classified as a
separate function, management has been tied to
budgeting through the imposition of management
systems designed to rationalize the budget process.

In adopting the role of guardian, the OMB regularly
reduces agency requests. This is necessitated by the fact
that combined agency estimates always exceed
acceptable ceilings and by the perception by the OMB
that implementing the President's policies means cutting
requests. OMB officials feel that advocacy is outside their
proper responsibility. Budget examiners and other
officials involved in the review process describe their role
as one of paring down agency requests, not adding to
them. As one official said, "I can't remember many cases
where we added on to an estimate. It happens but it's
exceedingly rare." In performing this role, the OMB is
frequently an obstacle to agency goals and desires. The
OMB wields the mightiest sword in budgeting, and the
cuts usually stick. Like the departments, they are
restrained in making cuts, however, since agencies are
not without their own resources or power base. Excessive
cuts can be appealed directly to the President if the agency
feels the OMB has been overzealous in "implementing"
the President's priorities on their budget. A more frequent
recourse for agencies is an appeal to Congress, where
agencies may attempt to get budget cuts restored. While
the Appropriations Committees often make additional
cuts of their own, they may react to excessive OMB cuts
and approve funding greater than requests. This practice
increased notably under Presidents Nixon and Ford.

The OMB must balance presidential priorities with
agency desires. This also entails resolving conflicts
between agencies competing for the same program or
similar programs, and a variety of other potential
disputes. The process of budget review is ultimately one of
mediation in the assignment of dollar totals to agencies.
In the absence of clear policy directions from the White
House, the OMB acts semiautonomously in this role.

In describing budget formulation, it is important to
recognize the routines of the process.[2] Budgetary actors,

the OMB in particular, routinize their activities and tend to develop stable relationships. While previous studies of budgeting have tended to overemphasize the stability of routines and neglect the non-routine sources of change, this remains an important characteristic. Because the budget is so complex, methodical procedures and patterns of interaction help simplify the normal process of decision making. This regularity leaves more room to maneuver in dealing with the special problems, salient new issues, and non-routine decisions which arise every year.

Formulation of the Executive Budget

Spring Preview

The process of budget review begins some nine months before the budget is submitted to Congress in January and eighteen months before the start of the fiscal year on October 1. (Appendix A summarizes the process of formulating the executive budget.) In the months of March through June, the OMB conducts the Spring Preview. Agencies are required to review their ongoing programs, plans for new activities, and major issues, as well as their compliance with OMB guidelines on management and program evaluation. The Spring Preview is largely unstructured, emphasizing large agencies rather than an across-the-board review of all agencies. It is focused primarily on policy issues rather than agencies *per se* and is designed to prepare OMB for the major budgetary issues that will arise in the autumn. There are usually no White House representatives present during the round-table discussions, which include budget examiners, OMB leaders, and agency officials.

The President establishes broad priorities and emphases at this stage, and reviews the condition of the economy. The OMB assists the Council of Economic Advisers and the Treasury in developing "economic assumptions," predictions of the trends in the economy for the next fiscal year. Since the economy has shown a tendency to be volatile over a period of months, let alone years, these assumptions are early "guesstimates" and are constantly revised throughout the formulation stage. In partial reaction to the economic turmoil of the 1970s, the overview session on the state of the economy was switched from the beginning of Spring Preview in March to the end of the process in June.

The months of spring are the most relaxed at the OMB; the frantic pace of budget preparation that occurs in the autumn is lacking. It provides the OMB leadership with a greater opportunity to innovate, to move in its own directions. Certain management techniques or legislative issues may be stressed; later in the process, these are relegated to a position of secondary importance. The OMB reports to the President at the conclusion of Spring Preview on general policy and major issues for the coming budget.

Agency Guidelines and Preparation of Estimates

Beginning in June, the OMB sends out guidelines to the agencies for budget preparation. This includes not only revisions to the technical procedures, but policy guidelines and specific ceilings for budget requests.[3] Again, all agencies are not treated equally. Smaller agencies are likely to receive only general instructions while the larger agencies are likely to receive more specific instructions on a spending ceiling and individual program totals. The Defense Department and several other agencies dealing with intelligence and national security do not receive written guidelines; by mutual agreement, their guidelines are given orally, not put in writing. During the summer, the OMB provides technical assistance to the agencies in the preparation of their estimates, and the individual budget examiners continue the process of oversight.

Fall Review

By September 15 most of the agencies are required to submit their formal estimates to the OMB. A few agencies may have until October 15 to submit their estimates. The agencies submit extensive materials. Besides providing specific requests for funds in the coming year, they provide background material (elegantly justifying their activities), five-year projections, special studies, cost-efficiency data, and a variety of supporting documents. The Fall Review is the most intensive period of OMB activity, referred to as "budget season."

The budget examiners play a crucial role in reviewing agency estimates. They are instrumental in the preliminary review and recommendations for funding. The examiners attempt to dig deeper into the program requests, seeking clarification and in some cases compiling independent background data. After the submission by the agencies in September or October, the budget examiners hold a series of separate meetings with the agency budget officials. One examiner reported preparing over 300 specific questions on the estimates for the agency to answer. After these meetings with the agency, the budget examiners begin to draft the initial memoranda for the Director's Review. This document contains notification of major changes in policy, staffing projections, and program breakdowns, as well as program support data. For the major agencies, the initial memoranda may be prepared in conjunction with an oral review where the budget examiners meet with higher level OMB officials and discusses the details of the agency program requests.

From November 1 to December 1 the Director's Review takes place. It consists of a number of sessions to arrive at the final figures for the budget. Unlike the intra-OMB sessions in the spring, these meetings often include members of the White House staff, Council of Economic Advisers, National Security Council, and other presidential advisers. At the same time as the Director's Review, OMB assists in arriving at a final set of economic assumptions and makes appropriate modifications in the totals.

During the fall budget season, the participation of the President is at the greatest. Although he has already expressed his general wishes, he may participate in deciding allocations between programs and must make last-minute decisions on totals. In December, after the completion of the Director's Review, the President must approve the OMB recommendations. Agencies are notified of the OMB allowances on requests to be included in the President's budget. At this time, agencies must revise their estimates to conform to the OMB decisions, although they may attempt to appeal directly to the President.

As the calendar of the budget formulation moves into late fall, the mechanical imperatives of the process begin to take over. The budget-preparation division of the OMB must have enough time to compile the thousands of pages of information that make up the budget documents. By late December, the final decisions must be made so that the budget can be printed in time for submission to Congress. The final job of OMB in the preparation stage is to draft the President's budget message, prepare the actual documents, and send them to the printing office.

Agencies and the OMB

While the process of budget review and preparation appears to be a formal one, the informal relations between the OMB and the agencies are equally significant. Budget examiners maintain continual contact with the agencies. As one examiner described it,

> A good budget examiner should never be surprised by anything the agency might submit or present in the formal process. Our relationship with the agency is less structured than it may appear in the sense that contact is maintained with the agency 365 days a year. You have to know the details. ... During oral review, a good budget examiner would not have to rely solely on information provided by the agency.

If the bulk of OMB-agency contact is informal, it becomes increasingly formal as one moves up the OMB hierarchy and towards the end of the formulation process. And in spite of the frequent contact, budget examiners are at a disadvantage, particularly when dealing with huge departments and agencies. For example, only four examiners are responsible for monitoring all the various activities of Housing and Urban Development (HUD). One examiner is assigned to the Peace Corps, domestic volunteer programs, and the Appalachian Regional Commission. In spite of their year-round efforts, it is impossible for the examiners to know their part of the budget nearly as well as agency officials know it. Besides informational advantages, agency budget officials do not hesitate to make a strong case with the budget examiners or to seek changes in their funding bases. As one examiner described it:

> NASA is fair with us but they're hard-hitting and tough. For example, they will point out that in constant dollars their budget has fallen from over $12 billion in the mid-1960s to $3 billion today. They have attempted to get the space shuttle on a multiyear funding basis, because it eats up more and more of their budget every year. They objected strenuously when we refused but we simply can't do it.

The range of contacts between agencies and the OMB is substantial. Some agencies encourage free contact with the OMB; others insist that official agency channels (the budget officer and staff) be used in dealing with OMB.[4] Examiners may attempt to bypass the agency budget office to get more accurate program information:

> In working with this department our major and normal channel should be the budget office. But we have mixed success in working with them. Their examiners are unlike ours; they don't deal with policy. They are only accountants, so I go directly to the bureau personnel. I try to keep the department informed of what I am doing.[5]

Budget examiners acknowledge and expect the gamesmanship and strategies of agencies. They know that agencies are trying to put their best foot forward and will pad their requests on occasion. Examiners attempt to deal with these strategies by seeking and developing their own independent sources of information. But there are severe limits to the extent they are capable of doing this. A more practical alternative is for the examiners to scrutinize the data and figures presented by the agency, attempting to draw their *own* conclusions, not those suggested by the agency. One budget examiner explained it like this:

> I look carefully for any changes in patterns. These shifts provide clues to important questions that may have been ignored in the discussions. Changes may indicate a legitimate shift in emphasis in programs, or that the Director wants to save some money to redecorate his office. I have had both happen.

The relationship between the OMB examiner and the agency often depends on whether examiners are perceived as sympathetic or antagonistic. Most often the examiners try to remain neutral and resist pressures to be co-opted. Examiners are usually viewed with a cautious respect and dealings are forthright. A few are seen as nit-pickers, others excessively critical, and personality conflicts are sometimes cited as a source of problems.

Regardless of the personal orientations of the budget examiners and their relationships with agencies, as representatives of the President they maintain the role of budget cutter. This results in an institutional conflict in the role orientations of the examiners and agencies. In good years, when there is a healthy economy and enough money to go around, the relationship is more congenial. As economic conditions deteriorate and presidential priorities call for spending reductions, the relationship becomes strained and morale suffers for both. One examiner stated,

> It's tougher for the examiners than the agencies in a cut-back year. We have to work harder, the negotiations get tougher and it's simply more difficult for everybody involved.

Agency officials tend to disagree; they become particularly upset when they perceive that Congress will surely reject the cuts the OMB and President are requesting. As one department budget officer observed,

> It gets reduced to a meaningless exercise. Nobody is taking it very seriously. We're not preparing a budget that Congress will adopt, we're preparing what the Administration will send up for Congress to add on to.[6]

The OMB and Politics

OMB Leadership

The director of the OMB can affect certain activities, but in other areas the process carries on regardless of the leadership. The OMB is headed by a director and a deputy director; since 1974 these appointments have required Senate confirmation. This change was symptomatic of the general congressional mistrust of the OMB and their desire to assert greater control after the Nixon years. In addition to the two top spots, there are four associate directors: economics and government; natural resources, energy and science; national security and international affairs; and human and community affairs.

Opportunities for leadership appear most promising during the spring and summer. As one branch chief related:

> From January until September the Director can have a great deal of influence. The process is more dynamic, more subject to improvisation and innovation on the part of the leadership. By fall the sheer necessity of having to compile a budget requires that the process oriented staff in the OMB dominates.

OMB directors tend to push the issues and themes the President thinks are important. This may take the form of particular issues or management techniques. Roy Ash, director under Nixon, initiated Management by Objective (MBO) during his tenure. James Lynn, director under Ford, let MBO drift but emphasized program evaluation. Under Carter, Bert Lance and James McIntyre attempted to implement Zero Base Budgeting, a reform the President had promised during his campaign.

As in any organization, the agency leadership affects the morale and performance of the agency. OMB had its leadership problems during the 1970s. Roy Ash was not particularly well liked by OMB staff and was seen as a pawn of the President. He was blamed for much of the criticism OMB was receiving from Congress. OMB directors are not usually front-page material, but in the first year of the Carter Administration, Bert Lance became a major embarrassment to the President, providing the first hint of scandal in the Administration. Lance, a close personal friend of Carter's from his home state of Georgia, had been a banker. Soon after his appointment and confirmation, a series of allegations concerning shady and illegal banking practices appeared in the press. Congressional hearings were held as the case against Lance grew, but the President refused to seek his resignation until the bitter end. The Lance incident not only damaged the President, but it continued the internal problems in OMB that had not been solved by Lynn during the Ford Administration. Carter appointed James McIntyre, another Georgian, as acting director and then director.

McIntyre was taken lightly when first appointed. *Newsweek* suggested that he had been written off as a "mere technician in the kindest appraisals — and as a timorous, provincial lightweight in the far more common gossip of the capital."[7] After several years on the job, however, McIntyre appeared to have won the respect of the President and many of his detractors.

The OMB director is not only the head of the agency but the top adviser to the President on budget matters. He must usually handle much of the heat from the executive branch, and the job is not always pleasant. It was reported that in McIntyre's first year as director, HUD Secretary Patricia Harris blistered the air with insults during their meeting. "She called him a white racist oppressor, a Fascist, a heartless monster — you name it — and all he said was, 'Now, Pat, you know you don't mean all that.' "[8] By relieving Carter of much of the detail, McIntyre, like some OMB directors before him, became a powerful man in Washington.

The Politicization of OMB

The Budget Office has always been political to the extent that it reflected the priorities and ideology of a particular President. Under Eisenhower, Kennedy, and Johnson the Bureau of the Budget was accused of partisanship, and was seen as being too powerful. Since the budget is a political document, such a reaction may be inevitable. The BOB and OMB have had to make hard choices and interpretations, step on some toes, and block the plans of numerous agencies and congressmen. The Congress has always been leery of the Budget Office; OMB officials agree that observers on Capitol Hill see them as much more powerful than they really are. The problems grew acute, however, when Nixon took over the White House in 1969. Nixon wanted a tough, loyal organization to do his bidding. The OMB became closely identified with Nixon's aggrandizement of power into the presidency at the expense of Congress. All this was accentuated by the partisan differences between the two branches and caused basic changes in the OMB itself.

OMB became not only an arm of the presidency but an agent of a particular President, "its operations increasingly dominated by short-term political appointees who had little understanding, appreciation, or patience for Congress as a co-equal branch."[9] The increase of political appointees reduced the prestige and influence of career civil servants in the agency. During the 1970s, turnover was high among senior staff. The new layer of associate directors, brought in from the outside, reduced the access of experienced career bureaucrats to the OMB leadership. While the reorganization did not succeed in reducing OMB's policy role, it did succeed in making the agency more political.

Part of the problem was the close identification of the OMB with the Nixon impoundment abuses (see Chapter 6). Although the reorganization of the Bureau of the Budget into the OMB was finally approved by Congress, there was substantial opposition. Some members of Congress felt they would have even less oversight control over the OMB. They believed the reorganization would centralize the executive branch around Nixon and further diminish their influence in domestic policy. Nixon's increasing willingness to impound money appropriated by Congress for domestic programs only exacerbated fears. However, after a vigorous lobbying campaign, Nixon was successful in gaining congressional approval of his plan.[10]

The desire to curb the President's budgetary powers continued to grow. Further fueling the discontent was Nixon's appointment of Roy Ash as director. Ash was president of Litton Industries, a multibillion-dollar defense contractor. This led Congress to pass a law requiring a Senate confirmation of the director and deputy director. The first bill allowed the Congress to remove Ash and Fredric Malek, then deputy director, and confirm the subsequent appointments. Nixon vetoed the bill on the grounds that it interfered with his removal power. The veto was sustained. Although it was too late as far as Ash and Malek were concerned, the revised legislation required that future appointees would have to be confirmed.

The tumultuous end of the Nixon Administration and the congressional Budget and Impoundment Control Act left the OMB in a tenuous position with lingering disfavor in Congress. The situation improved under Carter and Ford, but problems remain. While the OMB feels that they have made every effort at cooperating with Congress in the new budget procedures, they resist the additional congressional demands for information. As one OMB official remarked:

> Our role is to serve the President, not to be an information service for Congress. Some of their expectations and requests are unreasonable and threaten to alter our primary role as an arm of the executive branch.

While congressional leaders have not objected to the technical cooperation they have received, both Senator Muskie, chairman of the Senate Budget Committee, and Representative Adams, former chairman of the House Budget Committee, accused the OMB of "playing politics" with the budget totals to make Ford's budget look smaller than it actually was. Adams opened up the House Budget Committee hearings on the first budget resolution in March of 1976 by accusing the OMB of underreporting expenditures and overreporting revenues.[11]

The Office of Management and Budget remains an institution more politicized than its predecessor. While the storms of controversy that broke during the Nixon Administration have largely subsided, a residue of suspicion and resentment still lingers in Congress. On the whole, despite the Lance controversy, the image of OMB has improved under Carter. There have been fewer complaints from Congress as they have developed their own sources of budgetary information in the Congressional Budget Office and Budget Committees staffs. OMB has played an important role in keeping budget totals down for Carter, in implementing ZBB, and what little executive-branch reorganization has taken place.

By the end of the Nixon Administration, observers were noting the fundamental changes in OMB and its relationship to the President. Hugh Heclo described the declines in morale, increase in turnover, and changes in the relationship of the director to the President. Heclo commented that "there has been a fundamental shift in OMB's role away from wholesaling advice to the presidency towards retailing policy to outsiders."[12] Given the decline in visibility of OMB under McIntyre, and the closer working relationship with the President, it may be that the OMB is retreating from its highly politicized position of the early 1970s back to wholesaling advice to the President.

The OMB is primarily concerned with program-level budgeting decisions. In the annual review process, they are responsible for making a variety of decisions on the level of funding the agencies and their programs to be recommended to Congress by the President. In terms of the daily operations of agencies, the OMB plays an important role in the obligation of funds and monitoring agency spending.

In the interactive process of budgeting, the OMB is involved with both "top-down" and "bottom-up" decision making. The budget is formulated by aggregating the thousands of activities, programs, and agency requests into a whole. At the same time, priority decisions made by the President establish parameters for the totals to be determined, and the appropriate division between functions (although rarely are totals binding until the end). When a concrete ceiling is established by the President, the OMB proceeds to cut the various budget requests by the agencies into a final form that corresponds with the President's priorities. The key to understanding OMB influence is recognition of the limits of presidential control. The practical restrictions on presidential budgeting leave the OMB with considerable discretion.

FOOTNOTES

*Representative Joseph Addabbo (D-New York), as quoted in Joel Havemann, "OMB's New Faces Retain Power, Structure Under Ford," *National Journal,* July 26, 1975, p. 1072.

[1] Richard Neustadt, "Presidency and Legislation: The Growth of Central Clearance," *American Political Science Review* 48 (September 1954): 641-671; and Robert Gilmour, "Central Legislative Clearance: A Revised Perspective," *Public Administration Review* 31 (March/April 1971): 50-158.

[2] Ira Sharkansky, *The Routines of Politics* (New York: Van Nostrand-Reinhold, 1970).

[3] Circular A-11 contains the formal procedures for preparation of agency budget estimates; Office of Management and Budget, *Preparation and Submission of Budget Estimates,* circular no. A-11, rev., June 16, 1975.

[4] James W. Davis and Randall B. Ripley, "The Bureau of the Budget and Executive Branch Agencies," *Journal of Politics* 29 (1967): 749-769, reprinted in *Politics, Programs, and Budgets,* ed., James W. Davis, Jr. (Englewood Cliffs, N.J.: Prentice-Hall, 1969), p. 69.

[5] As quoted in Davis and Ripley, p. 69.

[6] Joel Havemann, "Budget Analysis," *National Journal,* January 31, 1976, p. 130.

[7] *Newsweek,* January 8, 1979, p. 21.

[8] *Ibid.,* p. 30.

[9] Louis Fisher, *Presidential Spending Power* (Princeton: Princeton University Press, 1975), p. 56.

[10] *Ibid.,* pp. 49-51.

[11] Committee on the Budget, U.S. House of Representatives, *Chairman's Recommendations for the First Concurrent Resolution the F/Y 1977 Budget,* 94th Congress, 2nd session., March 23, 1976.

[12] Hugh Heclo, "OMB and the Presidency — The Problem of 'Neutral Competence,' " *Public Interest* 28 (Winter 1975), 89.

The
President †

6

The federal budget is a dry, unfathomable maze of figures and statistics — thicker than a Sears-Roebuck catalogue and duller than a telephone directory.
—Lyndon B. Johnson*
I wish everybody in the country would read the budget.
—Harry S. Truman**

Budgeting confronts the President with both problems and opportunities. Although the budget bears his name as Chief Executive, he is by no means all-powerful in its preparation or execution. On the contrary, there are severe constraints — legal, economic, and political in nature. Because of the bulk and complexity of government, the President can rarely be immersed in the details of budgeting. His involvement centers on the highest levels of decision making. In establishing broad priorities, the President must balance domestic needs, the requisites of economic stabilization, the requirements of national defense, and pressures to curtail the growth of federal spending. Because past decisions carry into the current and future years, most of the budget is beyond the short-run control of the President. In the fragmented arena of budgetary politics, not even the President can impose his will on others; he most negotiate, mediate, and bargain with Congress and the executive branch.

Despite these limitations, the budget process offers the President promising opportunities to achieve his policy goals. The federal budget presents him with an opportunity to affect the economic health of the nation, to develop new programs and modify old ones, and over a period of several years, to make some changes in overall national priorities.

The Problems
of Presidential Budgeting

While the President may wish to initiate new programs, he must attempt to establish budget totals that promote economic stability. Because inflation is a problem that has confronted all modern Presidents, it often means cutting or holding back on spending. Fiscal considerations may dictate that an important new program cannot be funded. There is often conflict between equally deserving agencies and programs for limited budget dollars. The competition often pits defense requirements against demands for social welfare spending.

Public Expectations and Public Relations

All Presidents talk like fiscal conservatives: to be called "tight-fisted" is sweet music to their political ears. But while all Presidents must resist enormous pressure to increase government spending, not all are fiscal conservatives. In fact, most of them love to spend. Part of the tension between goals reflects an inconsistency in public attitudes and expectations. The public abhors a vacuum in the White House; Presidents are expected to provide proposals, policies, and solutions to problems. That usually demands money to fund existing programs and new programs. At the same time, an overwhelming majority of the public believes the budget should be balanced and is concerned with growth in federal expenditures. Voters are opposed to waste and duplication in government programs, paid for with their tax dollars. Presidents talk like fiscal conservatives because the public expects them to, even though at the same time they may be proposing massive new spending initiatives.

At least part of the President's response to budgeting is a public relations response that has proved to be remarkably similar for Republicans and Democrats alike. On one hand, they attempt to provide adequate funding for existing programs and to present new initiatives, even though they may be extremely modest proposals at the start. At the same time, they attempt to project an image of thrift and economy. Budget messages of the past 30 years are consistent in this regard. Although the issues and specific proposals change, the themes are congruent: attending to public problems while simultaneously attempting to hold down expenditures. Although Democrats most frequently are labeled "big spenders," only John Kennedy, in recent times, did not enter the presidency with talk of balanced budgets and holding down expenditures. And he attempted to stress his role as budget cutter at other times. Even Lyndon Johnson, reputedly a big spender, stressed the cuts he made in Kennedy's last budget upon assuming office in late 1963.

On closer inspection, however, the Presidents' goals in budgeting and the importance given to economizing are considerably different than their public exhortations would indicate. After repeated campaign attacks against the spending excesses of the Truman Administration, Eisenhower did not propose a balanced budget in the first year of his administration because he felt compelled to provide enough money to meet domestic and international needs.[1] Although Nixon campaigned against Johnson's excessive spending, in reality he was ambivalent about cutting Johnson's last budget because he harbored the notion that Eisenhower's failure to spend

in 1959-1960 cost him the election against Kennedy.[2]
Johnson's budget cutting in 1963 was overtly political as
later accounts of his decision-making process revealed.
After spending several weeks with Kennedy's budget,
projecting expenditures at $102 billion, Johnson sent a
surprisingly trimmed total request of $97.9 billion to
Congress. At the same time that Johnson was forcing
these painful cuts on the executive branch, he told his
advisers to quit lobbying for higher spending: "I want an
expanding economy, too, and I'd like a budget of $108
billion."[3] President Carter's promise to balance the
budget by the end of his first term was almost as well
publicized as later statements by his administration that
this goal was unlikely to be achieved.

Agencies, Interest Groups, and Congress

In addition to public pressure to economize and balance
the budget, organized interest groups make explicit
demands for greater spending. Presidential budgeting
must not only deal with the general public but with
attentive publics as well. These groups and individuals
are well informed, organized, and vocal. Veterans' groups
and military organizations lobby for greater defense
spending. Mayors, civil rights leaders, and organizations
like the Urban League lobby for more budget funds for
cities. The list and the demands also include business
leaders, bankers, and industrialists who urge less
spending (to promote business confidence) and tax breaks
for corporations (to stimulate the economy).

Some of the most prominent advocates of greater
spending are the agencies and departments of the
executive branch, and the President's Cabinet members.
Although most budget preparation takes place behind
closed doors at OMB, the President receives many direct
appeals for new programs and for more money for old
programs. Despite the fact that the bureaucracy is
supposed to defend the "unity" of the executive-branch
budget, agencies often work with allied interest groups
and their supporters in Congress to put pressure on the
President.

The Congress is a partner in shaping the national
budget but, from the President's perspective, may
represent an obstacle to his taxing and spending goals.

Historically, Congress has tended to trim the President's desires for specific items. With the new budget process implemented in 1975, Congress has sometimes disagreed with the President's fiscal policy and has specified different budget totals. The Appropriations Committees may slash key presidential proposals while approving pork-barrel projects the President feels are unnecessary.

Constraints on the President

Overall, the most significant problem of presidential budgeting is not the conflicting demands or the multitude of actors involved in the process, but the limits on what the President can do in the short run. As we saw in Chapter 3, about 90-95 percent of the budget is locked in a given year.

Perhaps no President felt the pinch of these constraints more than Gerald Ford. A lifelong fiscal conservative, advocate of a balanced budget, and opponent of public-sector expansion, he was confronted with the necessity of the largest budget deficit in history in fiscal 1976. After taking office in August of 1974, Ford announced his goal of balancing the federal budget. Six months later his administration was admitting that a deficit of $60 billion was inevitable. The severity of the recession and its sapping of federal tax collections caused the about-face. The reality of previous commitments was manifested to Ford during the summer and fall of 1975 while the estimates for fiscal 1977 were being prepared. In his initial meetings with Budget Director James Lynn, Ford was "horrified" by the 1977 figures and instructed Lynn to "get those spending numbers down."[4] Although the situation was more dramatic in 1975, such constraints have restricted presidential actions from Truman through Carter.

Another limitation in budgeting is imposed on a new President taking office. Since the outgoing President submits his last budget before the January inauguration of the new President, the incoming Chief Executive does not submit his first budget for a year. It does not take effect until October of the next year, almost two full years after his election. The new President may revise the old budget, distinguishing his priorities from those of his predecessor, but at the more detailed level of budgetary decisions, the

budget of the former President has an impact long after he
has left the White House.

The problems of presidential budgeting are many, and
the potential for frustration is great. Noting the
tremendous growth in uncontrollable spending and the
other limits on presidential discretion, Allen Schick
contends that budgeting is less useful to Presidents than
it once was.

> . . . the budget process tends to operate as a constraint on
> presidential power rather than as an opportunity for the
> development and assertion of presidential policies and
> priorities. Accordingly, contemporary Presidents may find it to
> their advantage to spend comparatively little time on budget
> matters and to insulate themselves from the process.[5]

Closer examination reveals, however, that the
constraints on presidential budgeting are not
significantly different today than they were 25 years ago,
and that there still are compelling reasons for presidential
involvement in the budgetary process.

The Potential
of Presidential Budgeting

Even with annual discretion of only about 5 percent
above or below current policy levels, there is much the
President can accomplish. Larger cuts or increases would
be disruptive to the economy, and would lead to
inefficiencies in programs implemented too quickly. Since
most spending decisions commit dollars for periods of
longer than one year, Presidents have significant
opportunity to impart their priorities over a period of
several years if they act in a consistent fashion. In spite of
the constraints imposed on President Ford in 1975, one
observer described how well the budget reflected the new
President's views:

> The President's fiscal 1977 budget was quintessential Ford. It
> stressed limited economic growth, a restriction on federal
> spending, a cut in taxes, incentives for business, a
> retrenchment in social programs, and an increase for national
> defense.[6]

Presidential complaints about fixed costs and budget
inflexibility are not new to the 1970s. In his memoirs,
Eisenhower described his difficulties in cutting the budget

during his first year in office. Although only 18 percent of outlays were considered uncontrollable (under the current definition) in 1953, another 71 percent were earmarked for national security, foreign aid, and atomic energy — items he considered virtually "uncuttable." This left $8.6 billion, or only 10 percent of all expenditures, to scrutinize for deep cuts. Eisenhower managed to make cuts of about $6 billion, and some eventually came from national defense, but his difficulties were similar to those faced by current Presidents.[7]

Despite the constraints, it would be unwise for Presidents to remove themselves from the budgetary process. Within limits, a President can assert his priorities and begin to implement his goals by proposing changes in taxes and in both controllable and uncontrollable spending.

Budget Preparation

The first thing to remember about the President's role in budget preparation is that, in terms of sheer quantity, about 99 percent of the work is done by the OMB, department, or agency. The President's involvement with details is extremely limited. But the President must approve the recommendations made by OMB that his previous instructions helped to shape. Therefore, the preparation of the executive budget for submission to Congress presents the President with perhaps his greatest opportunity to affect national priorities. It is also at this stage that he faces the most difficult choices in reconciling the many conflicts and competing interests. Presidents consider at least five types of priority-level decisions.

Total Spending This is the most visible number in the budget. Unlike budgetary decisions on programs and operations, these decisions are highly publicized and often take on great importance to Presidents. The pressure to keep spending totals down often leads to gimmicks and budgetary games on the part of the President and the Budget Office. In order to get a tax cut in 1964, Lyndon Johnson felt it was essential that his requests for fiscal 1965 remain under the $100 billion level.[8] This involved some real cuts but also some tricks to make the totals seem smaller. He cynically reassured those who felt the cuts were too severe that once he had the tax bill, he would do what Eisenhower did — talk economy, then spend.[9] Supplemental appropriation requests could be sent up after the 1964 elections.

No President is immune from the temptation to use budgetary gimmicks to keep totals down, although Carter requested $501 billion for fiscal 1979 when a sleight of hand could easily have kept the total below $500 billion. Ford's total requests of $395 billion for fiscal 1977 (after preliminary figures had pegged spending well above $400 billion) was attacked on Capitol Hill as deceptive. The new congressional budget staffs and legislative leaders suggested that the OMB had overestimated revenues and underestimated spending, for political purposes. Upon taking office in 1969, President Nixon cut Johnson's last budget by about $4 billion, but the cuts were described as "largely cosmetic."[10]

Juggling of totals is possible because of the imprecision of priority-level budgeting. Presidents know that when the fiscal year is completed, more than two years after they submit their budget, the totals may be significantly different anyway. In establishing total spending, they attempt to balance economic necessities with program demands *and* make the result look as favorable to them as possible.

Total Revenues and Tax Changes Since the bulk of the tax laws remain the same from one year to the next, Presidents tend to focus on specific changes in tax laws rather than to systematically review the sources of federal revenues. In this regard, working on a tax bill is easier for the President than dealing with an entire budget. It can be presented as a single bill and monitored more closely in Congress. Tax changes are proposed primarily for fiscal purposes but may be integral parts of other policies, such as Ford's proposed tax on gasoline and Carter's energy taxes.

Tax proposals are often tied to spending measures as in 1964. Another case involving President Johnson occurred in 1968, when House Ways and Means Chairman Wilbur Mills insisted that substantial cuts in expenditures would be necessary if Congress was to approve his tax surcharge.[11] Historically, it has been easier for Presidents to get tax cuts than tax increases passed by Congress. As former Budget Director Kermit Gordon explained, "Virtue is so much easier when duty and selfinterest coincide."[12]

Deficit or Surplus Despite the frequency of deficit budgets over the past 30 years, the sanctity of a balanced budget remains intact. Jimmy Carter is simply the latest in a line of successful presidential candidates to learn that a balanced budget is easier to promise than to produce. More important, it is not the ultimate consideration but only one of many important considerations in budgeting. Nonetheless, the reconciliation of revenues and expenditures is of great concern to Presidents. The rare surplus or balanced budget is announced as a sign of prudent management and sound fiscal policy. Deficit budgets are portrayed as necessary evils brought on by recession and essential to economic recovery.

Changes in Expenditure Trends While Presidents cannot pay attention to detailed changes in agencies and programs, they do focus on major trends and on specific proposals which will alter previous trends. In recent years, Presidents have been concerned with the downward trend in defense spending as a proportion of federal outlays, declining from 70 percent in 1950 to 25 percent in the late 1970s. Both Nixon and Ford attempted to reverse the decline in defense spending and, at the same time, to halt the rapid growth in income maintenance programs. While trends of defense versus social spending are the most salient, other trends are important and are highlighted by Presidents when they are perceived to be favorable.

New Programs and Initiatives For all the talk about budget cutting, even the tightest budget has room for new programs and presidential initiatives. Although the condition of the economy and revenue projections may determine the scope of new proposals, adding something new is an integral part of presidential budgeting. In this regard, Presidents may move from the priority level of budgeting to the program level on a very selective basis. The object of this presidential interest may be a "pet" program or highly favored agency. In spite of his primary goal of reducing federal expenditures, Eisenhower proposed major increases in foreign aid and for the U.S. Information Agency. In the economically healthy years of the early and middle 1960s, both Kennedy and Johnson included many major program initiatives in the budget. The demands of the war in Vietnam for more budget dollars curbed the proposal of new programs and the funding of others, but even in restrictive budget years, room for new proposals can be found. Criticizing the big-spending Democrats in Congress, Nixon nonetheless proposed major spending programs such as the family assistance plan and revenue sharing. In spite of Ford's problems in the recession years of 1974-1976, he proposed substantial increases in mass transit, energy research and development, and military spending. At one point, the Ford Administration considered a ten-year, $100 billion program in energy.[13] While President Carter refrained from proposing an expensive new program in national health care, he did offer a limited program with lower start-up costs. Although the difficulties and constraints are real, budget formulation offers a President a meaningful opportunity to affect national policy.

Achieving Budgetary Objectives

In addition to affecting policy through budget preparation, Presidents have subsequent opportunities to pursue their goals in the budgetary process. These include public statements, private lobbying, and a number of formal and informal decisions. Some of the subsequent opportunities for the President to pursue budgetary goals are required by law; others depend on his personal orientation.

State of the Union Address The President's annual January address before a joint session of Congress invariably contains a preview of his budget priorities and proposals. This forum offers him the opportunity to solicit support for his budget not only before Congress but the national television and radio audience as well.

Budget Message Following closely after the State of the Union Address, the President's budget is submitted to Congress in late January or early February. The message accompanying the budget is a partisan statement stressing the (perpetually) difficult choices and how important it is that Congress approve neither more nor less than his requests (for the good of the country). It is a political statement of priorities designed to portray the President's proposals as the only reasonable course, not as an objective invitation to debate national policy alternatives. The budget is released with hoopla and fanfare and usually a press conference where the President and his advisers explain the budget to reporters.

Economic Report of the President Submitted immediately after the budget, the Economic Report is required by the 1946 Employment Act. Prepared by the President's Council of Economic Advisers, this document describes the current state of the economy and more fully explains and justifies the fiscal policies proposed in the budget. It also contains recommendations for the Federal Reserve on proper monetary policy to correspond with the President's fiscal initiatives.

Press Conferences and Special Messages In addition to these statements issued annually by the President, special requests for tax legislation, substantive bills with spending implications, or supplemental appropriations may be sent down to Capitol Hill throughout the year. The President may take this opportunity to chide Congress about its action or inaction on the budget, or to amend his earlier requests. Periodic press conferences provide him with additional opportunities to lobby for his budget proposals. Budget reform has restricted his timing on special requests and messages and regularized the process of changing his initial budget figures.

Budget Updates Since 1975, the President is required by law to update his budget twice during the year, April 10 and July 15.[14] He must also provide Congress with a statement explaining all amendments or revisions to the original proposals made in January. This gives the President an opportunity to react to changing conditions or simply change his mind, but requires that it be done formally, rather than through informal channels or on a piecemeal basis. To some extent these requirements restrict his political maneuverability compared with past practices, although supplemental appropriations may be sent to Congress at any time.

Impoundment Impoundment is refusal by the President to spend what Congress has appropriated.[15] For all practical purposes impoundment, as practiced in the past, has been eliminated, but it remains historically important in the development of presidential budgeting. Impoundment dates back to early Twentieth Century Presidents and has been used by Republicans and Democrats alike. Historically, impoundment of funds was used in a reasonable fashion with only an occasional conflict. Certain appropriations might become unnecessary after being approved by Congress, making it absurd to spend money no longer needed. In 1905, the Anti-deficiency Act was passed to ensure that agencies did not make commitments above their appropriation limit; as amended, this gave the President the authority to establish reserves for contingencies. This was further affirmed in the 1950 Omnibus Appropriation Act, which gave the President the authority to withhold certain funds to effect savings and promote efficient management. Occasionally impoundments were controversial. President Truman impounded $735 million in funds for the air force when Congress appropriated funds for more air force groups than he thought necessary, and he withheld funds for an aircraft carrier.[16] Eisenhower impounded $137 million in procurement funds intended to build the Nike-Zeus missile bomber. President Johnson withheld $1.1 billion in federal highway funds and impounded substantial amounts appropriated for housing, urban development, education, agriculture, health, and welfare.[17] But under the Nixon Administration, impoundment was used and abused to an extent far beyond that of any previous administration.

Upon assuming office, Nixon used impoundment in the name of fiscal integrity to reduce grants for health, urban renewal, and Model Cities.[18] He was actually replacing congressional priorities with his own because at the same time he was proposing new expenditures in defense, space, revenue sharing, and the supersonic transport. This was followed by substantial impoundments of highway and sewer funds; later appropriations for control of water pollution, for housing, and for agriculture were withheld. The OMB underreported funds that had been impounded. Total impoundments are estimated to have been almost $18 billion, but a figure of only $8 billion was reported.[19]

Nixon defended impoundment on constitutional grounds. In response to a number of lawsuits to force the President to release funds, Nixon had his day in court and lost. The courts ruled that Nixon had exceeded his authority in impounding funds and was attempting to dictate his own priorities rather than effect savings and promote efficiency. Congress finally reacted strongly to the Nixon impoundments and passed the Budget and Impoundment Control Act only a month before Nixon's resignation. The new law put strict limits on the ability of a President to refuse to obligate funds appropriated by Congress. The new processes of rescission and deferral have created their own problems under subsequent Presidents, but the practice of impoundment as seen in the Nixon Administration is unlikely to reappear.

Rescission and Deferral The President still has an opportunity to reverse previous decisions and requests. If the President wishes to rescind budget authority (permanently eliminate) provided by Congress, he must send a special message to Congress requesting a rescission. This proposal is automatically rejected unless Congress passes a supporting rescission bill within 45 days. Ford, the first President to operate under these requirements, was uniformly unsuccessful in having proposed rescissions approved. If the President wishes to defer budget authority (temporarily delay spending) approved by Congress, he again must submit a special message to Congress. In contrast to rescission, however, deferrals are automatically accepted unless either house of Congress passes a resolution disapproving it. Deferrals are in effect only until the end of the current fiscal year. President Ford was more successful with deferrals than rescissions, as might be expected from the nature of law.

Veto of Appropriation Bills If the President is dissatisfied with amounts appropriated by Congress, he may veto that particular bill. In the 1970s, Republicans Nixon and Ford both used the veto to block what they considered excessive spending by Congress. Most of the vetos were upheld by Congress, the Democratic majority unable to muster the two-thirds needed to override. Some of the vetos were particularly onerous to Congress. Occasional use of the veto, however, helps minimize large congressional increases over presidential requests. Divided control of Congress and the presidency, the situation in fourteen years between 1952 and 1980, accentuates the partisanship of budgeting and the likelihood of presidential use of the veto.

Lobbying Congress In addition to his public statements, threats, and actual use of the veto, the President attempts to "sell" his proposals in a more positive way. Administration officials testify before the Budget Committees, the Joint Economic Committee, and other congressional panels to explain the President's program. Presidential liaisons attempt to garner support for the President's proposals in a variety of ways. Members of the President's party can be helpful to him, although less so when they are the minority party in Congress. Testifying before the Congress, each agency official is a representative of the President and defender of the "unity" of his budget. However, many agencies do all they can to strengthen their own position with Congress rather than worrying about the sanctity of presidential requests.

Reforming the Budget Process Several Presidents have attempted to eliminate waste, promote long-range planning, and make budgeting more rational by implementing budget reforms. Perhaps the most famous is Lyndon Johnson's initiation of Planning Programming Budgeting (PPB) in 1965. The President mandated that all agencies would use this new system under the guidance of the BOB. The story of the failure of PPB is complex and well told elsewhere,[20] but its initiation indicates a desire of Presidents to improve their control of budgeting. Similarly, under Nixon, Management by Objective (MBO) was implemented in the executive branch. Less ambitious than PPB, it nonetheless fell out of favor in a few years. The most recent presidential reform of the budgetary process was Jimmy Carter's imposition of Zero Base Budgeting (ZBB) in 1977. Claiming success with it in the state of Georgia, Carter promised to implement this new system during the campaign. Like the other reforms, ZBB is no panacea. Nevertheless, proposals for budget reform can be useful to Presidents both from a policy-management perspective, and from a political perspective.

Through a combination of statements and actions, Presidents attempt to support their budgetary priorities subsequent to the formulation and submission of the budget. Their success depends on the makeup of Congress, the political and economic environment, and their own political skills.

The President's Budget Advisers

Because budgets transcend a particular set of issues, budget discussions may arise in a variety of presidential forums such as the Cabinet, domestic-policy staff, and other advisory groups. OMB remains the most important source of budgetary advice for the President, and the budget director is usually the most important budget adviser.

Nixon's reorganization in 1970 was intended to reduce the policy-making role of the OMB. The new Domestic Council was to determine what was to be done; the OMB was to determine *how well* it was done.[21] In spite of this change in name and supposed change in function, the OMB has retained its important policy role. Under Nixon and Ford, the Domestic Council assisted the President in determining overall priorities and specific policy initiatives. As a body, it is closer to the President and deals more directly with day-to-day decision making. The council personnel are not budget experts, however, and must themselves depend on OMB for specific information on budgetary matters.

The importance of the budget director depends on his relationship with the President and on his knowledge and control of the OMB. Most budget directors have had close ties with the President and worked directly with him. Their expertise is essential in helping the President define and make his choices. Presidential support is also important in determining the strength of the budget director within the OMB. Occasionally, the relationship between the budget director and the President has been strained. Such was the case with Budget Director Robert Mayo and President Nixon. Mayo received little support from the President; many of his proposed cuts were not backed up by the White House. He became distant from the President and lost all standing in the White House. By late 1969 he had lost all actual contact with Nixon, receiving instructions from the President through John Ehrlichman.[22] This is an exceptional case; at the other extreme was the relationship between President Carter and his budget director, Bert Lance. Lance was not only a trusted political adviser and confidant of the President but a close personal friend as well. Lance enjoyed the complete confidence of the President and was a key adviser on a variety of foreign and domestic matters. As a newcomer to the OMB, however, Lance was not particularly strong within the agency, and some questions were raised concerning his ability to direct the formulation of the budget. McIntyre, his successor, had better standing within OMB but was not as close to the President.

The budget director is the most important adviser concerning the composition and details of the budget, but in providing fiscal advice he may be overshadowed by other more influential economic advisers. The chairman of the President's Council of Economic Advisers (CEA) and the secretary of the treasury, along with the budget director, form the economic "troika." This threesome meets with the President throughout the year to review economic trends and fiscal policy. With some exceptions, this informal group has played a key advisory role in the administrations of Truman through Carter. Deciding which of the economic advisers is currently most influential within the administration is a favorite game among reporters and can often change from month to month. Under Eisenhower, Treasury Secretary George Humphrey was considered ascendant. Under Kennedy, CEA Chairman Walter Heller was considered more influential than Budget Director Bell or Treasury Secretary Dillon. Under Carter, Budget Director Lance appeared to be dominant; after his resignation, most accounts suggested that Treasury Secretary Blumenthal was more influential than CEA Chairman Charles Schultz or Budget Director McIntyre, until Blumenthal was replaced in the 1979 Cabinet shakeup. Regardless of their individual relationships, the economic troika provides significant direction in determining presidential decisions on budget totals.

Although the Cabinet has declined significantly as an advisory body in the modern presidency, Cabinet members continue to play a key role in budgeting.[23] Some Cabinet members are closer to the President than others and may be part of the inner circle of White House staff that deal with the President on a regular basis. As a body, the Cabinet is an institution with divided loyalty. At the same time that they advise the President, they are department heads concerned with the programs of the bureaucracies under them. Despite good intentions, they have dual responsibilities and perspectives, unlike White House staffers who are responsible only to the President. Their own department budgets are often more important to them than the President's efforts at economizing. Carter learned this quickly after his Cabinet made combined demands that he felt were way out of line and when HUD Secretary Patricia Harris and HEW Secretary Joseph Califano went public with complaints about their budget allocations. Cabinet meetings to discuss the budget are rarely pleasant affairs. In preparing his fiscal 1971 budget, Nixon prevailed upon HUD Secretary George Romney to "voluntarily" accept a 5 percent cut in HUD's budget and announce it at the Cabinet meeting. "Nixon, in the manner of a pastor calling upon the faithful for contributions, challenged the other Cabinet heads to do likewise."[24] Their reluctance suggests that Kermit Gordon's earlier observations about duty and virtue are also operative in these situations.

Cabinet officials, the budget director, the secretary of the treasury, and the chairman of the Council of Economic Advisers assist the President in presenting his budget proposals to Congress and the public. These individuals testify before congressional committees, make speeches across the country, and meet privately with representatives of interest groups. The President sometimes meets personally with groups, but since he usually does not wish to accede to their demands, this task is generally delegated to others.

There is an abundance of budgetary advice available to the President, often too much. The President structures decision making in the way that best suits his personal taste and style. Some prefer to receive formal presentations, gather the data, and retire to make decisions alone. Others are comfortable thrashing out decisions in open sessions. Much of the work can be delegated to others. Presidents not only choose how they will formulate their budget decisions but also choose their own level of direct personal involvement in the process.

Presidential Involvement in Budgeting

It is worth reemphasizing that the incredible number of programs, functions, and accounts makes it impossible for the President to master the details of the budget, and that budgeting is only one of many important demands on his time. It is probably accurate to say that even without *any* presidential involvement, the budgetary process could proceed smoothly. Because the budget is perceived as important, however, Presidents choose to become involved. But the degree of involvement can differ significantly.

It is a difficult task to categorize recent Presidents by their involvement in budgeting, but we shall make a necessarily imprecise attempt. Good research materials are hard to come by and secondary works do not focus clearly on this dimension of the presidency. Changes in the political and economic environment may make budgeting a more salient concern in one year than another. There also appears to be a temporal phenomenon — a characteristic activism in the first year in office that transcends other differences across presidencies. Further, presidential activism can be expressed at either the formulation stage or in subsequent actions such as impoundment. Nixon, for example, presents a contradiction in his distaste for budget preparation and his active use of impoundment. Because of the current restrictions on a President's ability to impound funds and restructure appropriations, participation in the formulation of the budget is now a better measure of the degree of a President's interest than participation in the execution stage.

Presidents differ in their personal involvement in budgeting and their active pursuit of budgetary objectives, but in all cases, the budget bears their name as Chief Executive of the United States. Budgeting offers certain opportunities that some Presidents exploit and others ignore. In some instances, their performance in the budgetary process and the decisions they make reflect their leadership and ability to run the country.

It is possible to distinguish between budget *enthusiasts,* who maintain a high level of involvement in budgeting throughout the process; *reluctants,* who generally dislike budgeting and delegate as much as possible; and *periodic activists,* who occasionally become involved with particular phases of the budget or are particularly active in certain years. Before examining the individual Presidents, we shall consider the phenomenon of first-year activism, which is sometimes anomalous with the behavior of a President for the rest of his tenure in office.

First Year Activism

Presidential involvement with budgeting appears to decline over time and be greatest during the first year in office. Even reluctants like Eisenhower and Nixon took an active role in preparing their first budget. Filled with enthusiasm for the new job, the new President tackles the tasks of budgeting with great vigor. Some quickly learn that it is a difficult and often thankless task that can be delegated to others.

On the sixth day of his presidency, Harry S Truman summoned Budget Director Harold Smith to his office and recounts the meeting in his memoirs. Warned by Smith that the budget takes a great deal of time, Truman was not deterred. "I made it clear I would like it, for I had long been accustomed to dealing with facts and figures. I fully intended to plunge into the business of government."[25] After several sessions, even the minutiae of budgeting did not bother Truman. "This was to be my first budget as President, and I hoped to be able to justify every detail it contained."[26]

Similarly, Eisenhower recalled the work of putting together his first budget in 1953. "During the period of budget construction, Director Dodge and I worked together almost daily."[27] Eisenhower described the important decisions he faced, and the difficulty of balancing foreign and domestic spending with his overriding goal of balancing the budget.

Observers of the Kennedy Administration recall a similar activism as Kennedy dealt with his first budget, working closely with his economic troika in devising means for promoting economic recovery. Theodore

Sorensen has described Kennedy's role as budget cutter, scrutinizing every request and encouraging the budget director to say no.[28]

In his memoirs, Lyndon Johnson described his role in preparing budget requests in December of 1963, after only a month in office.

> I worked as hard on that budget as I have ever worked on anything. . . . Day after day I went over that budget with the Cabinet officers, my economic advisers, and the Budget Director. I studied almost every line, nearly every page, until I was dreaming about the budget at night.[29]

Nixon's first budget also has been described in terms of the President's high level of activity. One account described "a fortnight of frantic review" to get the totals down, with the President working "terribly hard" into the early hours of the morning.[30] Ford's great interest in the budget was consistent throughout his short administration. Carter plunged into the job of budget preparation enthusiastically in his first year in office, but his activity in subsequent years declined noticeably.

These apparent similarities in the Presidents' roles in preparing their first budgets actually veil some significant differences. For example, in his first meetings with the budget director, Truman was informed that Roosevelt had given the director a complete delegation of authority because he needed every available moment to deal with international affairs and the conduct of the war. Truman withdrew this delegation, believing that "since the budget involved matters of the highest policy, authority should properly be exercised by the President."[31] In contrast, Eisenhower delegated much of the budget-cutting authority to the budget director, even in his first year. He approved a memo that allowed the director to short-circuit direct agency appeals to the President, making it clear that Dodge's authority to cut was final with Eisenhower.[32]

The Reluctants: Eisenhower and Nixon

Of the last seven Presidents, Eisenhower and Nixon appear to have been the most reluctant to take a direct, active role in budget preparation. While neither felt the budget was unimportant, neither saw the tedious job of formulation as the main vehicle for achieving their policy goals. Eisenhower's delegation of authority in budgeting is consistent with his actions in other areas and with his generally passive decision-making style.[33] At one point in his second term, Eisenhower grew impatient with the continuing questions of his secretary of defense about the defense budget. Eisenhower finally admonished him that the defense budget was his job, not the President's, and not to bother him further about it.[34] In general he delegated the chores of budgeting to the Cabinet officers and the professionals in the Bureau of the Budget. Nixon, while more active in his overall style, disliked the conflicts inherent in budgeting. He insisted that the OMB officials directly mediate any executive-branch disputes over budget estimates, and refused to hear direct agency appeals. In spite of reports of his activities in preparing his first budget, others suggested that he felt the 40 hours he spent on the 1971 budget were squandered unproductively. Even the impounding of funds was delegated to OMB; he remained as isolated as possible, avoiding direct contacts with those most affected by the actions.

The case of Eisenhower's fiscal 1958 budget is instructive in demonstrating some of the pitfalls that may await a reluctant. The budget requests of $72 billion sent to Congress by President Eisenhower in January 1957 represented the more progressive trends of "modern Republicanism." Included were new initiatives in welfare, school aid, and defense. On the same day that Eisenhower presented his budget, Treasury Secretary George Humphrey was telling reporters that the new budget was disastrously excessive, and claimed it would lead to "a depression that will curl your hair."[35] Humphrey suggested that Congress should cut the President's budget wherever possible. This attack on the budget came from a high-ranking Cabinet official and key economic adviser. In an incredible response at a press conference several days later, Eisenhower agreed in principle with Humphrey that the budget should be cut. This political blunder caused confusion in the administration and Congress. In the months that followed, what came to be called "the battle of the budget" developed.[36] Eisenhower showed no inclination to clarify the confusion he had created and instead attempted to formulate a strategy for

dealing with criticism.[37] Even Sherman Adams,
Eisenhower's closest adviser, agreed that Eisenhower's
statements had "gummed up the sapworks."[38]
Congressional Democrats mirthfully exploited the
opportunity to embarrass Eisenhower and show they
could "out-economize" the President.

Richard Neustadt concludes that this was a
particularly costly sequence of events for Eisenhower,
damaging both his standing with the public and his
professional reputation.[39] Eisenhower did not know his
priorities and he did not know his budget. He failed to gain
consensus within his own administration and to control
his advisers. His handling of the 1958 budget led many to
question his leadership.

The Enthusiasts: Truman and Ford

At the other end of the spectrum are the Presidents who
seem to genuinely enjoy the process of budgeting and
maintain an active role throughout their administration.
Both Truman and Ford took a strong personal interest in
their budgets. Both Presidents brought valuable
congressional experience to the White House, Truman
from the famous "Truman Committee" that scrutinized
military expenditures during World War II and Ford from
his service on the House Appropriations Committee. An
avid reader, Truman spent many hours poring over
agency documents and budget figures. At the conclusion
of one of Truman's press conferences on the budget, a
reporter commented that the presentation was very
interesting. Truman replied, "It is interesting to me. That
is one of my hobbies."[40] Although Presidents tend to
exaggerate their knowledge of details (Truman and
Johnson in particular), Truman and Ford appear to have
had much greater familiarity with their budgets than
other Presidents.

Ford's activism in budgeting was a change from his
predecessor's role. One OMB official put it like this:

> Ford has surprised a lot of people. He is the most active
> President since Truman, and the contrast with Nixon is
> tremendous. And he really knows the numbers. He spent weeks
> going over figures that Presidents usually pay no attention to.

In contrast to the reluctants, the enthusiasts take an
active role in resolving agency conflicts and in dealing
directly with department complaints. Truman engaged in

a struggle with Secretary of the Navy James Forrestal over the navy budget. When Forrestal claimed Truman's cuts would endanger national security, Truman, in a "crisp reply," informed him that the cuts would stick, and added the further requirement of a monthly report on actual and projected expenditures that he would personally monitor.[41] In 1975, Ford met personally with representatives of 16 agencies to hear appeals over the final OMB figure. The President acting as the magistrate of final appeals was in sharp contrast to previous practices.

President Ford's presentation of the fiscal 1977 budget is a dramatic counterpoint to Eisenhower's 1958 budget problems. Eisenhower had just been elected by a huge popular landslide while Gerald Ford was an "accidental" President. Appointed by Nixon, he was the first non-elected President. Yet Ford, with his own personal style and abilities as a budget enthusiast, was able to enhance his professional reputation in presenting the fiscal 1977 budget. The contrast between Ford's press conference explaining his budget proposals and Eisenhower's acceptance of criticisms undercutting his own proposals is unmistakable. One observer described the scene of Ford's press conference as follows:

> Ford played the role of impresario, backed by his full Cabinet, top OMB officials and senior White House aides. Standing at a podium, Ford conducted the performance like a virtuoso, with impressive familiarity with intricacies of the budget, rattling off figures and elaborating with detailed analyses. Physical grace may have been missing on the Vail ski slopes, but not here in a forum with which he was more at ease. Only rarely did Ford turn to members of the supporting cast, and then it was less for assistance than for the purpose of getting them into the act.[42]

A majority of Congress disagreed with Ford's fiscal policy and his budget proposals. Despite his lack of success, Ford earned respect among the Washington establishment for his handling of the budget. He knew his priorities and he had done his homework. Despite more general difficulties with his reputation as a leader, he won praise for this performance.

Because Ford was President for only two and a half years, it might be argued that his categorization as an enthusiast may simply reflect the early activism discussed above. While there is less certainty concerning

Ford because of his short tenure, the other factors seem
unmistakably clear. His actions, his attitudes, and his
satisfaction in working with the budget strongly suggest
this categorization.

The Periodic Activists: Kennedy, Johnson, and Carter

The final group of Presidents fall between the other two,
and may demonstrate elements of both. As a group, their
role in budgeting seems to vary by issue and over time.
Kennedy and Johnson are considered active Presidents
but their budget activity was sporadically directed
towards particularly controversial items and programs of
personal interest. For example, Kennedy was concerned
over the rapid growth in agriculture programs,
particularly crop subsidies, that were draining resources
from other priorities. In response, he became personally
involved in the details of the agriculture budget and in
seeking reductions.

Johnson's activism seemed to come earlier in his
administration, when revenues were growing and choices
were easier. He was not afraid to impose his priorities on
his economic and budget advisers. In explaining his goal
of getting expenditures below $100 billion for fiscal 1965,
one participant summed up the meeting: "He pulled all of
us to his way of thinking and left not the slightest doubt
which way he was going . . . With that meeting out of the
way, Johnson took over the budget as his personal
property — cutting, patching, and splicing."[43] In
subsequent budgets, his participation was more limited.
He faced the difficult cuts in his domestic programs in the
late 1960s by relying more on across-the-board cuts than
on selective cuts that demanded more careful scrutiny.

Carter also seems to fit the mixed category. Like others,
his enthusiasm for budgeting seems to have cooled after
he had gone through it once. He was reported to be
"getting over his penchant for trying to decide every
aspect of every program."[44] In 1977, Carter immersed
himself in the preparation of the budget, carefully
scrutinizing 25 briefing books of about 150 pages each,
and encouraging meetings with agency officials to
discuss the budget figures.[45] The decline in activity and
the increased delegation of authority in subsequent years
suggests that Carter fits the category of periodic activist.

Presidential Impact

Why do Presidents differ in their performance in budgeting and what difference does it make? Although the reasons are as diversified as the men who have held the office, it is possible to make some generalizations. A President's involvement in budgeting appears to be related to three main factors:

(1) perception of the budget as important to the achievement of policy goals
(2) affinity for conflict resolution in the executive branch
(3) general decision-making style

Presidential involvement in budgeting has an impact on the parameters of subsequent decisions. The greater the personal involvement of the President, the greater the constraints on subsequent decisions in the bureaucracy. On the other hand, the less active the President's role, the greater the discretion of other actors (White House staff, OMB, agencies) and the more the budget is built from the bottom up by aggregating components, with less reshaping from the top. Despite the limits and constraints on presidential budgeting, consistent personal involvement can have an important impact on national policy and the executive branch.

It should be mentioned that the budget activism is not an unmitigated good. A President may become too involved with small details and minor programs. Delegation of authority is essential, but the proper balance must be found by the individual. Overall, the budget enthusiasts probably have an advantage over the other types, and the reluctants sacrifice opportunities for influence.

Budgeting presents a great many difficult choices for Presidents, and they are severely constrained in what they can do. However, the budget still offers potential for the President to express his political philosophy and pursue his policy goals. At the same time, it is a test of his political skills. Despite the fact that most of the work is delegated to OMB, the President plays a crucial role in agenda setting. Congress, since budget reform, is a more equal partner in budgeting, but the President and the executive branch are clearly still dominant. Over the course of four or eight years, a President can affect the scope and role of the federal government. It is this potential that compels presidential involvement in budgetary politics.

FOOTNOTES

†Portions of this chapter are taken from "The Fiscal Chief: Presidents and Their Budgets," in Steven A. Shull and Lance T. LeLoup, eds., *The Presidency: Studies in Policy Making* (Brunswick, Ohio: King's Court Communications, 1979).

*Lyndon Baines Johnson, *The Vantage Point* (New York: Holt, Rinehart & Winston, 1971), p. 34.

**Harry S Truman, remarks at dedication of GAO Office Building, September 11, 1951, in Louis Koening, *The Truman Administration* (New York: New York University Press, 1956), p. 76.

[1]Dwight D. Eisenhower, *Mandates for Change 1953-1956* (Garden City, N.Y.: Doubleday, 1963), p. 296.

[2]Rowland Evans, Jr., and Robert Novak, *Nixon in the White House* (New York: Random House, 1971), p. 187.

[3]Rowland Evans, Jr., and Robert Novak, *Lyndon Johnson, The Exercise of Power* (New York: New American Library, 1966), p. 392.

[4]Joel Havemann, "Budget Analysis," *National Journal,* January 31, 1976, p. 129.

[5]Allen Schick, "The Budget Bureau That Was: Thoughts on the Rise, Decline, and Future of a Presidential Agency," *Law and Contemporary Problems,* 35 (Summer 1970), reprinted in Aaron Wildavsky, *Perspectives on the Presidency* (Boston: Little, Brown, 1975), p. 342.

[6]Dom Bonafede, "From Bungler to Budget Juggler," *National Journal,* January 31, 1976, p. 152.

[7]Eisenhower, p. 129.

[8]The actual budget was significantly above $100 billion because in 1964 the "administrative" budget excluded trust-fund transactions. The "unified" budget, adopted in 1969, now includes these expenditures.

[9]Evans and Novak, *Johnson,* p. 393.

[10]Evans and Novak, *Nixon,* p. 187.

[11]Johnson, p. 449.

[12]*Ibid.,* p. 440.

[13]John J. Casserly, *The Ford White House* (Boulder: Colorado University Press, 1977), p. 123.

[14]*Budget and Impoundment Control Act* (1974), Public Law 93-344.

[15]Louis Fisher, *Presidential Spending Power* (Princeton: Princeton University Press, 1975), chapters 7 and 8.

[16]*Congressional Quarterly Weekly Reports,* February 3, 1973, p. 213.

[17]*Ibid.*

[18]Fisher, p. 169.

[19]*Ibid.,* p. 172-173.

[20]Allen Schick, "A Death in the Bureaucracy: The Demise of Federal PPB," *Public Administration Review,* 33 (March/April 1973): 146-156.

[21]Office of Management and Budget, Domestic Council, *Public Papers of the Presidents,* 1970, p. 260 (Reorganization Plan no. 2).

[22]Evans and Novak, *Nixon,* p. 187.

[23]Richard Fenno, *The President's Cabinet* (New York: Vintage, 1959).

[24]John Osborne, *The Second Year of the Nixon Watch* (New York: Liveright, 1971), p. 17.

[25]Harry S. Truman, *Years of Decisions: Memoirs,* vol. 1 (Garden City, N.Y.: Doubleday, 1955), p. 59.

[26]*Ibid.,* p. 99.

[27]Eisenhower, p. 296.

[28]Theodore Sorensen, *Kennedy* (New York: Harper & Row, 1965), p. 415.

[29]Johnson, p. 36.

[30]Osborne, p. 18.

[31]Truman, p. 59.

[32]Eisenhower, p. 297.

[33]James David Barber, *The Presidential Character* (Englewood Cliffs, N.J.: Prentice-Hall, 1977).

[34]*Ibid.,* p. 163.

[35]*New York Times,* January 27, 1957.

[36]Evans and Novak, *Johnson,* p. 196.

[37]Robert Branyan, *The Eisenhower Administration 1953-1961,* vol. 2 (New York: Random House, 1971), p. 833.

[38]Evans and Novak, *Johnson,* p. 196.

[39]Richard Neustadt, *Presidential Power* (New York: Wiley & Sons, 1976), chapter 4.

[40]*Public Papers of the President,* January 19, 1946, p. 36.

[41]Richard Haynes, *The Awesome Power* (Baton Rouge: Louisiana State University Press, 1971), p. 120.

[42]Bonafede, p. 152.

[43]Evans and Novak, *Johnson,* pp. 393-394.

[44]*Time,* January 30, 1978, p. 21.

[45]*Ibid.*

Congress:
The Budget
Process

Perhaps the most important aspect of the resolution is the fact it contains the budget of Congress and not that of the President.
—Representative Brock Adams

Throughout the Twentieth Century, the congressional power of the purse slowly eroded. Congressional budget procedures remained static, while the powers of the President and the executive branch increased to match the growing complexity of the federal budget. By the early 1970s the situation had become critical. Nixon freely impounded congressionally approved funds. Congress simmered in frustration, unable to control expenditures, unable to pass appropriations bills on time, unable to establish national priorities.

The situation was finally changed in 1974 when

Congress passed the Budget and Impoundment Control Act. After two years of concerted legislative effort, a bipartisan majority approved legislation for budget reform. It established a mechanism allowing Congress to take an overview of the budget, created two new committees to formulate budget resolutions, and provided a strict timetable for congressional action.

The imbalance between Congress and the presidency had become apparent during the Nixon Administration, even before the impeachment hearings in 1974. During this period Congress moved on a number of fronts to correct the legislative-executive imbalance that had developed in both foreign and domestic policy, including war powers, executive agreements, impoundment, and the budget. But the weaknesses inherent in the authorization-appropriations process were not being discovered for the first time in the 1970s. The deficiencies had been recognized 50 years earlier.

After passing the 1921 Budget and Accounting Act creating the first national budget, it was the intention of Congress to approve the President's budget as a whole. The House and the Senate designated the Appropriations Committees to consider the budget and report a single appropriations bill. But the centralization never came about.[1] Old habits were hard to break, and Congress continued to approve spending measures individually. Congress tried again to centralize consideration of the budget after World War II. The 1946 Legislative Reorganization Act created a Joint Committee on the Budget, composed of all members of the House and Senate Appropriations Committees, the House Ways and Means Committee, and the Senate Finance Committee.[2] The period was marked by sharp partisanship; the Republicans had taken control of Congress in 1946 for the first time in a decade and missed no opportunities to try to embarrass President Truman. Compromise was difficult in this divisive atmosphere.

In 1947, this bulky panel of over 100 members was unable to agree on an overall ceiling for the budget. In 1948, Congress tried again. This time they adopted a budget ceiling, but it was virtually ignored in subsequent spending actions. In 1949, Congress did not even try to pass a budget. The last effort at a legislative budget came in 1950, when the House passed an omnibus appropriations bill. The effort again failed because of late Senate action and the numerous supplemental appropriations that had to be passed later. Serious efforts towards a congressional budget were dead until the 1970s.

The old system was rife with defects. Rapid growth in federal spending in the 1960s and early 1970s was attributed to inadequate congressional control. Unable to take an overview of the budget at any stage of the process, Congress was unable to make fiscal policy. There was no way to consider national priorities, since each bill was considered in isolation from other actions and the merits of one proposal could not be weighed against those of another. There had been a gradual disintegration of the appropriations process causing chaos in the executive branch. With no independent source of budgetary information, Congress had no way to verify OMB estimates. These long-standing defects merged with Nixon's impoundment abuses, crystallizing congressional sentiment to act. After decades of self-imposed paralysis and decline, the congressional budget process was born.

The Congressional Budget Process

Budget Decisions

Like the entire national budget process, the congressional budget process is fragmented and complex. As a decentralized institution, Congress uses committees as the dominant decision-making centers. The committee system allows specialization in substantive policy areas, and the seniority system encourages stability in committees. In analyzing taxing and spending decisions in Congress, committee roles and jurisdictions are key. There are five main types of congressional decisions.

Establishing totals Since 1975, Congress must approve budget totals for revenues, expenditures, and deficit or surplus. The House and Senate Budget Committees recommend two concurrent resolutions specifying these totals, the first in May establishing targets, and the second in September establishing binding totals. The resolutions are in effect for the next fiscal year unless Congress revises its estimates and passes an additional resolution.

Authorizations Before budget authority (usually in the form of appropriations) can be created, a program must be authorized. Legislation setting up an agency or program for a certain period must be passed. It often includes a maximum amount that may be appropriated for the program. The authorizing committees are the standing committees of the House and Senate such as the Education and Labor, Agriculture, and Interior and Insular Affairs Committees in the House, and the Armed Services, Judiciary, and Foreign Relations Committees in the Senate. Entitlement legislation is included in the jurisdiction of certain authorizing committees. Authorizations may be annual, multiyear, or indefinite (permanent), although most programs do not require yearly authorizations.

Appropriations The most familiar and traditional congressional spending action is the passage of appropriations. Once a program is authorized, money may be appropriated creating budget authority and allowing agencies to spend money. The House and Senate Appropriations Committees were considered two of the most powerful committees in Congress and the bulwark of the old budgeting system. The authorization-appropriations process was left intact under the new system, but the Appropriations Committees must now act within the confines of the concurrent resolutions.

Revenues Congress is responsible for raising money as well as spending it. The tax laws are like indefinite spending programs in that they are permanent until Congress changes them. In practice, annual budgeting involves both short-term actions (such as surcharges or rebates) and long-term actions (such as increasing the standard deduction). Revenue decisions fall within the jurisdiction of the House Ways and Means Committee and the Senate Finance Committee. Both committees also have important spending responsibilities as authorizing committees as well.

Oversight The final actions taken by Congress in the budget process involve oversight and program review. Congress attempts to insure that funds are spent in

Table 7-1 Congressional Budgetary Decisions

Levels of Budgeting	Congressional Budget Decision	Key Congressional Actors	Type of Congressional Action	Predominant Duration of Actions
PRIORITY	(1) Budget Totals	Budget Committees	Concurrent Resolutions on the Budget	Annual
	(2) Authorizations	Authorization Committees	Legislative Authorizations, Entitlements	Annual Multiyear Indefinite
PROGRAM	(3) Appropriations	Appropriations Committees	Individual Appropriations Bills	Annual
	(4) Revenues	Ways and Means & Finance Committees	Permanent Tax Code Changes Short-Term Tax Changes	Annual & Indefinite
OPERATION	(5) Oversight & Review	Appropriations Committees — Authorization Committees — CBO — GAO	Authorization Hearings — Program Evaluation — Audits	Periodic

accordance with the intent of Congress. Oversight and review take place in both authorization and appropriations hearings. The Congressional Budget Office (CBO) and the General Accounting Office (GAO) also are involved with oversight and review. CBO engages in budget and program evaluation, while GAO selectively audits certain agencies and issues periodic studies on agency operations.

Table 7-1 summarizes the five types of congressional decisions including the level of budgeting, main participants, type of action, and duration of actions. Most actions are taken at the program level, but since budget reform, the priority level has become increasingly important. The actions taken by individual committees are no longer as isolated from each other as they once were; the congressional budget process has helped to integrate these actions. In the past, the congressional budget was simply made from the bottom up by aggregating individual measures. Although this is still the dominant mode, the Budget Committees and the budget resolutions now provide some shaping of the budget from the top down.

Budget Timetable

Before the passage of the 1974 budget act, the congressional timetable of budgeting was often erratic. By the 1970s, most appropriations bills were not passed by the start of the fiscal year, and agencies had to operate on a continuing resolution at the previous year's level of funding. Many bills were passed as much as six months late; on several occasions, an appropriations bill was never passed.[3] The new timetable was ambitious in setting rigid deadlines for committee actions, but despite the doubts of many skeptics Congress has been able to meet the deadlines. Table 7-2 summarizes the congressional budget timetable.[4]

The process actually begins before the President submits his budget. By January the Office of Management and Budget is required to submit to Congress the current services budget. This document estimates what the budget would look like for the next five years without any changes in programs. This provides Congress with a baseline total to work from and a figure

Table 7-2 Congressional Budget Timetable

Action to be completed	On or before
President submits current services budget to Congress	January
President submits annual budget message to Congress	15 days after Congress meets
Congressional committees make recommendations to Budget Committees	March 15
Congressional Budget Office reports to Budget Committees	April 1
Budget Committees report first budget resolution	April 15
Congress passes first budget resolution	May 15
Legislative committees complete reporting of authorizing legislation	May 15
Congress passes all spending bills	7 days after Labor Day
Congress passes second budget resolution	September 15
Congress passes budget reconciliation bill	September 25
Fiscal year begins	October 1

for what a "standpat" budget would look like. This
current services budget submitted by the OMB is
complemented (or contradicted) by the current policy
budget prepared by the CBO. The current policy budget
has the same purpose but uses "congressional"
assumptions instead of "presidential" assumptions, and
can sometimes differ by as much as $10 billion.

First Concurrent Resolution

The Budget Committees begin to hold hearings after the
President submits his budget in January. Their task is to
gather information on economic conditions, fiscal policy
alternatives, and national budget priorities. The Budget
Committees take testimony from the administration,
members of Congress, outside experts, and interest-group
representatives. By March 15, all the standing
committees in the House and Senate are required to
submit "views and estimates" of what their legislative
plans are for the coming year to the Budget Committees.
These are estimates of the amount of new budget
authority and outlays to be approved in the coming year.
This gives the Budget Committees some idea of overall
legislative plans for the coming year and forces the
committees to take an overview of their prospective
agenda and likely results. Experience to this point has
shown that the committees tend to estimate higher than
they will actually approve, to insure that they retain
flexibility in their subsequent legislative actions.

By the first of April, the Congressional Budget Office
submits its annual report to the Budget Committees. The
exact format of this report varied over the first five years
as the CBO sought a format most suitable to
congressional needs. The purpose of the report is to
specify a number of budget alternatives for Congress.[5]

By April 15, the House and Senate Budget Committees
are required to report the committee version of the first
concurrent resolution to their respective houses. The
resolution is to specify:

(1) outlays
(2) budget authority
(3) revenues
(4) surplus or deficit
(5) public debt

(6) budget authority and outlays for 19 functional categories.

May 15 is the next deadline for Congress; it is a crucial one in two respects. Standing committees must report all legislation recommending new budget authority. Any such legislation reported after May 15 may be considered only if an emergency waiver is adopted. Second, May 15 is the deadline for passage of the first concurrent resolution. Prior to the adoption of the resolution, neither house of Congress may consider any revenue, spending, entitlement, or debt legislation. When the House and Senate resolutions do not agree (virtually always the case), they are considered by a conference committee that reports back to each house. The totals in the first resolutions are *targets,* not binding ceilings; only the figures in the second resolution are binding.

An accompanying statement provides for distribution of allocations to committees of the totals included in the resolution. One of the problems in congressional budgeting is crosswalking between the functional categories and the jurisdiction of congressional committees. The resolution allocates to the committees the amount approved in a functional area. The Appropriations Committees divide totals among their subcommittees.

Second Concurrent Resolution

Although the Appropriations Committees will have begun before May, the summer months between May and September are the period of their greatest activity. Most of the work of the Appropriations Committees is carried out in the subcommittees. In the subcommittee hearings, agency officials defend their budget requests, justify their programs, and explain their anticipated future directions. Consistent with specialization and reciprocity, the full committee usually follows the recommendations of the subcommittee, and the House and Senate usually follow the recommendations of the committee.[6] During these months, the Congressional Budget Office issues periodic reports on the status of the various appropriation bills. This "scorekeeping" function of the CBO compares amounts and changes in the legislation with the levels specified in the first resolution.

By the seventh day after Labor Day, Congress must complete action on all bills providing new budget and spending authority. Action must be completed by early September to enable Congress to pass a second resolution and complete the process of reconciliation before the fiscal year begins on October 1. Attention shifts back to the Budget Committees in September. By the fifteenth of September, Congress is required to pass the second concurrent resolution. This document reaffirms or revises the targets in the first resolution. On the basis of new information, different economic assumptions, or approved spending actions, Congress adopts binding totals for budget authority, outlays, revenues, deficit, and public debt. The second resolution may be at variance with previous actions; therefore, it may contain instructions to certain committees to alter their previous actions including rescinding or amending appropriations, raising or lowering revenues, or any other such actions. This process is called reconciliation and must be completed in 10 days, by September 25. The fiscal year begins five days later.

Congress may not adjourn for the session (adjourn *sine die*) until the second resolution is approved. After passage of the second resolution, neither house may consider any legislation that would exceed the approved totals or reduce revenue. Congress may at any time, however, pass another resolution. This might be in conjunction with a supplemental appropriation bill or in response to sudden changes in the economy or other extenuating circumstances.

Many observers were pessimistic about the prospects for successful implementation of budget reform in Congress. Because of the record of past delays and obstruction, the statutory deadlines appeared too rigid for Congress to meet. Congressional leaders agreed to a trial run in 1975, implementing only part of the procedures, with full implementation not required by the law until 1976.

Battles of the Budget

Although the budget act was passed by substantial majorities in both the House and the Senate, the driving force for reform was an unholy alliance of fiscal conservatives and spending liberals.[7] This coalition was convinced of the need for radical changes in congressional budget procedures, but for different reasons. Most members of Congress shared the view that they had lost the power of the purse to the executive; members of both parties wanted to do something to regain it. Beyond this common desire to reassert legislative authority, supporters had divergent objectives in pursuing budget reform.

Conservatives saw reform as a way to reduce federal spending. The new procedures would set binding limits, control "backdoor" spending, and force Congress to go on record publicly if they wanted to approve a deficit. Liberals concerned with domestic needs saw reform as a means to publicly debate national priorities. The new procedures would allow them to question the billions of dollars spent on defense and to identify social problems in need of attention. These divergent expectations created a tenuous and volatile environment and set the stage for a number of budget battles.

Since the adoption of the congressional budget process, sharp disputes over the direction of fiscal policy and budget priorities have erupted, with noticeable differences between the House and the Senate. From the outset, the budget process was a divisive, partisan issue in the House. In the Senate, members of both parties worked together more harmoniously. In the first five years of implementation, many issues have divided the House (and to a lesser extent the Senate), but the major budget battles have been fought over three main concerns: (1) the amount of expenditures and spending growth, (2) the budget deficit and the issue of a balanced budget, and (3) the relative allocations in the budget to defense versus domestic spending.

The House and Senate began their markup of the first budget resolution in the spring of 1975. House Budget

Committee Chairman Brock Adams and the Democratic leadership in the House soon recognized the difficult task that awaited them. House Republicans had already stated that the trial run was meaningless and they would have no inhibitions about voting against the first resolution. Taking the side of President Ford, House Republicans objected to the increases proposed by the Democrats and the size of the deficit. The deficit — projected at the time to be over $70 billion, the largest in history — was the real sticking point. But as the following excerpts from the debate in 1975 indicate, total spending and defense versus domestic shares in the budget were also disputed.[8]

> MR. LATTA (R-Ohio): We will have acquired by fiscal year 1976 $600-plus billion in debt since the beginning of our history but we are going to acquire one-sixth of that in one single year. That is scary. That is scary.... We are passing this tremendous debt onto our children and their children. I think that is downright immoral.

> MR. WRIGHT (D-Texas): As an abstract proposition, I suppose anyone would say "no" to that kind of debt. I do believe if we look at the historic movement of the Federal debt in connection with the historic movement of the Gross National Product, we may see the estimated figure of a $73.2 deficit in slightly less terrifying perspective.

Attempts were made to amend the resolution to balance the budget:

> MR. ROUSSELOT (R-California): Mr. Chairman. I will offer at the appropriate time an amendment to ... call for a balanced budget at roughly a $300 billion expenditure level. I rise in opposition to the House Concurrent Resolution 218 as reported by the House Budget Committee. In my estimation the Federal spending and the deficit ... would result in giving the economy another dose of inflation-recession — an action which I do not think the economy can tolerate and an action which I do not believe the citizens of this nation can tolerate.

Some suggested that the evils of unemployment far outweighed the evils of a deficit budget:

> MR. BADILLO (D-New York): An increase of 1 percent in unemployment brings about a $16 billion increase in the Federal deficit ... but providing for 1 million public service jobs would cost only $10 billion. Therefore, we are actually reducing the budget deficit by providing more for public service employment.

Spending levels were too high for some and too low for others:

> MR. CONYERS (D-Michigan): Congress could set no higher goal for itself than to restore the economic health of our Nation, but the Report of the Budget Committee does not foresee our

doing this. . . . In fact, the committee did not even consider a budget which could have been part of a full employment economy. Although I commend the committee for its hard work . . . I feel I must vote against the resolution. The people of Detroit and of other hard-pressed areas need to know their Representatives in Congress will not abandon them.

MR. GOLDWATER (R-California): If House Concurrent Resolution 218 is any indication . . . of what the taxpayer can expect in the way of immediate help in fiscal matters from this Congress they had better hold on to their wallets real hard.

Too much for defense or not enough?

MS. HOLTZMAN (D-New York): It seems to me that in time of peace that [subtotal for defense] is an extraordinarily high amount to be devoting to the defense budget. It is about time we begin to look at the defense budget from the point of view of waste. Waste and inefficiency in the defense budget must be eliminated if we are to control future deficits and have the Federal funds needed for domestic programs.

MR. LATTA: For a number of years there has been a constant erosion of the U.S. Defense effort while at the same time there has been a steady increase in defense spending by the Soviet Union. The Congress simply cannot keep spending for practically every imaginable type of domestic assistance program and assume that we can shake down the defense budget. . . . Someone has calculated that if the erosion in our defense program continues at its present rate, in 10 years we will be down to the Secretary of Defense, no soldiers, sailors, airmen, or marines at all, just the Secretary of Defense, and he would be armed with a single rifle. . . . We cannot allow a continuation of this erosion of our forces.

The issues raised in the House in the first two years provided a preview of the conflicts that would recur throughout the decade. Using their full powers, the House leadership and the Democrats on the Budget Committee managed to pass the first resolution in May of 1975 by a slim four-vote margin, 200-196. In the fall, the second resolution (conference report) squeaked through by only two votes. The budget-reform coalition that had passed the Budget and Impoundment Control Act by a margin of 401-6 in 1974 had broken down when numbers were applied to the process. The result was a fragile coalition in the House, made up primarily of moderate and liberal Democrats, supporting the budget process.

The situation across Capitol Hill in the Senate was quite different. While only three of 131 Republicans in the House supported the first resolution in 1975, Senate Republicans voted in favor of the resolution by a margin of 19-18. Senate Budget Committee Chairman Edmund

Muskie (D-Maine) worked cooperatively with Ranking Minority Member Henry Bellmon (R-Oklahoma). They presented a united front on the floor of the Senate, supporting the compromises reached in committee and opposing amendments to the resolution proposed from the floor. Like the patterns of conflict in the House, the patterns of support for the budget resolutions in the Senate remained relatively stable over the next five years. The House continued to struggle to win majority support for their resolution, while the Senate continued to win approval by a better than 2-1 margin.

Despite the difficulties encountered in the House, the budget process survived the trial run in 1975. Congress had produced its first legislative budget and had made some changes in the President's requests. In 1976, the complete provisions of the act were implemented, including the September deadlines. On the House side, Adams was concerned with the survival of the process. In the Senate, Muskie and Bellmon were interested in increasing their impact on budget totals by challenging "budget-busting" legislation that was reported to the Senate. The unemployment rate had begun to decline, and the recovery from the severe 1973-1975 recession was under way, but difficult fiscal decisions remained. The deficit was still estimated in the range above $50 billion and was still unpalatable to fiscal conservatives. In addition, 1976 was an election year. Many senators and all members of the House faced reelection.

The macroeconomic issues again dominated the debate, but defense spending was more of an issue than it had been in 1975. The previous year, Congress had made sizable cuts in the defense requests submitted by President Ford. But — facing elections in November increased pressure from the Pentagon, and the threat of a veto from the President — Congress approved a sizable increase in military spending. Tax reform and proposals for a tax cut to stimulate the economy were also at issue in both houses. Several actions taken by the House and Senate resulted in tangible savings. They removed a provision from Social Security that increased benefits faster than the Consumer Price Index, and a ceiling on spending from the Highway Trust Fund was imposed.

In the first full year of implementation, Congress met all the deadlines. Perhaps the most impressive accomplishment was that all regular appropriations bills were passed before the start of the fiscal year for the first time in decades. The resolutions in the House had passed with slightly more comfortable margins than in the previous year, and all were optimistic that the process was more secure.

That was not to be the case, however. In May of 1977, the budget resolution reported by the House Budget Committee was defeated on the floor. The first defeat of a budget resolution was blamed partially on President Carter, who had taken office in January. During the House debate, an amendment to increase the subtotal for defense was offered with the support of the administration. The Budget Committee Democrats were enraged because the President had not given them prior notice of this move. When the amendment passed, the balance struck in committee began to waver. Other amendments were passed, and when the final vote was taken, the resolution was overwhelmingly defeated, 84-320.

The House Budget Committee and House leaders regrouped to salvage a budget resolution and save the budget process. Leaders attempted to convince members of the importance of the still-fledgling budget process to Congress, and urged members to support the resolution despite their dissatisfaction with some of the policies it contained. Budget Committee Chairman Robert Giaimo (D-Connecticut), who had replaced Adams in the 95th Congress, and the Democratic leaders were successful in their efforts. The same amendment to increase defense spending was turned down when the budget resolution came to the floor again, and the coalition was maintained. The budget process had survived its most serious threat. Most observers felt afterwards that the incident actually strengthened the process, by demonstrating that a floor defeat would not automatically doom the process.

In 1978, Proposition 13 in California and the growing tax revolt came to the fore as issues in the budget process. House Republicans continued to oppose the committee's recommendations and began to develop alternatives of their own. One of those alternatives almost passed the House in 1978. In the Senate, Bellmon was under increased pressure to break with Muskie and establish an independent Republican alternative. Bellmon and his allies resisted these pressures, however. By 1979, the conservative mood dominated the country and the Congress. Congress was heading for a balanced budget by 1981, partly in response to the growing movement for a constitutional convention to propose an amendment to balance the budget.

This left liberals in the House dissatisfied and alienated. They had supported budget resolutions in the House for four years, despite the fact that they were not always happy with the figures. Faced with even more restrictive proposals for the FY 1980 budget, the liberals revolted. Led by the congressional black caucus, liberals teamed up with conservative Republicans to defeat the conference report of the first concurrent resolution for 1980. The bill went back to conference, and some concessions were made. But more than anything, this group that had faithfully supported the budget resolutions wanted a symbolic gesture to make it clear that their future support could not be taken for granted.

The history of the budget process in Congress has been one of recurrent battles over fiscal policy and budget priorities. The divisive issues that are hammered out in the White House behind closed doors are debated openly in the Congress. With inflation, unemployment, tax reform, defense spending, social welfare programs, and many other divisive issues merged in the budget, conflict is almost inevitable.

House-Senate Differences

Partisanship and Voting Alignments

Why has the budget process been more controversial and partisan in the House than in the Senate? The answers lie in a number of factors: constituency pressures, committee organization and membership, committee leadership and decision making, and the nature of coalitions in the House and Senate. Table 7-3 examines the voting alignments in the House and Senate on the first concurrent resolutions during fiscal years 1976-1979. The contrast in support for the budget resolutions is apparent. In most cases House Republicans

Table 7-3 Budget Resolution Votes: House of Representatives and Senate, 1975-1978

HOUSE Date	First Concurrent Resolution	Vote Y-N	Republicans Y-N	Democrats Y-N	Northern Democrats Y-N	Southern Democrats Y-N
5/ 1/75	Committee Report, FY 1976	200-196	3-128	197-68	151-33	46-35
5/14/75	Conference Report, FY 1976	230-193	5-138	225-55	164-28	61-27
4/29/76	Committee Report, FY 1977	221-155	13-111	208-44	159-20	40-24
5/13/76	Conference Report, FY 1977	224-170	10-125	214-45	161-21	53-24
4/27/77	Original Committee Report, FY 1978	84-320	2-135	82-185	50-132	32-53
5/ 5/77	Revised Committee Report, FY 1978	213-179	7-121	206-58	142-39	64-19
5/17/77	Conference Report, FY 1978	221-177	29-107	192-70	122-53	70-17
5/10/78	Committee Report, FY 1979	201-197	3-136	198-61	152-25	46-36
5/17/78	Conference Report, FY 1979	201-198	2-133	199-65	134-47	65-18

SENATE Date	First Concurrent Resolution	Vote	Republicans	Democrats	Northern Democrats	Southern Democrats
5/ 1/75	FY 1976 Committee Report	69-22	19-18	50-4	36-1	14-3
5/14/75	FY 1976 Conference Report	—	—	Voice Vote	—	—
4/12/76	FY 1977 Committee Report	62-22	17-16	45-6	32-4	13-2
5/12/76	FY 1977 Conference Report	65-29	16-20	49-9	34-6	15-3
5/ 4/77	FY 1978 Committee Report	56-31	15-17	41-14	36-3	5-11
5/13/77	FY 1978 Conference Report	54-23	17-12	37-11	29-4	8-7
4/26/78	FY 1979 Committee Report	64-27	16-19	48-8	35-4	13-4
5/12/78	FY 1979 Conference Report	—	—	Voice Vote	—	—

Source: *Congressional Quarterly Weekly Reports, 1975-1978.*

have voted against the resolutions as a bloc, with only a
few defectors. Senate Republicans, on the other hand,
have split their votes frequently with a majority
supporting the resolutions. House Democrats have
generally supported the budget resolutions by a margin of
about 4-1, with about 50 votes against the resolutions.
Most of the "nay" votes have come from Southern
Democrats and conservatives; except in 1979 only a few
liberals have voted against the resolutions. In most cases
Senate Democrats have displayed strong support for the
resolutions.

Constituency factors may explain some of the
differences in House and Senate support. Political
scientists generally conclude that constituency pressures
are greater on representatives than on senators.[9]
Senators represent larger, more diverse areas and run for
reelection only every six years. House members must run
every two years, and the spending-deficit issues appear to
be more conspicuous in their campaigns. Public pressure
to balance the budget makes it difficult for members to go
on record in support of deficits. House members fear
electoral reprisals, even though they may realize that
deficits are inevitable given the national economic
conditions. Senators seem to express less concern over the
dangers of a vote in favor of a deficit.

As the budget approached a state of balance in 1979 and
1980, it became apparent that deficits were not the only
reason for Republican opposition in the House. One
member of the House Budget Committee commented,
"Even if the committee reported a balanced budget, the
Republicans would oppose it, trying to balance it at a
lower level." Although partisanship and party discipline
are the exception rather than the rule in Congress, House
Republicans see fiscal policy and the budget as an issue on
which they can clarify party differences.

Committee Structure and Membership

The budget act reflected differences in the original
House and Senate versions of the bill. In the Senate, the
Budget Committee was established on the same footing as
any other standing committee. In the House, by contrast,
tenure on the committee was limited to four years out of
10, and provision was made for direct representation of

the Ways and Means Committee, the Appropriations Committee, and the party leadership. This structure was the result of concessions to the powerful money committees in the House, who wanted to insure that the new Budget Committee remained weak.[10] It also reflected the reformist sentiment in the House in 1974, the desire to limit seniority and block the establishment of a new committee power.

The tenure and membership restrictions on the House Budget Committee affected the norms of behavior and careerism usually operative in the House. Membership on the House Budget Committee became a secondary assignment, since members could not build up seniority and develop a congressional career as they could on other committees. It also reduced the incentives to protect committee reputation and prestige, norms that usually restrict partisanship on committees.[11] One of the results is that the House committee has been characterized by significantly more partisan bickering and dispute than the Senate committee.

Divisions on the House Budget Committee have been fostered by the selection of members. The Democrats have tended to place liberals on the committee. The Republicans have tended to choose conservatives, achieving what one observer called "the largest concentration of right-wingers in the House." The ideological cleavage fostered through the selection of members has increased the divisiveness on the House committee. Although the Senate Budget Committee includes both liberal Democrats and conservative Republicans, other norms have restrained the level of partisanship and conflict.

At the start of the 96th Congress, the Democratic caucus in the House changed the rules regarding Budget Committee membership, allowing members to stay on the committee six years rather than four. This allowed Robert Giaimo to remain as chairman in 1979-1980. If this trend continues, the House may remove all restrictions from committee membership in an attempt to strengthen the committee and its ability to enforce the budget resolutions.

Committee Strategies

The Senate Budget Committee, finding itself in a stronger institutional position than its House counterpart, has pursued somewhat different strategies than the House.[12] Because of its relative weakness and the divisive environment in the House, the House Budget Committee has been process oriented. In attempting to arrive at a set of figures that can pass the House, Adams and Giaimo have stressed the importance of the process, downplaying policy, because they realize that no member will be completely satisfied with the totals.[13] The Senate Budget Committee, more secure in terms of process, has been able to focus its attention more on policy. This has manifested itself in several ways. Assisted by Bellmon, Muskie was able to mount challenges to bills from other committees on the Senate floor. In the first year of operation of the new Senate Budget Committee, Chairman Muskie took on Senator John Stennis and the powerful Armed Services Committee, urging the defeat of an authorization bill that violated the targets in the first resolution. Much to the surprise of many observers, the Senate upheld Muskie's position.[14] The more aggressive strategy of challenging bills on the floor marked the budget process in the Senate in the first five years. The Senate Budget Committee has been defeated on a number of occasions, particularly on tax measures, but has also gained some impressive victories.

A more indirect strategy has been pursued in the House. Neither Adams nor Giaimo directly challenged bills from other committees. Instead, they attempted to work behind the scenes, trying to have the desired changes made in committee before a measure reached the floor for a vote. Avoidance of direct conflict was consistent with the process emphasis of the committee in the first years. Both Budget Committees have generally practiced accommodation and deference to the standing committees, since their survival depends on the support of these committees. This is reflected in the fact that most of the spending desires of the standing committees have been included in the budget resolutions. The difference is that accommodation and deference in the Senate have been punctuated with more aggressive challenges.

Committee Leadership

Some of the differences in House-Senate patterns may be explained by differences in leadership, but to some extent they merely reflect the environment of each house. Brock Adams, Chairman of the House Budget Committee in the 94th Congress, was not particularly senior or well known at the time of his appointment. Nonetheless, he received high marks for his careful attempts to insure the continuation of the budget process. Senator Muskie, Chairman of the Senate Budget Committee, had more seniority and was a nationally known figure. The combination of Muskie, a liberal, and Bellmon, a conservative, presenting a united front, proved to be effective. In contrast, the ranking minority member on the House Budget Committee, Delbert Latta (R-Ohio), was a reluctant and part-time supporter of the process, and a constant opponent of the resolutions. The opposition of Republican leadership in the House posed a continual threat to the budget process.

Adams began the practice of offering the chairman's "mark" at the beginning of budget markup: a set of recommendations for the budget resolution that serves as the agenda for the committee deliberations. In the Senate, Muskie has not used a chairman's "mark." Instead, the committee has proceeded by looking at the President's requests and considering one function at a time. With this fuller participation of the committee members, decision making is less conflictive in the Senate than in the House.

Decisions

The budget process has followed a different pattern of development in the House and Senate. The decisions reached by each house reflect the variations in environment, voting alignments, partisanship, leadership, and strategies. Table 7-4 summarizes the congressional budget resolutions from FY 1976-1980. The aggregate totals provide only a partial view of the decisions made by Congress but allow some comparisons. In the first two years, Congress demonstrated a willingness and ability to change the totals recommended by the President. In FY 1976 and 1977, Congress provided for outlays greater than those requested by President

Table 7-4 Comparison of Budget Totals (1976-1980)
(in billions of dollars)

	President's Budget	First Resolution			Second Resolution		
		House	Senate	Final	House	Senate	Final
FY 1976							
Total outlays	$349.4	$368.2	$365.0	$367.0	$373.9	$375.6	$374.9
Total budget authority	385.8	395.9	388.6	395.8	408.0	406.2	408.0
Total revenues	297.5	298.1	297.8	298.2	301.8	300.8	300.8
Deficit	51.9	70.0	67.2	68.8	72.1	74.8	74.1
FY 1977							
Total outlays	$394.2	$415.4	$412.6	$413.3	$413.2	$412.8	$413.1
Total budget authority	433.4	454.1	454.9	454.2	452.6	447.5	451.5
Total revenues	351.3	363.0	362.4	352.5	362.5	362.0	362.5
Deficit	43.0	52.4	50.2	50.8	50.7	50.8	50.6
FY 1978							
Total outlays	$459.37	$464.5	$459.2	$460.95	$459.57	$459.9	$458.25
Total budget authority	507.3	502.3	504.6	503.45	508.0	501.4	500.1
Total revenues	401.62	398.1	395.7	396.3	397.93	394.8	397.0
Deficit	57.75	66.4	63.5	64.65	61.64	65.1	61.25
FY 1979							
Total outlays	$499.4	$500.9	$498.9	$498.8	$489.8	$489.5	$487.5
Total budget authority	565.6	569.5	566.1	568.85	561.0	557.7	555.65
Total revenues	439.8	443.0	443.3	477.9	450.0	447.2	448.7
Deficit	59.6	57.9	55.6	50.9	39.8	42.3	38.8
FY 1980							
Total outlays	$532.3	$529.9	$532.6	$532.0	$548.2	$546.3	$547.6
Total budget authority	615.0	605.1	600.3	604.4	631.8	636.6	638.0
Total revenues	503.9	509.0	503.6	509.0	519.3	514.7	517.8
Deficit	28.4	20.9	29.0	23.0	28.9	31.6	29.8

Source: *Congressional Quarterly Weekly Reports.*

Ford. The totals have been more similar to presidential requests under President Carter, but congressional independence is still in evidence.

The resolutions that passed the House have been slightly more liberal than the Senate versions. The fact that the budget coalition in the House is made up of moderate and liberal Democrats helps explain this phenomenon. With Republican participation in the Senate, the resolutions have tended to be slightly more conservative. This is revealed in several ways. The overall House totals have tended to be slightly higher for outlays and authority, and the deficits slightly larger. Differences can also be found in comparing the functional subtotals within the budget (not shown). The House has tended to approve higher totals for income security and lower totals for national defense than the Senate. Over the first four years, the Senate versions of the budget resolutions called for $8.8 billion more for defense than the House versions. In contrast, the House versions of the resolutions called for $15.7 billion more for income security than the Senate.[15] The differences in the various versions have been worked out in conference.

In the conference committee, the House has not been dominated by the Senate. Although conferees most frequently settle on a figure somewhere between the two versions, the final figures have actually been closer to the House report in more cases.[16] In some instances, the relative weakness of the House can be used as a bargaining tool in conference. The argument that certain concessions from the Senate are essential if the resolution is to pass the House can be persuasive. Despite some major policy differences, the conferees have usually been able to resolve their differences in a matter of days.

Evaluating the Congressional Budget Process

A large majority of Congress agreed to procedural changes without agreeing on specific policy objectives. Differing expectations about the system mean that there can be no single judgment about the results of budget reform. It is possible, however, to assess its impact on a number of dimensions.

Procedures and Timetable A precondition for any impact is the survival of the process. Given the history of previous failure and the reluctance of Congress to embrace change, survival of the congressional budget process was by no means assured. On this dimension, the budget process has been a success. It has survived a number of tests and challenges, and the deadlines have been met with regularity. Although some appropriations bills have not been passed by September because of tangential issues (for example, federal funding of abortions), the record is excellent compared to results under the old system. Committees have grumbled about the difficulty of the March 15 and May 15 deadlines but have gone along for the most part. Both the House and the Senate have been relatively generous about granting waivers, but not to the extent of undermining the process. In general, Congress has adapted well to the new procedures. Budgeting in Congress, if still complex and confusing, is more orderly than in previous decades.

Impoundment Control The impoundment-control provisions of the budget act were never used on President Nixon, their main target. He resigned in 1974, a few months before implementation began. The procedures for rescission and deferral described in Chapter 6 have successfully eliminated the previous impoundment abuses, although not without creating some new problems of their own. Of the $9 billion of rescissions requested by President Ford during his administration, 86 percent of the requests were rejected.[17] He was more successful at deferring spending; only 24 percent of these proposals were rejected. New problems arose from a lack of clarity in the act in classifying presidential requests, and in the number of rescissions submitted by Ford. The initial volume threatened to overload the system. Under the Carter Administration, most of the impoundments that carried over from the Nixon Administration are gone. The volume has receded to manageable levels, and the system seems to be working. No longer can Presidents impound funds at will and thwart the intentions of Congress.

Improving Congressional Information One of the objectives of budget reform was to improve the quantity and quality of congressional information. By the 1970s, Congress had become dependent upon the OMB and the executive branch for all its budgetary information. With Nixon in the White House, there was increased doubt on Capitol Hill that the information they were receiving was either complete or accurate. Three organizations were created by the budget act to improve congressional information: House Budget Committee staff, Senate Budget Committee staff, and the Congressional Budget Office (CBO).

Conferees in 1974 rejected the idea of a joint budget committee staff, opting instead for individual staffs and the CBO to serve all of Congress. The House and Senate approached the question of staff in different ways. The House Budget Committee developed a staff with an emphasis on technical expertise, while the Senate Budget Committee hired a staff with as much political experience as budgetary know-how. Both staffs help the committees prepare the budget resolutions by providing various studies and analyses. The Senate has used the CBO more than the House has, and some competition has developed between the House Budget Committee staff and the CBO. The relatively greater political skills of the Senate staff have assisted the committee in accurately gauging the mood of the Senate and may have contributed to the greater margin of passage in that body. The addition of committee staff has clearly increased the information available to both houses.

The CBO was created to provide budgetary and policy analysis. Because they do not formulate the legislative budget, they reject being characterized as a "congressional OMB." Their role is to provide the Congress with:

- *scorekeeping reports:* comparisons of pending and enacted legislation with targets and ceilings specified in the budget resolutions
- *"costing-out" bills:* projections of the costs of spending bills to specify the long-term costs of current legislation
- *five-year projections:* reports on current policy levels of taxing and spending projected for five years
- *budget alternatives:* alternative levels of taxing

and spending, their implications, economic
assumptions, analyses of fiscal policy choices
  • *policy studies:* special reports on current issues
    that affect the budget.

CBO encountered difficulties in their early years of
operation. They were criticized for policy advocacy, for
gaining too much publicity, and for requesting a
limousine to transport CBO officials. Some of these
problems were the result of poor judgment by CBO but
much of it was the inevitable outcome of engaging in
research on controversial issues. Overall, congressional
appraisals of CBO work have been favorable.[18] They have
increasingly tailored their reports to the needs of the
congressional committees, and have raised the level of
awareness of members about the multiyear consequences
of budget decisions.

With the addition of the committee staff and the CBO,
Congress has substantially improved both the quantity
and quality of information. Although Congress still
receives much of its information from the executive
branch, they have a check on its accuracy, and they have
access to data previously not available. In terms of
facilitating more informed decisions on priorities and
programs, budget reform has succeeded.

Impact on the Budget

The question of whether Congress has had a greater
impact on the federal budget since 1975 is more difficult to
answer. With the trend towards fiscal conservatism in
Congress and the country, budget control has
increasingly been defined as budget cutting. Has the
budget process resulted in less spending than would have
occurred without the new procedures? Most members feel
that some savings have been realized. Some estimate that
as much as $15 billion has been saved, but others are more
cautious in their estimates. One member commented that
"a few billion don't mean much when you've got a half a
trillion dollar problem." Only a few of the most
conservative members claim that the process has resulted
in no reductions in spending.

It is difficult to document evidence of substantial
reductions, and it is questionable to attribute all but a few
reductions to the process itself. Public pressures to reduce
spending would have been as great without the process.

But the new procedures have provided a much more workable vehicle for Congress to respond to public pressures. Despite the new budget process, there are still strong spending pressures in Congress. The authorizing committees continue to act as advocates of additional outlays in their own areas, and the Budget Committees have been only partially successful in holding back these demands. Test votes compiled by the Senate Budget Committee reveal that on a number of occasions the Senate has approved additional spending over the objections of the committee.[19]

If the most salient objective of reform was to "control" the budget, many liberals wanted to restructure national priorities. Since 1975, however, virtually no restructuring has occurred. In fact, the relative shares within the budget have been more stable than in the years immediately preceding implementation. Most members agree that there has been little transfer from one part of the budget to another. Representative John Conyers (D-Michigan) expressed his disappointment with this aspect of the budget process:

> The most serious shortcoming of the budget process has been the neglect of its priority-setting purpose. We have not done nearly enough to define and order priorities according to national needs, or to anticipate and plan for future needs so that we may judge the desirability and effectiveness of existing programs. Obviously, there will always be several priorities reflected in the budget. But unless we focus on concrete goals and targets, we will not be in a position to determine what has to be traded off, sacrificed, and how the several priorities are related to one another.[20]

One must conclude that most members are satisfied with current allocations, or at least that no alternatives are more desirable to a majority. The process, per se, cannot restructure priorities. The problem may be not in setting priorities, but in whose priorities are being set. On the other hand, taking an overview of the budget may have rigidified current allocations. With the scarcity of resources, participants may have fought harder to keep their current share. Budget reform has not changed the political nature of budgeting. Reallocation is more likely to occur by a differential allocation of new resources than by taking from one and giving to another. This means advocates of reallocation are likely to remain disappointed until new resources become available.

With the emphasis on preserving the process, Congress

has not attempted change priorities. The reconciliation process has not been used, and the ceilings in the second resolution tend to ratify spending decisions already made. But if and when Congress is ready to alter national priorities, it will have a system that hypothetically makes it possible.

The congressional budget process has had a negligible impact on the revenue side of the budget. Most of the concern during the formulation of the budget act was on expenditures. The provisions for integrating revenue and spending decisions are weak; the only relevant item in the budget resolution is a target figure for receipts. Attempts by the Budget Committees to affect changes in the tax laws have been opposed by the Finance and Ways and Means Committees. A number of new tax expenditures (or tax loopholes) have been approved in recent years. Congress can escape the restrictions of the budget resolutions by moving the effective date of the provisions to the next fiscal year. Yet these weaknesses on the revenue side may have saved the budget process in its early years. An additional area of controversy may have made compromise on the budget resolutions impossible. But the lack of control of revenues limits the responsiveness of the congressional budget process and its ability to integrate fiscal policy with taxing and spending decisions.

Independence from the Executive

Putting controls on impoundment and improving congressional information were both related to the more general objective of increasing congressional independence and redressing the imbalance in budgetary power. In the first two years after the passage of the budget act, Congress proved that it could alter the fiscal priorities of the President. It also demonstrated that it could be responsive to the President by passing the third resolution for FY 1977 to encompass President Carter's stimulus package.

Congress is clearly more capable and independent in budgeting than it was before 1975. Presidents are now restricted in their ability to impound funds, and Congress plays a greater role in establishing fiscal policy. But complete "independence" from the executive is undesirable. Conflict between institutions, where rivalries and jealousies outstrip the recognition of mutual purpose, does not serve the best interests of the nation. The President remains the most important participant in budgetary politics, but the congressional budget process has helped to restore the traditional system of checks and balances.

After many decades using antiquated procedures, Congress reversed the erosion of fiscal power to the executive. The congressional budget process has been successfully adopted; the timetable and procedures have resulted in a stronger and more orderly process. Because the choices are difficult, the budget remains a controversial issue in Congress. If the procedures become more secure and established in the 1980s, Congress may be able to de-emphasize process goals and emphasize policy goals, further increasing their impact in budgetary politics.

FOOTNOTES

For a more detailed study of budget reform and the congressional budget process see Lance T. LeLoup, *The Fiscal Congress: Legislative Control of the Budget* (Westport, Conn.: Greenwood Press, 1980).

[1]Louis Fisher, *Presidential Spending Power* (Princeton: Princeton University Press, 1975), pp. 36-37.

[2]Louis Fisher, "Experience with a Legislative Budget," in U.S. Senate, *Improving Congressional Control Over the Budget*, 93rd Congress, 1st session, pp. 250-251.

[3]See George Gross, "The Congressional Budget and Impoundment Control Act of 1974: A General Explanation," Committee on the Budget, U.S. House of Representatives, October 1975.

[4]*Ibid.*

[5]*Congressional Quarterly Weekly Reports,* June 5, 1976, pp. 1430-1432.

[6]Richard Fenno, *The Power of the Purse* (Boston: Little, Brown, 1966), chapter 8.

[7]The terms *liberal* and *conservative* can be used for different purposes, and may not represent a clear dichotomy of attitudes and behavior. They are used here in reference to a member's orientation towards government spending. Conservatives tend to favor less spending but more for defense. Liberals tend to favor more spending, but less for defense.

[8]The excerpts were selected from the lengthy 10-hour House debate on the First Concurrent Resolution on the Budget, FY 1976; *Congressional Record,* H3404-H3405, H3552-H3591, April 29-May 1, 1975. See also Committee on the Budget, U.S. Senate, *Concurrent Resolutions on the FY 1976 Budget: Compendium of Materials Leading to Passage,* 94th Congress, 1st session, October 1975, pp. 687-986.

[9]Aage Clausen and Richard Cheney, "Comparative Analysis of

Senate and House Voting on Economic and Welfare Policy: 1953-1964," *American Political Science Review,* 64 (March 1970): 151. For a general discussion of constituency influence on members of Congress see Roger Davidson, *The Role of the Congressman* (New York: Pegasus, 1969).

[10]Allen Schick, "Budget Reform Legislation: Reorganizing Congressional Centers of Fiscal Power," *Harvard Journal on Legislation,* 11, no. 2 (February 1974): 310-311.

[11]Richard Fenno, *Congressmen in Committees* (Boston: Little, Brown, 1973), chapter 1.

[12]John Ellwood and James Thurber, "The New Congressional Budget Process: The How's and Why's of House-Senate Differences," in *Congress Reconsidered,* eds. Larry Dodd and Bruce Oppenheimer (New York: Praeger, 1978).

[13]Lance T. LeLoup, "Process Versus Policy: The U.S. House Budget Committee," *Legislative Studies Quarterly,* May 1978.

[14]Joel Havemann, *Congress and the Budget* (Bloomington: Indiana University Press, 1978).

[15]LeLoup, *Fiscal Congress,* chapter 3.

[16]*Ibid.*

[17]Havemann, *Congress,* p. 182.

[18]*Ibid.,* p. 114.

[19]Data on "test votes" compiled by Senate Budget Committee, reported in LeLoup, *Fiscal Congress,* chapter 7.

[20]Committee on the Budget, U.S. House of Representatives, *Oversight of the Congressional Budget Process,* 95th Congress, 1st session, pp. 128-130.

Congress:
Authorization
and Appropriation

*Never lose sight of the fact that the
Appropriations Committees are the saucers
that cool the legislative tea.*
—Appropriations Committee Member*

I n addition to approving budget totals, Congress must
still approve authorizations and appropriations. Behind
the radical changes instituted by budget reform, the
process of authorization and appropriation continues to
operate much as it has for decades. The most dramatic
difference for the committees is the existence of targets
and ceilings which make their subsequent decisions more
accountable to the overall priorities of Congress.

No money may be appropriated unless previously
authorized by law. An authorization is a statement of
legislative policy; an appropriation is the funding of that

policy. Periodic conflicts have emerged between the
authorizing and appropriating committees. The standing
committees may attempt to pressure the Appropriations
Committees to fund the programs they have authorized.[1]
On other occasions, they may admonish members of the
Appropriations Committees to "appropriate, don't
legislate," objecting to what they see as usurpation of
their legislative prerogatives.

Authorizing committees have bypassed the
Appropriations Committees with the passage of
entitlement and "backdoor" spending programs. In a few
cases, annual authorizations have been required, such as
for foreign aid, atomic energy, space, and weapons
programs. A classic battle between authorization and
Appropriations Committees' influence took place in 1958
over the creation of the space program.[2] Proponents of
annual authorization saw it as an opportunity for
congressional oversight and control, while opponents
saw the move as an obstacle to the orderly process of
budgeting.

Budget reform in Congress helped to increase the
coordination of these sometimes disparate stages of
budgeting. But two tendencies are still apparent after
budget reform. First, many spending decisions are made
directly by the authorizing committees. Second, in the
appropriations decisions, Congress still relies almost
exclusively on agency presentations and testimony in
determining effectiveness and need. Congress does not
have the capacity to evaluate programs on its own and
must depend on an annual review that is less thorough
than many feel is necessary. Some basic questions must
be explored. What spending and taxing decisions are
made by the standing committees in Congress? How do
the Appropriations Committees review agency programs
and requests in deciding what to appropriate? Finally,
how are program decisions in Congress related to priority
decisions?

Committee Jurisdiction and Advocacy

Committees are not equal in terms of the amounts of money they control in the authorization and appropriation process. Table 8-1 shows Senate committee jurisdiction over the FY 1979 budget (figures are comparable for the House). Also shown are the relative shares of the budget assigned to the various committees. Authorizing committees have both direct spending jurisdiction and indirect control of entitlements funded through appropriations. Therefore, the final column in Table 8-1 shows the actual spending jurisdiction of the committees. While the Appropriations Committees have jurisdiction over the largest portion of the budget, it is less than 50 percent. The Senate Finance Committee (and House Ways and Means Committee) control 40 percent of the budget, only slightly less than the Appropriations Committees. They play a significant role in both the spending and revenue sides of the budget. Other authorizing committees have jurisdiction over the remaining 14 percent. The figures change from year to year, but the general shares are fairly typical.

Although Congress traditionally has played the role of guardian in the budget process, advocacy by the authorizing committees and the Appropriations Committees has increased in recent years. On March 15, the committees in both the House and the Senate are required to submit their views and estimates to the Budget Committees: the committees can only surmise what subsequent actions will be and whether the full House or Senate will concur. The tendency for the committees, however, is to come in high: to make sure they include all possible spending that they might want to pass that session. Once a lower level is included in the first resolution, their policy objectives might be more difficult to achieve. Table 8-2 shows the combined estimate of outlays recommended by the House committees in comparison with the President's requests and the recommendation of the House Budget Committee chairman. The total of all committee estimates was $442

Table 8-1 Spending Jurisdiction by Senate Committees, Fiscal 1979

(New Budget Authority)

(in millions of dollars)

Committee	Direct Spending Jurisdiction	Entitlements Funded Through Appropriations	Total	Proportion
Appropriations	$354,953	(-$70,453)*	$284,500	46%
Finance	213,588	34,289	247,877	40%
Other Authorizing Committees	60,300	30,200	90,500	14%

Subtotals, Other Authorizing Committees

Government Affairs	$26,117	—	$26,117
Veteran's Affairs	1,062	13,752	14,814
Foreign Relations	11,424	—	11,424
Armed Services	-190	10,279	10,089
Agriculture, Nutrition, & Forestry	616	9,206	9,822
Environment & Public Works	8,226	—	8,226
Human Resources	4,237	2,613	6,850
Commerce, Science, & Transportation	1,248	199	1,447
Energy & Natural Resources	1,038	58	1,096
Select Committee on Indian Affairs	256	—	256
Banking, Housing, Urban Affairs	240	—	240
Judiciary	173	57	230
Rules & Administration	46	—	46

*Since the appropriations are mandatory, they are deducted from total.
Source: *Second Concurrent Resolution, FY 1979; Senate Budget Scorekeeping Report,* 79-9, October 2, 1978.

billion, almost $50 billion greater than the President's requests, and $30 billion greater than the Budget Committee recommendations. In every function, the committees' estimates of outlays were higher; only for science, space, and technology was the total the same. The largest percentage increases were in the areas of commerce and transportation (40 percent higher than the President's requests) and in education and social services (70 percent higher than the President's requests). The same pattern has been repeated in subsequent budgets.

**Table 8-2   A Comparison of Recommended
Spending by the President, Standing Committees,
and House Budget Committee**
(Outlays by function, dollars in billions)

Function	President's Request	FY 1977 Standing Committee Views & Est.	Budget Committee Chairman's Recomm.
National Defense	$101.1	$102.9	$ 99.6
International Affairs	6.8	7.2	6.5
General Science, Space, and Technology	4.5	4.5	4.5
Natural Resources, Environment, and Energy	13.8	16.6	15.7
Agriculture	1.7	2.9	2.0
Commerce and Transportation	16.5	23.4	17.8
Community and Regional Development	5.5	7.0	6.2
Education, Training, Employment, and Social Services	16.6	27.6	22.8
Health	34.4	39.3	38.2
Income Security	137.1	144.1	140.1
Veteran's Benefits and Services	17.2	19.8	18.2
Law Enforcement and Justice	3.4	3.7	3.5
General Government	3.4	3.7	3.5
Revenue Sharing and General Purpose Fiscal Assistance	7.4	8.0	7.4
Interest	41.3	44.3	42.0
Allowances	2.3	2.6	.8
Undistributed Offsetting Receipts	-18.8	-15.6	-15.9
Total	$394.2	$442.0	$412.8

NOTE: Detail may not add to totals because of rounding.
Source: House Budget Committee, *Chairman's Recommendation for First Concurrent Resolution, FY 1977.*

Why are the estimates for outlays by the committees so much higher than the President's requests or the eventual congressional totals? Committee advocacy is at work. An equally important reason is that each committee estimates its share of the budget in isolation from other committees. They are not concerned with total spending; that is the job of the Budget Committees. There is no pressure in the initial stage to hold down their estimates. In addition, the committees have no direct role in determining total budget outlays.

While evidence suggests that committees adopt the role of advocate, many still behave like guardians when confronting agencies anxious to undertake new programs. The role of advocate is possible, however, because they are not directly accountable for budget totals, and can afford to be the main force for spending initiatives and policy advocacy in the Congress.

The appropriating and authorizing committees are differentiated by their degree of advocacy. The Appropriations Committees have stronger traditions and norms of budget cutting and guardianship regarding executive-branch requests. But within the congressional budget process, even the Appropriations Committees may promote greater spending. Senator William Proxmire, chairman of a Senate appropriations subcommittee (and a self-proclaimed budget cutter) described the lessons of experience in making the March 15 estimates:

> I made a low estimate and I lived to regret it, I fought for the estimate, but I lost. Ever since then ... I have attempted to come in high rather than low. They [the estimates] can contain everything including the kitchen sink. It is easier and safer to suggest a high figure so that in the end one will look good by coming in under it rather than submitting a lower figure which may be exceeded.[3]

Advocacy by the standing committees places them in direct conflict with the Budget Committees and makes it difficult for the Budget Committees to keep the committees happy while restraining spending growth in the aggregate.

The Authorizing Committees

One of the targets of budget reform was the authorizing committees. Using various forms of "backdoor" spending, entitlement programs, and multiyear spending commitments, they had increased their own influence on budgeting while decreasing overall congressional control. By writing mandatory outlays into substantive legislation, the authorizing committees guaranteed the stability and growth of social welfare expenditures, protecting them from the President and from possibly antagonistic appropriations subcommittees. The consequence, however, was less annual flexibility. The Budget and Impoundment Control Act put restrictions on the authorizing committees by restricting backdoor spending. Budget reform has also affected the committees in other ways.

Types of Authorizations

Authorizations include both broad grants of legislative authority and specific limits on the amounts that may be appropriated. There are three types of authorizations.

Annual authorizations require reauthorization of a program every year. They are a relatively recent phenomenon, developing since World War II. Though annual authorizations were established to improve congressional scrutiny of agency programs, some were instituted as a result of dissatisfaction with Appropriations Committee oversight. Agencies and programs requiring annual authorization include the Atomic Energy Commission, National Aeronautics and Space Administration, Energy Research and Development Administration, foreign assistance programs, National Science Foundation, and military procurement, research, and development.[4]

Annual authorizations increase congressional oversight and improve short-term control. Since they require agencies to endure four hearings per year, the result is an increase in workload, and some duplication. If authorizing committees continually authorize more than is appropriated, an "authorization-appropriations gap" may develop.[5] As the gap grows, it may create conflict between authorizing and appropriating subcommittees and stimulate further advocacy on the part of the legislative committees.

Despite the recent popularity of annual authorizations, they compose only about 15 percent of the budget.[6] Although some benefits in terms of legislative control result, there are significant costs to annual authorizations.

Multiyear authorizations establish an agency or program for a fixed period of time, usually between two and five years. A number of federal assistance programs to state and local government are on multiyear authorizations. Revenue sharing, for example, was first passed in 1972 and authorized for four years. In 1976, it was reauthorized for another four years with a few variations. It was scheduled for reauthorization in September of 1980, but in an environment of controversy and some sentiment to discontinue the program.[7]

Multiyear authorizations represent a compromise between annual and permanent authorizations. Congress retains periodic control but avoids an annual review. This is particularly useful for state and local governments who need to know ahead of time how much federal aid is forthcoming for their own budget planning. Multiyear authorizations create more certainty for other levels of government while still allowing a congressional review. In a single year, multiyear authorizations coming up for review constitute about 10 percent of the budget. About one-fourth of the budget is on a multiyear cycle.[8]

Permanent (or indefinite) authorizations establish legislative authority for agencies and programs with no fixed date of termination. Congress may review and alter permanent authority, but they are not required to do so. Permanent authorizations usually do not specify a dollar figure as annual and multiyear authorizations usually do. Instead, it is specified that sums "necessary and proper" to carry out the program should be appropriated.[9] Oversight and control of these programs is left to the Appropriations Committees. Permanent authorizations create stability in federal programs, such as Social Security. Other items with indefinite authority include fixed costs such as interest on the national debt, although this is subject to debt-ceiling limitations. As the major changes in Social Security in 1977 suggest, Congress can and does make significant changes in programs with permanent authorizations.

Over half the budget is currently under permanent authorization, somewhat less than it has been in previous decades. While the stability is important in many programs, many members of Congress feel the permanent authority shields much of the budget from control, and many programs from careful scrutiny.

Crosswalking

Budget resolutions specify targets and ceilings on the basis of budget functions, but authorizing decisions are

Table 8-3   House Agriculture Committee Jurisdiction
(Budget Functions That Include Authorizations from Agriculture Committee)

Budget Function	Example of Agriculture Programs Included in Function
International affairs	Agriculture trade assistance
Natural resources, environment, and energy	Land and water conservation
Agriculture	Farm subsidy program
Commerce and transportation	Commodities futures trading commission
Community and regional development	Rural waste disposal
Health	Control of pesticides
Income security	Food stamp program
Revenue sharing and general purpose fiscal assistance	Agriculture assistance to states
Interest	Agency borrowing

Source: House Budget Committee, *Views and Estimates of Standing Committees,* FY 1977, pp. 1-56.

made in the traditional agency and program categories. Allocations in the budget resolutions must be translated into committee subtotals by crosswalking. The House Agriculture Committee presents a good example of crosswalking. Table 8-3 shows that nine of the functions listed in the resolutions are partially under the jurisdiction of the Agriculture Committee. This is almost half of the 19 functions (there were only 16 until 1979). Besides the "agriculture" function, the committee authorizes programs in the international affairs, health, income security, and commerce and transportation functions. This breakdown must be made for every authorizing committee in order to implement the resolutions, and one must go in the other direction to monitor compliance with the targets.

Changes in the Authorizing Process

Although they play a central role in the budgetary process, the standing committees in Congress consider themselves legislative, not budgetary, units. Their primary interest is in their substantive specialization and the legislation they must consider. The timetable established by the 1974 budget act required that they act more quickly and more regularly, instead of at their own pace. Some members of the authorizing committees feel the deadlines are too rigid, allowing too little time to adequately consider their legislation.[10] Because of the uncertainty at the time of the March 15 reports, committees have tended to come in high in the estimates. But the March 15 reports require all committees in Congress to participate in a regular yearly budget cycle, and this is an improvement over past practices.

The May 15 deadline also has posed some problems for the authorizing committees, but most have reported legislation by this date. One of the results is a disproportionate number of bills reported right before the deadline, and more bills reported than previously was the case, some without extensive hearings. This is another outcome of the uncertainty and the timetable. Overall, budget reform has improved the authorizing process. Backdoor spending has been reduced, and decisions are better coordinated.

The Ways and Means and Finance Committees

Not only do the House Ways and Means and Senate Finance Committees control the revenue side of the budget, but they are the two most influential authorizing committees. Table 8-1 showed that they had about 40 percent of annual outlays under their jurisdiction. Table 8-4 examines the specific spending programs that the two committees oversee. Included are Social Security, medicare, medicaid, welfare (ADC), unemployment compensation, and revenue sharing. Both the House and the Senate have turned back attempts to carve up the jurisdiction of the two committees. Recent congressional battles, such as changes in Social Security, have taken place in the somewhat misnamed "tax-writing" committees. Future battles, such as the adoption of national health insurance, will also take place there.

The policy influence of the Ways and Means and Finance Committees is not limited to the big expenditure

Table 8-4   Finance Committee Spending Jurisdiction
Fiscal Year 1979, New Budget Authority

Programs	Direct Spending Jurisdiction	Entitlements Funded Through Appropriations
Social Security	$102,727	
Federal hospital insurance	21,894	
Federal supplementary medical insurance	9,751	
Unemployment insurance	15,994	$ 885
Social Service		2,578
Medicaid		11,253
AFDC		6,663
Supplemental security income		5,558
Revenue sharing	6,855	
Interest on debt	54,700	
Refundable earned income credit	841	
Other	524	
Total — Fiscal 1979*	$213,588	$ 34,289
Grand Total†		$247,877

*Allocation in second resolution FY 1979.
†Total does not reflect certain actions completed in 2d session, 95th Congress.
Source: *Senate Budget Scorekeeping Report*, No. 79-11, November 13, 1978, p. 47.

items. Control of tax policy and federal revenues affects policy in a multitude of ways. One result of the actions of these committees is the growth in tax expenditures. Chapter 10 examines the concept of tax expenditures in greater detail. They represent special tax provisions such as exclusions, exemptions, deductions, and credits. By recommending a variety of tax benefits, many behavioral objectives can be achieved: spending or saving more, investing, insulating, owning a home, driving an economy car, and so forth. The cost to the Treasury of these special tax provisions increased almost 200 percent in the last decade.

Changes in the Committees

The House Ways and Means Committee is considered one of the most powerful committees in Congress. A decade ago, Chairman Wilbur Mills (D-Arkansas) was called the second most powerful man in Washington. He ran the committee firmly but with the support of the members. Mills had abolished subcommittees in the late 1950s, and centralized the power around himself.[11] As an expert in the highly technical area of the federal revenue code, Mills was able to dominate decision making through both expertise and compromise.

Committees tend to be less dominant in the Senate, and the Finance Committee was not considered as powerful as its House counterpart. Nonetheless, led by Senator Russell Long (D-Louisiana), it is one of the more powerful committees in the Senate. In the 1970s, both committees faced challenges to their autonomy and power.[12] In the House, the Democratic caucus adopted a number of reforms aimed specifically at the Ways and Means Committee, such as requiring open hearings. (Mills had kept most of his hearings closed.) In 1973, the caucus limited the committee's ability to use a closed rule on the floor to prevent amendments. A rule requiring all committees with more than 20 members to have at least four subcommittees was aimed exclusively at Ways and Means. Even more significant changes were imposed in 1974. The committee was stripped of its power to make assignments of members to other committees (Ways and Means had served for decades as the Democratic Committee on Committees). The caucus acted to enlarge the committee from 25 to 37 members and created a fifth subcommittee. All these changes were made easier by the personal decline of Mills, who was involved in the "Tidal Basin" affair and revealed a problem with alcoholism. Representative Al Ullman was selected as the new chairman in December of 1974, just as the budget process was first implemented.

The Senate Finance Committee was not the target of reform as much as the House Ways and Means Committee had been, but there were several challenges. Committee sessions were opened, and printed transcripts of the proceedings were produced. But other reforms were turned back. Long was able to keep a steady grip on the committee and hold back the reformist tides of the mid-70s. Significantly, both committees rebuffed attempts to reduce their jurisdiction over several of the large spending programs.

Changes in the Revenue Process

Of all the participants in the congressional budget process, the tax-writing committees have been affected the least by budget reform. They may actually have gained power under the new system. Coordination of tax decisions with spending decisions remains loose and vague. There are no figures in the budget resolutions dealing with revenues with the exception of a revenue floor. Resting on this one figure, almost any combination of tax provisions can be devised, if it produces approximately the right amount of money. Tax expenditures are not approved in the budget resolution, so unlike the functional totals on the spending side, there is no way to take an overview of the revenue provisions. Because the tax benefits are individually popular, they are difficult to vote against. But the result is further tax losses, further fragmentation of the tax structure, and no systematic overview of revenue policy.

Some additional constraints have been imposed on the Ways and Means and Finance Committees. They have been involved in several losing battles with the Budget Committees over tax issues. Although there is greater coordination of taxing and spending than previously, there is still room for improvement.

The Appropriations Committees

Of all the participants in congressional budgeting, the House and Senate Appropriations Committees had the most to lose through budget reform. They had been the dominant force in spending decisions, but many of the failures in the congressional system were attributed to them. Recognizing their own shortcomings, the Appropriations Committees supported the new budget process.

In contrast to the Ways and Means Committee and the Finance Committee, the Appropriations Committees are decentralized; most of the work (about 95 percent) is done in subcommittee. The 13 subcommittees control various portions of the allocation. Table 8-5 shows the 13

Table 8-5   Appropriations Subcommittees and Allocation U.S. Senate, FY 1979

(in billions of dollars)

Subcommittee	New Budget Authority	Share
Defense	$120,300	34.1%
Labor; Health, Education and Welfare	73,687	20.8%
HUD; Independent Agencies	70,356	10.9%
Agriculture	22,184	6.2%
Interior	11,962	3.5%
Public Works	10,462	2.8%
Transportation	9,873	2.7%
Treasury, Post Office, General Government	9,714	2.7%
Foreign Operations	9,273	2.6%
State, Justice, Commerce, Judiciary	9,192	2.6%
Military Construction	3,881	1.0%
Legislative Branch	1,127	.3%
District of Columbia	287	.05%
Total, Appropriations Committee	$353,076*	100%*

*Totals vary because of rounding.
Source: *Senate Budget Scorekeeping Report*, No. 79-11, November 13, 1978, 95th Congress, 2nd session.

subcommittees for the Senate in the 95th Congress, their allocations, and relative share. Subcommittees and allocations are comparable for the House. Reflecting the major budget items, the Defense and Labor-HEW subcommittees have the largest amounts of executive requests to approve.

As the budget has become more complex, the categories in line-item appropriations encompass larger and larger accounts.[13] But the Appropriations Committees have other devices to assert control over the bureaucracy.[14] The committees may write financial restrictions into the spending bills, limiting or prohibiting certain expenditures. Specific policy directives may be included in the bill or in the accompanying report. The committees may also require the agencies to submit more detailed budget estimates for certain activities and projects.

Changes in the Committees

The traditional view of the Appropriations Committees portrayed them as "power" committees, oriented to maintaining their internal influence within Congress.[15] Traditionally, the committees adopted the role of budget guardian, cutting executive-branch requests. Richard Fenno extracted the language of guardianship from his interviews with Appropriations Committee members:

> The action verbs most commonly used are 'cut,' 'carve,' 'slice,' 'prune,' 'whittle,' 'squeeze,' 'wring,' 'trim,' 'lop off,' 'chop,' 'slash,' 'pare,' 'shave,' 'shack,' and 'fry.' The tools of the trade are appropriately referred to as 'knife,' 'blade,' 'meat axe,' 'scalpel,' 'meat cleaver,' 'hatchet,' 'shears,' 'wringer,' and 'fine tooth comb . . .' Budgets are praised when they are 'cut to the bone.'[16]

At the same time, they sought to provide adequate funding for major programs. The general ideological consonance between Republicans and Democrats over their budget-cutting role has tended to facilitate consensus. There remains today an atmosphere of bipartisanship on the committees.

The Senate Appropriations Committee differed from the House Appropriations Committee in several ways.[17] The House, as originator of spending bills, historically has had a primary position in the appropriations process. The committee in the Senate, more oriented to constituent service, was less integrated and powerful. The House tended to have longer, more detailed hearings on the agency requests and to make deeper cuts in requests. Because the House acted before the Senate, agencies had a better idea of where they stood before the Senate review. As a result, agencies were in the habit of appealing cuts made in the House to the Senate committee, counting on the Senate to recommend slightly more than the House in a majority of cases. The Senate Appropriations Committee has been characterized as a "court of appeals" for agencies. With the development of the budget process, however, the differences in both the timing and the actions of the two committees have been reduced.

By the end of the 1960s, it had become apparent that the decentralized appropriations process was not capable of dealing with the changes in the national budget. In the minds of many members, they had fallen short in their role as guardian of the public purse. In the 1970s, the House Appropriations Committee appears to have developed more of a constituency orientation, emphasizing benefits to their districts. This is consistent with more general changes in Congress and the reduction in the number of marginal districts and incumbent defeats.[18] The increase in committee advocacy in the 1970s was reflected in Table 8-2. This trend also was fostered by a change in how members are assigned to subcommittees. Member self-interest has increased because farmers now sit on the agriculture subcommittee, and so forth.

The results of these changes in the committee and the implementation of the budget process have reduced the power and autonomy of the Appropriations Committees. Although they are still among the most powerful in Congress, their reputations have declined. The budget resolutions have added a set of external constraints that were not present before. Despite the changes, the Appropriations Committees remain the most important stage for congressional scrutiny of executive-branch programs and activities.

Committee Review of Agency Programs

What kind of information do the Appropriations Committees seek and what kinds of questions do the members ask? While each agency, program, and subcommittee may be very different, some regular patterns emerge. In reviewing agency operations, committee questions may focus on one or several of the following: (1) existence — is this program or agency necessary? (2) objectives — what are the goals of the agency; are they the correct goals? (3) results — can the agency show benefits and justify previous program spending? (4) line-item changes — why does it cost this much to operate these programs; what will new programs cost? Why does the agency need more or less than last year's appropriations for a particular expense? As listed here, these lines of inquiry are ranked from *least* frequent to *most* frequent focus of questioning.

Existence Most agencies do not have to justify their existence or the existence of major programs. At any given time the consensus is that the vast majority of federal activities are justified and should continue. A few agencies and programs, however, are the exceptions to this rule, and usually face the most difficult appropriations situation. Even in most of these cases, only one or two subcommittee members will be antagonistic in questioning an agency's existence.

Although NASA retains a supportive coalition in Congress, some members call the space program a national luxury. These critics argue that too much is spent for space when so many social needs go unfunded or underfunded. Foreign aid programs have continually been opposed by some members of Congress. Representative Otto Passman, former chairman of the Foreign Operations Subcommittee of the House Appropriations Committee, opposed foreign spending for decades. In grilling ACTION officials over their foreign budget,[19] Passman questioned the need for the Peace Corps. He delighted in pointing out how much they contributed to the national debt, how they were partially responsible for public works projects being stopped, and how they duplicated the work of other agencies:

> REPRESENTATIVE PASSMAN (D-Louisiana): Can you tell the Committee what has been accomplished by the Peace Corps which would justify this large investment that could not have been done equally well or better by the AID (Agency for International Development) technical assistance programs?[20]

Despite opposition that questions their basic existence, NASA, the Peace Corps, and foreign aid programs have survived. Such questioning often takes place with the full realization that the programs will continue. Still, such explicit opposition is rare; most appropriations hearings operate on the premise that the agency and programs are here for the foreseeable future. Investigation centers on what they have done and want to do. While some agencies have been put out of existence, this is extremely rare.

Objectives Acknowledging the continued existence of an agency, the subcommittee members may question the goals and objectives of the agency. Members may be antagonistic if they feel the agency priorities are not in line with those of Congress:

> REPRESENTATIVE FLOOD (D-Pennsylvania): Doctor, in the budget justification for the Heart and Lung Institute, here is this statement:
>
> For more than 50 years heart and blood vessel diseases have

> been the major causes of death in this country. . . . This is
> three times the deaths from cancer, the next highest.
>
> In light of that statement, how do you explain the fact that the
> Heart Institute budget is only 50 percent of the investment in
> the Cancer Institute . . .?
>
> DR. LAMONT HAVERS (National Institutes of Health):   The first
> factor . . . determining the budget of NIH is the societal
> pressures and concerns as reflected primarily through the
> political process. . . . As I look over the history of the past 40
> years or so, our society first fears cancer, and the next fear is
> heart, and that is where they put their priorities.[21]

The case of heart disease versus cancer is a good
example of the difficulty of specifying and debating
objectives. While elimination of both are perhaps equally
worthy goals, budgetary participants find it easier to
agree on spending for heart and cancer research than
deciding how much more important one is than another.
In the appropriations process, the money allocated
represents an implicit set of program objectives rather
than an explicit statement on value to society. While the
subcommittees often discuss goals and objectives, for the
most part these are not the main concern of the hearings.
Like an agency's continued existence, program objectives
are generally left unspecific and assumed to be clear. More
attention is paid to results, costs, and changes from
previous budgets.

   Results   Agencies like to prove to the subcommittee
that they are doing a good job and summon all the
supportive data they can find. Showing positive results is
more difficult for some agencies than others. Compare the
differences in testimony between the Peace Corps and the
domestic components of ACTION:

> MR. HESS (Peace Corps):   There are benefits that accrue to
> those people in the countries where we serve, in terms of
> manpower training. A second benefit is that the volunteers
> who serve in the Peace Corps become much better acquainted
> with the problems in foreign countries, and are . . . able to put
> America in a little bit better perspective in the World. Third,
> Mr. Congressman, benefits accrue to the people in those
> countries who associate on a daily basis with Peace Corps
> volunteers and gain a much better familiarity with
> Americans.[22]

Before a different appropriations subcommittee, the
benefits from domestic volunteer programs are described
in terms of cost-benefit analysis.

> MR. MOULD (ACTION):   In the case of the foster grandparents'
> program using fiscal year 1971 in which a total of $12.2 million

was invested, the return on that was $13.8 million, or a net excess of economic benefits of $1.6 million. In the case of the RSVP (Retired Senior Volunteer Program), the volunteers produced man-hours of service evaluated at a 2-to-1 benefit to cost ratio.[23]

Members of Congress want to see results for the money they appropriate. Even supporters of an agency like to have tangible evidence to help rationalize their support. Committee members may be put off by results that look foolish and will draw attention to consequences that seem to be of questionable value to the public. The following observations during the NIH hearings are suggestive:

> REPRESENTATIVE SHRIVER (D-Kansas): Sometimes NIH-supported projects make it difficult for some of us to understand the benefit derived by the people who are paying the bills — our taxpayers. . . . This project, which apparently stretched over about a year, supposedly proved that baby monkeys will accept mongrel dogs as substitute mothers. I have read this release carefully — it even included a picture of a monkey clinging to a dog — and I can't find any potential help for human health problems. The main findings seem to be that the monkey reached the point where they preferred the company of dogs rather than other monkeys, although any old dog would do. I'm not sure this is a step forward.[24]

Agencies facing more programmatic queries but lacking tangible evidence of results must be innovative. NASA, for example, computes a cost benefit of seven to one for its spending. In presentations to the committees, it details how NASA programs benefit consumer and capital goods manufacturing, environmental products, food production and processing, petroleum and gas industries, construction, transportation, and health, among others.[25] Almost all hearings include some inquiries about results. Some agencies are able to provide better responses than others.

Line-item changes Subcommittee members seem to be most confident and comfortable when talking about money. They can relate all agency activities to the common denominator of dollars. Appropriations hearings usually focus not on an agency's existence, objectives, or even performance, but on the cost of its programs. If costs are running high, something must be wrong.

> REPRESENTATIVE TALCOTT (R-California): Name me one large local housing authority that did operate effectively and without an operating subsidy.

> SECRETARY CRAWFORD (Assistant Secretary, HUD):   The most
> efficient, well-managed housing authority in the country is
> New York City. However, they require operating subsidies
> because of inflationary factors and other reasons.[26]

Subcommittee Chairman Boland stated the committee's
objections to inefficiency and confusion more succinctly:

> REPRESENTATIVE BOLAND (D-Massachusetts):   One thing is
> clear, unless the management of HUD is improved, unless the
> right hand knows what the left is doing, the appropriation of
> billions of dollars of program funds is going to be wasted.[27]

When the subcommittee, committee, and Congress
support certain policies, they are reluctant to punish
inefficiency and mismanagement by cutting the budget.
Congress is limited in its ability to improve management,
so the hearings are often an opportunity to lecture
agencies to do a better job. Despite the complexity of the
budget, members of the subcommittees sometimes show a
remarkable eye for detail.

> REPRESENTATIVE ROONEY (D-Pennsylvania):   You suggest an
> increase in limitation to $1.8 million for administrative
> expenses. You actually need, you say, but $1,782,900. You have
> delightfully rounded this out so as to increase the amount of the
> limitation by $17,100. Did you know that this was done?[28]

Appropriations subcommittees, in spite of their
specialization, rarely undertake extensive program
review. Instead, they focus on changes in an agency's
request. This provides the committee with a cue that
something meriting their attention is taking place.
Committee members want to know the purpose of a
proposed increase or the reason for a decrease. Like the
OMB budget examiner, being unable to review
everything, the congressmen look for clues to problems in
program operations or for substantive policy changes.
The Department of Defense (DOD) budget demonstrates
the dilemma of subcommittee review. There are no
members who question the need for national defense;
hearings focus on projected costs for a certain military
capability, funding new weapons systems, and meeting
the increasing costs of the military establishment.
Committee members have shown an increasing
understanding of more technical points than in the past,
and are sometimes suspicious of padding by DOD
officials. In spite of the fact that most of the controllable
dollars are in defense, the majority of the budget is not
discretionary and is not actively reviewed. The main

focus is on changes in proposed expenditures, new programs, and increased costs.

Patterns of Appropriations

Congress still tends to make marginal cuts in executive requests for appropriations, although congressional increases are more prevalent than in the past. Table 8-6 shows the percentage of requests appropriated by Congress from 1969 to 1979 at the department level plus major independent agencies. As a word of caution, this level of aggregation conceals many variations in individual agency budgets, as well as agency programs. It does, however, provide an impression of overall appropriation patterns. The differences between fiscal 1969 and 1970 are quite noticeable; Congress approved a higher proportion of requests for every department in 1970 than in 1969, with the exception of the Defense Department. In the first year of the Nixon Administration, Congress began to back off from its role as budget cutter, a behavior pattern that continued through the Ford Administration. While defense averaged 94 percent approval of requests from 1970 to 1975 (i.e., an annual cut of 6 percent by Congress), health, education, and welfare agencies (excluding most uncontrollables) averaged 102 percent (i.e., an annual increase of 2 percent over the President's requests).

The record of appropriations change shown in Table 8-7 also reveals some interesting patterns. While the State Department displays a stable growth pattern (but recall the high inflation, particularly 1974-1975), other departments, like Labor, had a fluctuating pattern of appropriations change. So much lies behind each figure that it is impossible to convey the many budgetary and policy issues negotiated in this period. For example, the Labor Department changes are the result of fluctuating spending for manpower programs; Agriculture Department appropriations include commitments for crop subsidy payments that vary widely from year to year. Housing appropriations for 1971 included new congressional programs in housing. The change would have been even greater had Nixon not vetoed the original higher version of the HUD appropriations bill. It is obvious that major appropriations changes do occur, as a

Table 8-6 Congressional Action on Executive Requests
(percentage of requests approved by Congress)

Department or Agency	1969	1970	1971	1972	1973	1974	1975	1976	1977	1978
National Aeronautics and Space Administration	91.4%	99.5%	98.0%	99.9%	100.0%	99.5%	98.9%	99.9%	99.6%	99.5%
Veterans Administration	92.6	100.4	101.2	101.8	100.7	100.4	99.9	100.4	100.4	100.1
Housing and Urban Development	44.3	91.5	111.7	128.0	86.6	115.4	95.1	89.6	96.7	96.1
Defense	93.2	92.5	96.8	95.9	93.4	96.1	94.8	96.6	97.6	98.3
Labor	94.8	97.8	97.5	98.2	99.9	100.1	111.9	106.4	89.0	100.3
Health, Education, and Welfare	97.1	98.0	101.4	103.2	106.8	103.8	97.2	107.4	100.2	97.6
Atomic Energy Commission	93.3	93.9	96.6	98.1	99.1	96.2	96.5	98.0	98.7	97.5
Agriculture	105.5	115.4	116.6	100.2	103.7	98.0	96.8	100.7	98.7	101.1
Transportation	84.5	102.5	95.1	101.6	98.6	96.2	93.1	100.8	98.6	94.4
Interior	88.6	99.0	99.0	99.5	100.0	102.5	100.1	98.1	99.9	90.2
Treasury—Post Office	98.9	99.6	98.9	97.4	98.7	99.1	97.5	103.9	98.5	97.6
State	94.3	98.9	98.0	97.2	97.1	97.7	94.8	99.3	98.5	97.8
Justice	92.3	95.5	99.3	98.4	99.4	99.0	97.3	103.9	96.8	100.1
Commerce	91.8	95.7	93.7	94.6	102.3	101.0	97.1	112.8	101.8	90.8

Source: Congressional Quarterly Almanac, 1968-1975.

Table 8-7 Appropriations Change

(percentage change in appropriations from previous year)

Department or Agency	1970	1971	1972	1973	1974	1975	1976	1977	1978
National Aeronautics and Space Administration	-7.5%	-11.6%	.9%	3.3%	-11.9%	6.8%	4.5%	8.8%	8.2%
Veterans Administration	10.5	17.7	20.6	8.9	3.0	14.0	3.1	-3.3	3.2
Housing and Urban Development	-12.0	78.8	-2.0	23.2	-23.3	-2.5	-2.6	93.8	-15.0
Defense	-3.1	-4.4	5.9	5.4	-.2	11.3	15.3	5.1	6.8
Labor	41.6	100.8	-33.2	125.5	-73.4	326.0	190.8	-43.9	-56.4
Health, Education, and Welfare	3.1	-4.8	24.5	41.3	15.2	-6.9	42.8	17.8	-0.2
Atomic Energy Commission	-13.7	2.9	.5	14.8	-11.3	-25.4	13.4	15.1	14.5
Agriculture	23.8	47.7	75.5	1.2	-13.3	22.9	4.4	10.4	43.4
Transportation	31.2	21.7	11.4	3.2	-3.4	11.7	36.1	16.9	41.1
Interior	14.3	40.8	16.9	11.0	-8.5	30.5	33.2	76.8	-16.0
Treasury—Post Office	6.8	15.2	25.3	7.5	4.6	30.8	31.6	-10.0	20.1
State	3.6	16.2	11.2	11.7	11.7	14.1	29.1	17.9	-0.03
Justice	59.8	38.6	39.5	12.9	4.3	13.9	4.9	2.8	7.4
Commerce	2.5	21.3	26.1	14.5	-10.3	12.3	-4.4	26.8	14.4

Source: Congressional Quarterly Almanac, 1968-1975.

result of both executive and legislative initiative. Tables
8-6 and 8-7 provide a rough indicator of some of the fronts
for budgetary battles in the 1970s although the figures
alone fail to detail their precise nature. While the budget
will always look much like last year's budget, and many
agencies have very stable funding patterns, significant
changes in the budget do occur.

The outcomes of the appropriations process depend on a
number of factors:

(1) the nature of the program
(2) the assertiveness of the agency
(3) subcommittee relationships with the agency
(4) the political environment and member goals
(5) constraints imposed by the budget resolutions

Certain popular programs may be destined for budget
growth regardless of what the agency officials may do. In
more normal cases, shrewd and forceful agency
leadership may pay dividends. In their dealings over the
years, agency officials tend to establish fairly stable
relationships with the Appropriations Committees.
Individual members vary from enthusiastic support to
vehement opposition with the majority of members being
"skeptically supportive."

As the political climate in the country and in the
government changes, committee behavior may change.
Developments in the executive branch led to differing
patterns of appropriations in the 1970s. The movement for
budget reform represented a new set of demands for
budget control that had not been forthcoming in the
previously fragmented system.

A number of changes in the appropriations process
have occurred over the past two decades. The
Appropriations Committees tend to be less stringent
guardians than they once were, evidencing more frequent
advocacy. The committees have lost some of the
institutional power they once enjoyed. The Senate
Appropriations Committee is now more nearly the equal
of the House Appropriations Committee. The budget
process itself has reduced the autonomy the committees
once had on the spending side of the budget. But the
changes have been gradual, and the Appropriations
Committees have cooperated fully with the Budget
Committees.

Budget reform has changed the nature of congressional budgeting, including the authorization, revenue, and appropriation processes. The system is still fragmented, but it is more structured and timely. Congressional budgeting is still predominantly a "bottom-up" process, but the budget resolutions have begun to shape decisions from the top down. Yet there are still gaps in legislative control and oversight of executive-branch spending. Additional reforms, such as multiyear budgeting and sunset legislation, are examined in Chapter 12. And as the next chapter suggests, agencies still retain considerable discretion in executing the enacted budget.

FOOTNOTES

*As quoted by Aaron Wildavsky, *The Politics of the Budgetary Process* (Boston: Little, Brown, 1964), p. 100.

[1]Wildavsky, p. 99.

[2]John S. Saloma III, "Legislative Effectiveness: Control and Investigation," in *Congress and the President: Allies and Adversaries,* ed. Ronald C. Moe (Pacific Palisades, California: Goodyear Publishing Co., 1971), pp. 192-194.

[3]Committee on the Budget, U.S. Senate, *Hearings, Can Congress Control the Power of the Purse?,* 95th Congress, 2nd session, March 6, 1978.

[4]Allen Schick, *Congressional Control of Expenditures,* Committee on the Budget, U.S. House of Representatives, CP-95-1, January 1977, p. 24.

[5]*Ibid.*

[6]*Ibid.,* p. 22.

[7]Richard Nathan and Charles Adams, *Revenue Sharing: The Second Round* (Washington, D.C.: Brookings Institution, 1977).

[8]Schick, p. 24.

[9]*Ibid.,* p. 19.

[10]Committee on the Budget, U.S. House of Representatives, *Hearings, Oversight of the Congressional Budget Process,* 95th Congress, 1st session, October 5-6, 1977.

[11]John Manley, *The Politics of Finance* (Boston: Little, Brown, 1970).

[12]Catherine Rudder, "Committee Reform and the Revenue Process," in *Congress Reconsidered,* ed. Laurence Dodd and Bruce Oppenheimer (New York: Praeger, 1977), p. 119.

[13]Louis Fisher, *Presidential Spending Power* (Princeton: Princeton University Press, 1975), pp. 59-63.

[14]Schick, pp. 33-35.

[15]Richard Fenno, *Congressmen in Committees* (Boston: Little, Brown, 1973).

[16]Richard Fenno, *The Power of the Purse* (Boston: Little, Brown, 1965).

[17]Fenno, *Power,* p. 143.

[18]Morris Fiorina, *Congress: Keystone of the Washington Establishment* (New Haven: Yale University Press, 1977).

[19]Committee on Appropriations, Subcommittee on Foreign Assistance and Related Programs, House of Representatives, *Hearings,* 92nd Congress, 2nd session, 1972, p. 888.

[20]Committee on Appropriations, Subcommittee on Foreign Operations, U.S. House of Representatives, *Hearings, Peace Corps,* 93rd Congress, 2nd session, 1974, p. 946.

[21]Committee on Appropriations, Subcommittee on Labor, Health, Education and Welfare, U.S. House of Representatives, *Hearings, National Institutes of Health,* April 9, 1975, 94th Congress, 1st session, p. 16 (thereafter cited as *NIH Appropriation Hearings*).

[22]Committee on Appropriations, U.S. Senate, *Hearings, Foreign Assistance and Related Programs, Fiscal Year 1974,* 93rd Congress, 1st session, 1975, p. 411.

[23]Committee on Appropriations, U.S. House of Representatives, *Hearings Before a Subcommittee on Appropriations,* 93rd Congress, 1st session, 1973, p. 946.

[24]*NIH Appropriation Hearings,* p. 64.

[25]Committee on Appropriations, Subcommittee on Housing and Urban Development, U.S. House of Representatives, *Hearings, National Aeronautics and Space Administration,* 94th Congress, 2nd session, February 18, 1976, pp. 114-129.

[26]Committee on Appropriations, Subcommittee on Housing and Urban Development-Independent Agencies, U.S. House of Representatives, *Hearings, Department of Housing and Urban Development,* 93rd Congress, 2nd session, May 21, 1974.

[27]*Ibid.*

[28]As quoted in Wildavsky, p. 109.

Budget
Execution

Chapter IX

In many cases the decisive commitment to spend funds is made not by Congress but by executive officials.*

Budgetary politics does not end with the final passage of appropriations bills and the second resolution in Congress. Rather, a new phase begins. The process of disbursing and spending money makes up the third level of budgeting — the operation level. Agency budgets are not self-executing. The operation of agency programs involves decisions on purchasing goods and services, timing of obligations, and the reallocation of funds within and between appropriation accounts. The politics observed in the process of executive preparation and congressional approval continue into this phase of budgeting.

Unlike decisions made in cyclical fashion, operations budgeting takes place on a continuous basis. Decisions are limited by allocations made at earlier stages and by a number of formal legal requirements, OMB regulations, and agreements with the appropriations subcommittees. Yet, within the constraints imposed by higher-level decisions, agencies retain latitude for considerable discretion. As obligations are incurred and expenditures made, agencies may discover a different situation than originally anticipated in formulating their requests. As administrators implement the current budget, they may need to reallocate funds within their operations. They may make supplemental requests or petitions to transfer funds and they may alter the substance of future budgets based on current operations.

Agencies must decide how much to spend. The legal requirements governing the expenditure of funds may result in tactics by agencies such as attempts to spend money very quickly before the fiscal year expires. If they have a large carry-over, Congress may reduce their budget next year; if they run out of money early, they may be accused of using the tactic of "coercive deficiency," and supplemental funds are not guaranteed.[1] How agencies spend their funds affects not only the programs they administer but their subsequent stance in the budgetary process.

This chapter examines several basic questions concerning the implementation of a budget. How is the budget executed, reviewed, and audited? How much discretion do agencies have in spending money? The politics of budget execution reveal a basic conflict between legislative control and administrative discretion. Agencies have a variety of means available for increasing their own control over expenditures, while Congress, in turn, can attempt to impose greater restrictions on the agencies. The case of covert funding provides an example of extreme agency control over its own budget. All these questions surround the budget at its final stage, when the billion-dollar totals of national priorities become discrete, observable implementing actions taken by the bureaucracy.

Implementing the Budget

Disbursement and Apportionment

Appendix C displays graphically the execution of the enacted budget. After the appropriations bills have been passed, appropriation warrants are sent to the agency by the U.S. Treasury. At this time, the agency revises its operating budget for the coming year, even though the passage of the second concurrent resolution could require last-minute changes. Agencies also prepare requests for OMB indicating how they would like their money apportioned to them in the coming year.

The OMB is responsible for distributing money to the agencies by an agreed upon apportionment system. Most agencies receive their funds on a quarterly basis; this serves to make expenditures more uniform over the fiscal year. Some agencies may operate under different time periods or by activities; for example, an agency may have a particularly large purchase in a certain month. Funds are obligated when the agency spends them under a system analogous to the use of a large checking account. The OMB does not put all the money for the year in at once; it is doled out in portions so that there is some left towards the end of the year. Funds are obligated by drawing on the accounts in the 12 Federal Reserve banks. The OMB is empowered to withhold certain funds in order to establish reserves. As Chapter 6 showed, the practice of impoundment, reaching its height under the Nixon Administration, involved withholding billions of dollars for policy reasons, not just to establish reserves. Under the Impoundment Control Act this is now illegal, although OMB may still withhold funds "for contingencies, to effect savings and to promote greater efficiency of operations."[2] The President may request that budget authority approved by Congress be rescinded or deferred. Both of these actions require congressional approval, although deferrals are automatically approved unless either house objects.

Agency budget officers must see that they spend within the apportioned limits, whether it be to purchase goods and services, make necessary payments on contracts, buy supplies, or pay utility bills, transportation expenses,

salaries, or benefits. Agency officials must file reports
with OMB (as frequently as every month for some
agencies) on their expenditures. The OMB also uses this
stage to promote management goals, requiring the
agencies to report on program objectives, manpower
improvements, and other cost-efficiency information. The
monies are actually paid out after the proper vouchers
have been signed and the Treasury issues checks.

Review and Audit

The final stage in the process consists of audits of
agency operations to insure that obligations and outlays
follow the provisions of the authorizing and
appropriating legislation and all other rules governing
the expenditure of funds.[3] The General Accounting Office
(GAO) serves as the main auditor of the federal
government. The comptroller general, head of GAO,
audits, examines, and evaluates agency programs. The
GAO does not audit every agency account every year.
Rather, it does so selectively on a sampling basis. Reports
on violations, findings, and recommendations for
correction are reported to Congress, OMB, and the
agencies themselves. The GAO is also responsible for
monitoring the rescission and deferral process. The
comptroller general reports any withholding of funds not
reported by the President and may bring civil action
against the President if he fails to comply with the law.[4]

The process of budget review and audit takes up to 12
months after the end of the fiscal year. This means that an
annual budget finally becomes history more than three
years after its initial preparation. Some of its provisions
and decisions may have implications for many more
years. The process of budget execution and audit involves
many more subtleties than this brief description implies.
There are various ways for agencies to manipulate
expenditures to serve their own needs and sometimes to
frustrate the desires of Congress.

Agency Control of Spending

The Limits of Congressional Control

Congress has always recognized the need to allow some agency discretion in spending because the situation can change between the time money is appropriated and later when it is spent.[5] Historically, Congress has fluctuated between very specific line-item appropriations and broader grants of money.[6] During periods of national emergency, Congress has been more willing to appropriate lump sums to the executive branch. Although the appropriations process does not review every program from the ground up every year, the subcommittees do closely examine the line-item requests. In fact, the degree of congressional control is greater than appears in the actual appropriations bills. The Appropriations Committees often earmark parts of a budget item for specific purposes, and agencies are expected to follow these directives. Such information is often contained in the hearings, committee reports, and floor debate. Agencies are also bound by agreement to maintain expenditures within the line-items in the President's budget, as approved by Congress, even if not written into the appropriations bill. The committees may go further and require an agency to submit a more detailed budget before initiating a program.

In spite of the constitutional principle of congressional control over the budget and the specific controls exercised by Congress and the Appropriations Committees, it is increasingly difficult for them to maintain a thorough oversight of agency spending. Agencies have available a number of techniques to increase their own discretion. While Congress must be a willing partner in some of these methods, an opportunity for abuse exists that can unnecessarily weaken legislative control.

Contingency Funds

Since unforeseen events may require sudden expenditures, Congress has often provided emergency or contingency funds.[7] Agencies have periodically misused these funds or used them to substitute for funds they failed

to have appropriated. Contingency funds in foreign aid
have particularly been used to circumvent congressional
action.[8] Congressman John Rhodes (R-Arizona)
described the foreign assistance contingency fund as
being used for only one contingency, "that the House and
Senate did not appropriate as much money for this
program as the people downtown would like."[9] President
Kennedy used such funds to start the Peace Corps and
President Johnson used some to pay for a commission on
civil disorders.[10] Congress responded by slashing the
fund and forbidding its use for any project that had been
submitted to Congress. Yet the fund continued to be
abused; President Nixon spent money on projects that
would hardly qualify as an emergency, including the gift
of a $3 million helicopter to Egypt in 1974.[11]

As such funds are misused, Congress may respond by
reducing their size and use. Yet disasters like the
Guatemalan earthquake in 1976 show the need for readily
available funds to meet foreign emergencies. The same is
true for domestic programs. Unless Congress is willing to
eliminate all discretion, contingency funds are necessary
and the potential for abuse remains.

Reprogramming

Reprogramming consists of shifting funds *within* an
appropriation account. Unlike the transfer of funds
between accounts (see below), reprogramming is not
statutorily based but rather depends on "agreements"
with the Appropriations Committees.[12] These
agreements, however, are not always honored by the
agencies. The Army Corps of Engineers, the District of
Columbia Government, and the HEW Department were
all chastised by the Appropriations Committees for
disregarding congressional instructions. The GAO
reported that Internal Revenue had reprogrammed over
$40 million without approval of the Appropriations
Committees.[13] Reprogramming in the Defense
Department averaged over $2.5 billion a year between
1956 and 1972.[14] Congress first asked to be informed, later
required reports to be submitted, and finally required
DOD to obtain prior approval for reprogramming. In spite
of this, hundreds of shifts in funds take place without
congressional knowledge or approval. While

reprogramming itself is necessary and legitimate, as with contingency funds, it can be misused. An agency can pad a popular program and then reprogram it to another activity that might not receive congressional approval. In 1971, the Defense Intelligence Agency (DIA) tried to negate a $2 million cut imposed by the House Appropriations Committee by persuading the Pentagon to request reprogramming of $1.3 million to them.[15] Since reprogramming below a certain level does not require congressional approval, projects may be started with amounts below the thresholds. Congress is then approached for funding with the program already under way. Such circumvention of thresholds has been used by the Defense Department to undertake new research projects and to start new weapons systems.

While the appropriations review process in Congress may not be as thorough as some would like, it is very thorough compared with reprogramming decisions. Billions of dollars of reprogramming receives barely any attention at all. Unlike appropriations, most decisions on reprogramming need only be approved by committee, not by the entire Congress.

Transfer Authority

Unlike reprogramming, transfer authority allows agencies to shift funds from one appropriation account to another. Such actions must be approved by Congress. One of its most controversial uses was President Nixon's transfer of funds from foreign assistance accounts to the Defense Department to use in bombing Cambodia.[16] Previous congressional action allowed him to transfer up to 10 percent of foreign assistance money for "national security reasons." Although many members of Congress objected vehemently between 1970 and 1973, Congress continued to grant transfer authority to the President. In many cases Congress had little choice, since the actions had already been taken, and administration officials threatened to continue the operations regardless of what Congress did.[17] The ultimate result of the transfer of funds to finance operations in Cambodia was litigation filed by members of Congress against the President and a potential impeachment article against Nixon that was drafted in 1974.

Timing of Expenditures

In addition to shifting funds within their budget, agencies must also decide when to spend their money. They possess considerable latitude in these decisions. When Congress makes funds available for a specific period of time, any unobligated funds will lapse at the end of that period. "No year" appropriations can be obligated at any time by the agency. When agencies are not required to spend all the money in one year, there is a tendency to carry over large balances. This provides agencies with greater control over expenditures and reduces the relationship between appropriations and outlays. However, most agencies want to be sure to spend any funds that would lapse at the end of the fiscal year. The problem with large carry-over balances is that Congress makes subsequent reductions in appropriations. As a Pentagon official noted, there is "nothing as difficult as going asking for money when you've already got a pile of unused money."[18]

A rash of spending at the end of the fiscal year looks suspicious to Congress. Besides the OMB apportionment system, some appropriation bills limit the amount that can be spent at the end of the year. One the other hand, if agencies spend every nickel, Congress may feel they are not economizing. The optimum spending pattern would leave the agency with a small balance at the end of the year.[19]

One strategy employed by agencies is to underestimate the size of the unobligated balance that will be carried over that year. In 1961, the navy estimated a carry-over of $26 million; at the end of the year, actual carry-over was five times that.[20] Agencies may also recover funds that have been previously unavailable or may try to underestimate those gains. In both cases, the tactic of underestimation may backfire the next year and result in an appropriations cut by Congress.

Agencies may actually engage in illegal accounting practices to conceal transfers and carry-overs. In 1972 the U.S. Office of Education (USOE) failed to award some $55 million in contracts before the end of the fiscal year.[21] USOE proceeded to backdate actions in the previous fiscal year so as not to lose the funds. When these illegal expenditures were discovered, the agency was charged for the money in the current year, leaving them $55 million short. This put the Appropriations Committee in the unenviable position of being able to punish the agency by refusing to grant a supplemental appropriation — but at the expense of education programs for handicapped children. Congress finally required HEW to submit a reprogramming plan to cover these programs out of existing funding.

Agencies sometimes manipulate their expenditure decisions simply to reduce uncertainty caused by congressional delay in appropriations decisions and to balance relatively lean years with the more plentiful years. Having operated with a relatively tight budget from a continuing resolution throughout most of 1976, the Peace Corps suddenly found itself with more money than anticipated after the foreign operations appropriation finally passed. In addition, the prospects for the transition quarter (the unique period during the changeover in the start of fiscal years in 1976 and 1977) looked better. Agency officials were then concerned with being able to spend the money before the end of the fiscal year. One solution was to "forward-fund" certain expenses: pay for it this year and use it in future years. The Peace Corps paid for charter flights to be used in the next year and forward-funded several million dollars of contracts to train volunteers. Such practices on a large scale might be highly suspect, but Peace Corps budget officials reported that no objections to this practice had been raised in the past.

The desire of agencies to spend money before it lapses sometimes produces ill-conceived and hasty decisions that can plague an agency program for many years. One such case is the Economic Development Agency (EDA) and the Oakland projects in the 1960s.[22] In attempting to create permanent private-sector jobs for the hard-core unemployed, the EDA administrators were forced to approve projects and commit funds within a period of months:

> Only four months remained in which to process nearly $300 million worth of projects, since any not completed and approved by the end of May could not go through the required legal and fiscal machinery in time to be funded.[23]

Agency officials feared that if they failed to spend allotted funds they would be penalized in the subsequent year:

If EDA failed to use all of its current appropriation, the next
year's appropriation would almost certainly be cut by the
Budget Bureau and Congress.[24]

The decision was to spend all the money in one city
rather than divide the money among several. This
allowed EDA to commit all its funds before the deadline
and offered the possibility of a dramatic success. Because
of this hasty action, however, there was inadequate
investigation of alternatives, assessment of the political
situation, and consideration of the potential obstacles
involved in getting participants to fulfill their
responsibilities. The projects in Oakland were chosen and
the funds committed in time, but the results in most cases
were unspectacular if not outright failures.

Decisions on how much to spend and when to spend
have considerably more importance than might appear at
first glance. It becomes apparent that congressional
appropriations do not translate directly into
expenditures; many billions are manipulated to give
agencies greater autonomy in their operations.[25] While
the detailing of abuses may give a sinister aura to these
agency techniques, some discretion is essential to efficient
policy implementation.

Shortfalls and Overruns

The budget totals recommended by the President and
approved by the Congress are necessarily imprecise. They
are a mixture of a forecast of receipts, an estimation of
entitlement expenditures, and a prediction of agency
outlays. Actual expenditures by agencies often reflect
significant variation from what was approved. Although
individual agencies may have strategic objectives in
deciding what to spend, in many cases factors beyond
their control make it impossible to spend what was
anticipated. In the aggregate, this imprecision at the
operation level can affect general priorities and the fiscal
impact of the budget.

In the first years of the congressional budget process,
outlays were consistently below levels specified in the
budget resolutions. The shortfalls in spending amounted
to $10.1 billion in FY 1976, $7.8 billion in the transition
quarter, $7.3 billion in FY 1977, and $8.4 billion in FY
1978.[26] The shortfall during the transition quarter

suggests that this temporary change caused some confusion among budgetary participants. Of the underspending in 1976, approximately $4.8 billion was the result of faulty estimates for uncontrollable outlays for medicare and public assistance. The remainder was the result of the failure of agencies to commit funds as rapidly as anticipated. The Defense Department alone underspent in 1976 by $4 billion.

A favorable result of the shortfall was a reduction in the 1976 budget deficit. But of greater concern to economists was the fact that the underspending was linked to the economic slowdown in the fourth quarter of 1976. Underspending from 1976 to 1978 resulted in a reduction of stimulus to the economy of $32.6 billion from the amount approved.

Shortfalls are sometimes balanced by overruns. In 1978, for example, farm price supports were $4.5 billion more than was estimated.[27] By FY 1979, the increase in inflation was pushing both receipts and expenditures above the totals in the budget resolution. Between the first and second resolutions of FY 1980, CBO estimated an $8 billion overrun in spending, but a $10 billion increase in receipts.[28]

The margin of error in projecting outlays and revenues can be as great as 2 percent in a year. This reduces the ability of policy makers to fine-tune the economy or to direct national priorities. This again suggests the inherent limits on priority decisions and "top-down" budgeting. While agencies are constrained individually, their combined actions can have an impact on priorities.

Covert Budgeting

The area of greatest executive-branch discretion in budgeting is in intelligence operations. The operation of intelligence activities takes place without most members of Congress having an idea how much the U.S. spends on this function. Estimates run from $6 billion to as high as $10 billion.[29] The U.S. budget in the past has not listed spending requests of the Central Intelligence Agency (CIA), Defense Intelligence Agency (DIA), National

Security Agency (NSA), or any other intelligence-gathering agency. It would be impossible in such a short space to delve into the many controversies surrounding the intelligence community. But covert budgeting is of interest because it presents a contrast to the process of budget formulation and implementation in other agencies and an example of almost total budgetary autonomy.

Covert funding can take place in several ways.[30] One is the provision of confidential funds. These are appropriation accounts for an unnamed purpose, hidden in an appropriations bill. There are many agencies with confidential funds that can draw from the Treasury without the usual voucher and approval. Unvouchered expenditures can be drawn upon the approval of a single individual, usually the head of the agency. Second, funding may be totally secret, at no point appearing in the public record. The intelligence community is supported by both types of covert funding. The intelligence budget is mysterious because it is hidden in so many places and has so many sources. Funds from a variety of government agencies are transferred to the CIA through the Defense Department and other channels.[31] While Congress was a full partner in establishing the statutes that require secrecy of the intelligence budget, dissatisfaction has arisen because of CIA involvement in domestic affairs and a variety of questionable overseas activities. While most members of Congress support the principle of a strong intelligence-gathering capacity, many resent their inability to get even rudimentary information on how the money is being spent.

How does covert funding affect the process of budget execution and audit? Since reprogramming depends on identification of line-item expenditures which are absent from intelligence appropriations, reprogramming takes place at the discretion of the agency.[32] Similarly, transfers from other appropriation accounts are made freely at the will of the agencies under the provision of existing statutes. The OMB is informed of major transfers, but has no control over them.[33]

If the sources of funding the intelligence budget are known only to a handful of persons in the executive branch, the question remains as to who monitors or oversees the expenditure of funds and the operation of intelligence activities. A handful of members of Congress

are privy to certain information that is denied to other
members of the Appropriations Committees and the rest
of Congress. In response to Budget Director Lynn's
statement that Congress is informed of the intelligence
budget, one member replied:

> REPRESENTATIVE GIAIMO (D-Connecticut):   I have been on the
> Appropriations Committee since 1963, and I am on the Defense
> Subcommittee which deals with the intelligence community.
> . . . Up until last year I was never even privy to the briefings of
> the intelligence community. Your statement that the
> Appropriations Committee has performed oversight is just not
> so. . . . It is not Congress who is informed. It is a certain few
> members.[34]

During the Pike Committee hearings on the intelligence
community, the budget director suggested that the CIA
goes through the same internal review procedures, on a
confidential basis, as other agencies. However, OMB is
familiar only with "large expenditures of money on
particular projects."[35]

> MR. GIAIMO: Can you reassure us — the Committee and the
> American people — that there are no unwarranted
> expenditures of money, illegal in nature, involved in the
> intelligence community budget which would deal, for example,
> with assassinations?
>
> MR. LYNN (Budget Director):   We cannot give that assurance,
> sir.

A similar lack of information was evidenced by the GAO
in discussing its program review and audit procedures.

> CHAIRMAN PIKE (D-New York):   Does the General Accounting
> Office, which has the responsibility for representing the
> Legislative branch of our government in overseeing the
> expenditures of the public money, know how much we spend on
> intelligence?
>
> MR. STAATS (Comptroller General):   No, sir, we do not.
>
> CHAIRMAN PIKE: Because of the restrictions which have been
> placed on your access to information, does the GAO know
> whether there is duplication in the realm of our intelligence-
> gathering activities?
>
> MR. STAATS: We would have no way of finding out, Mr.
> Chairman.[36]

Covert budgeting represents a degree of agency
autonomy unmatched in the other budgetary phenomena
examined. While there is a legitimate need for secrecy in
the intelligence budget, the situation seems to have gotten
out of balance. Many members of Congress want to see
that balance restored.

Congressional approval of agency budgets does not put

an end to budgetary politics; rather, it "signals the start of another, more complex round of games."[37] Agencies have available to them a number of techniques and methods to exert control over their own programs and expenditures. While agencies are limited by program decisions, they have latitude to operate and ability to influence upper-level decisions. The operation level is of crucial importance. It is in spending the money that the government acts, that people are affected, and that the response to demands is made.

The key relationships are clearly between the agency, the Appropriations Committees, and the OMB. As in budget preparation, the assertive agency strives for increased autonomy while the OMB and the Appropriations Committees strive for control and agency accountability. Louis Fisher concludes that, "instead of laws determining how taxpayers' funds are spent today, the crucial commitments are often made by administrative officials."[38] The case of covert budgeting in intelligence activities demonstrates a situation of imbalance between administrative autonomy and accountability. While the majority of the agencies do not display such an imbalance, unwarranted agency discretion can easily expand without careful oversight.

FOOTNOTES

*Louis Fisher, *Presidential Spending Power* (Princeton: Princeton University Press, 1975).

[1]Aaron Wildavsky, *The Politics of the Budgetary Process,* 2nd ed. (Boston: Little, Brown, 1974), p. 31.

[2]Office of Management and Budget, *Instructions on Budget Execution,* circular A-34, July 10, 1971, rev., pp. 19-22.

[3]Office of Management and Budget, *Budget of the United States Government, Fiscal Year 1977,* p. 172.

[4]*Ibid.*

[5]The best available work on this stage of budgeting is Louis Fisher, *Presidential Spending Power* (Princeton: Princeton University Press, 1975). This chapter relies heavily on his research.

[6]Fisher, pp. 59-63.

[7]*Ibid.,* pp. 66-71.

[8]James Nathan and James Oliver, *U.S. Foreign Policy and World Order* (Boston: Little, Brown, 1976), p. 493.

[9]*Congressional Record 21477, 1961,* as quoted in Fisher, p. 67.

[10]Fisher, p. 68.

[11]*Ibid.,* p. 67.

[12]*Ibid.*, p. 76.

[13]General Accounting Office, "Appropriations Committees Not Advised on Reprogramming of Funds by the Internal Revenue Service," B-133373, May 1, 1973.

[14]Fisher, p. 86.

[15]*Ibid.*, p. 90.

[16]*Ibid.*, p. 107-119.

[17]*Ibid.*, p. 90.

[18]Robert Moot, Pentagon comptroller, as quoted in Fisher, p. 139.

[19]Wildavsky, p. 31, and Fisher, p. 140, agree in this conclusion.

[20]Fisher, p. 141.

[21]This account is reported in Fisher, p. 142-143.

[22]Jeffrey L. Pressman and Aaron B. Wildavsky, *Implementation* (Berkeley: University of California Press, 1973).

[23]Pressman and Wildavsky, p. 12.

[24]Amory Bradford, *Oakland Is Not For Burning* (New York: McKay, 1968), p. 123, as quoted in Pressman and Wildavsky, p. 12.

[25]Empirical evidence for this conclusion is found in Steven A. Shull, *Interrelationship of Concepts in Policy Research,* Sage Professional Papers in American Politics, 1976, and "The Relationship Between Budgetary and Functional Policy Actions," in *Policy-Making in the Federal Executive Branch,* ed. Randall B. Ripley and Grace A. Franklin (New York: Free Press, 1975), pp. 91-116.

[26]Congressional Budget Office, *The Economic Outlook for 1979-1980: An Update,* July 1979, 96th Congress, 1st session, p. 32, note.

[27]Office of Management and Budget, *Budget of the United States Government, FY 1980,* p. 329.

[28]Congressional Budget Office, p. 32.

[29]Select Committee on Intelligence, U.S. House of Representatives, *U.S. Intelligence Agencies and Activities: Intelligence Costs and Fiscal Procedures Hearings,* July 31-August 8, 1975 (hereafter cited as *House Intelligence Hearings*). Also see "Report of the House Select Committee on Intelligence" (Pike report), *Village Voice* (New York), February 11, 1976.

[30]Fisher, pp. 205, 213.

[31]*Ibid.*, p. 215.

[32]*House Intelligence Hearings,* pp. 56-57.

[33]*Ibid.*, p. 88.

[34]*Ibid.*, p. 62.

[35]Budget Director James Lynn's Statement, pp. 55-89.

[36]*Ibid.*, p. 12.

[37]George Hale and Scott Douglas, "Discretionary Politics and the Budgetary Process." (Paper presented at the Annual Meeting of the Midwest Political Science Association, Chicago, Ill., April 29-May 1, 1976.)

[38]Fisher, p. 257.

Taxes:

Who Pays?

*One man's loophole is another man's divine right.**

F or decades, reformers have been complaining about the tax system in the United States. Proponents of tax reform point out that some millionaires pay no federal taxes or very little, including five persons with annual incomes over $5,000,000.[1] They cite giant corporations receiving "welfare for the rich," such as an oil company that made $400 million and paid no corporate income taxes.[2] But why no sweeping tax reform? Senator Russell Long, chairman of the Senate Finance Committee, commented several years ago on what still holds true today.

> Tax reform is change; it is generally controversial and is apt to be destructive to certain interests. . . . Broad tax reform, though important, just does not possess the air of urgency necessary to seize the concern of the nation.[3]

Every provision of our patchwork tax laws is of vital importance to some segment in society in a place where it is felt most — the pocketbook. Any proposed change hits home to some group, some well organized and powerful. It took 20 years, for example, to pass a partial elimination of the oil depletion allowance.[4] The tax system seems to be in perpetual need of reform, but attempts always seem to fall short.

Taxes have several important policy impacts: they may provide incentives or disincentives for public behavior, they affect fiscal policy, and they have implications for the distribution of income in society. In attempting to answer the questions of who pays and who benefits, this chapter focuses on tax incidence, tax expenditures, and current taxes in the United States.

Taxes

Taxes transfer control of resources from one segment of society to another. The transfer may take place between private individuals and the public sector, or from one private group to another. Economists have defined certain goals and principles of taxation.[5] The first principle is that of *equity:* treating persons in the same economic situation alike (horizontal equity) and persons in different economic situations differently (vertical equity).[6] Horizontal equity means that after accounting for the ability to pay (based on the number of dependents, for example), families with the same income should pay the same amount of tax. Vertical equity is more controversial; it involves the question of how much more wealthier persons should pay than poorer persons.

The second principle of taxation is *economic efficiency:* obtaining from a given amount of resources the highest possible output.[7] In the days of laissez faire economics, the most efficient tax was seen as one that was neutral. Today, the government uses non-neutral taxes to achieve both economic and social goals.

A good tax system should be *fiscally efficient;* its implementation and compliance should be at the lowest possible cost. Taxes should be characterized by *simplicity,* both to foster efficiency and to promote equity. A good tax system should also be characterized by *certainty;* its provisions and application should be straightforward and clear, with as little "grey area" as possible.

The vertical equity of a tax depends on its impact on different levels of income. The federal tax system is a combination of state, local, and national taxes, all with a different impact. There are three basic types of taxes.

Progressive Tax A tax is progressive if it taxes upper-income categories at a *higher* rate than lower-income categories. If a family with an annual income of $10,000 pays 10 percent (or $1,000 in taxes) while a family with an income of $100,000 pays 60 percent (or $60,000 in taxes), the tax is progressive. The federal income tax is a progressive tax; as income rises, not only do taxes rise but the rate of taxation rises also.

Proportional Tax A tax is proportional if it taxes all income categories at the *same* rate. If the family with an annual income of $10,000 pays 15 percent (or $1,500 in taxes) and the family with an income of $100,000 pays 15 percent (or $15,000 in taxes), the tax is proportional. While the upper-income family pays ten times as much tax, the *proportion* of income paid in taxes by each family is the same. Certain flat-rate state income taxes and some city payroll taxes are examples of proportional taxes.

Regressive Tax A tax is regressive if it taxes upper-income categories at a *lower* rate than low-income categories. If both the family with an income of $10,000 and the family with an income of $100,000 pay $200 in tax on the purchase of a new car, the tax is regressive, since the effective rate for the first family is 2 percent of their income but only 0.2 percent for the second family. Sales taxes are regressive since they have a higher incidence on lower-income groups than higher-income groups.

The Impact of Taxes

Growth of Tax Burdens

Leaving the existing tax rates alone, inflation pushes families and individuals into higher tax brackets every

Figure 10-1   Growing Tax Burdens

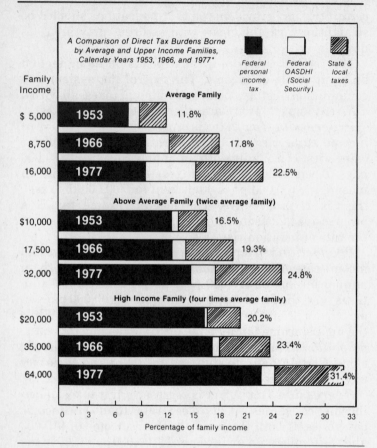

*These estimates assume a family of four and include only: federal personal income taxes, federal OASDHI, state and local personal income and general sales taxes, and local residential property taxes.
Source: Advisory Commission on Intergovernmental Relations, 1979.

year. Although there have been a number of tax cuts at the federal level in the last two decades, the tax burden has gradually increased at all levels. The tax revolt, Proposition 13 in California, and the various proposals to limit taxes are in part of response to this increasing load. Figure 10-1 compares the average tax burdens for three income classes in 1953, 1966, and 1977. By 1977, the average family paid almost as much in taxes as the high-income family paid in 1966. The figure also indicates that by 1977, Social Security payroll taxes (OASDHI) made up a significant proportion of the tax burden for the average family. The combination of high inflation and growing tax burdens contributed to the public dissatisfaction with taxes and the movement to curtail tax collections.

The automatic growth in receipts from the progressive income tax adds pressure for tax cuts at a time when there is a strong sentiment to balance the budget. In the past, Congress has usually not allowed individual income tax receipts to exceed 11 percent of personal income.[8] Without a tax cut, receipts from this tax will exceed 14 percent by 1984. If the budget is balanced, or if a recession develops, pressure on Congress and the President for a tax cut will escalate.

Tax Incidence

Comparisons of the distribution of burdens imposed by federal taxes can be made using the two major federal taxes, individual income tax and Social Security payroll tax. Table 10-1 displays the two taxes as a percentage of adjusted gross-income class for calendar year 1977.[9] Comparing average tax payments across income categories, the difference in the two taxes is apparent. The personal income tax is progressive; it taxes persons earning over $100,000 a year at a higher rate (38 percent) than all lower-income categories. On the other hand, the Social Security tax is proportional below $25,000 but regressive overall, since it taxes the highest-income classes at the lowest rate. The combined effect of the two major taxes is still a progressive scale, but not as progressive as the personal income tax alone.

Unfortunately, understanding the effect of taxes is a more complex task. One must consider the *incidence* of taxes, which is, by definition, the reduction in real income that results from a tax. Real income may be reduced in two ways: individuals have less money because of direct taxes, or taxes may result in higher prices for goods that individuals buy, thereby reducing their purchasing power.[10] A tax is not always borne by the group on which it is initially levied. Certain taxes are shifted. Corporate income taxes are partially shifted from stockholders to consumers, who must pay more for products. Property taxes may be partially shifted from landowner to renter in

Table 10-1 Tax as a Percentage of Adjusted Gross Income
(tax dollar amounts in billions)

Adjusted gross income ($ in thousands)	—Existing Law—		
	Individual income tax $	Social security payroll tax $	Total $
0-3	-.4	5.5	5.1
3-5	1.6	4.9	6.5
5-10	6.7	5.2	11.9
10-15	9.6	5.6	15.2
15-20	11.5	5.5	17.0
20-25	13.4	4.9	18.3
25-50	17.0	3.8	20.8
50-100	26.6	1.7	28.3
100 and over	38.1	.6	38.7
All classes	13.6	4.6	18.2

Source: *Congressional Budget Office*, January 23, 1976.

the form of higher rents. To gauge the actual effect on taxes, one must examine not just where the tax is levied, but who actually pays.

Economists studying this topic disagree about the incidence of taxes. It is difficult to determine with precision the actual shifting of taxes. As a result, different studies may make different incidence assumptions and therefore arrive at different conclusions about the effect of taxes. In presenting the most reliable recent findings, two sets of incidence assumptions will be used: most progressive assumptions, which suggest less shifting to lower-income levels, and least progressive assumptions, which suggest a greater shifting of burdens back to lower-income classes.[11]

When all federal, state, and local taxes are considered, a different pattern emerges than in Table 10-1.[12] Table 10-2 looks at the effective tax rate under two sets of incidence assumptions. Under both, the effective rates for the lowest-income categories are remarkably high; under the least progressive assumptions, persons in the lowest-income category bear a greater tax burden than all but the wealthiest persons. How is this possible? First, it assumes that portions of the property tax and corporate income tax

Table 10-2   Effective Rates of Federal, State, and Local Taxes by Adjusted Family Income Class, 1966

Adjusted Family Income Class ($ in thousands)	Effective Tax Rate (Percent)	
	Most Progressive Assumptions	Least Progressive Assumptions
0-3	18.7%	28.1%
3-5	20.5	28.3
5-10	22.6	25.9
10-15	22.8	25.5
15-20	23.2	25.3
20-25	24.0	25.1
25-30	25.1	24.3
30-50	26.4	24.4
50-100	31.5	26.4
over 100*	46.5*	29.6*
all classes	25.2	25.9

*Estimated from three categories to preserve comparability with table 10-1.
Source: Pechman & Okner, p. 49.

are shifted to consumers. Second, it reflects the fact that regressive sales and excise taxes hit the poorest groups in society particularly hard. Third, it reflects the relatively low amounts of income of the poor before taxes.

It is possible to go a step further and examine the overall effective tax rate across the population percentiles from the poorest to the wealthiest. This is shown in Figure 10-2. For the vast majority of the population, the combined effect of all taxes was approximately equal to a proportional tax of 25 percent. That means if, in a single stroke, all existing taxes were eliminated and replaced with a flat-rate tax of 25 percent the total impact would be the same for approximately 90 percent of the population. The proportional rate in 1980 would be over 30 percent.[13] Broken down into components, the progressive federal income tax *alone* prevents the entire system from being regressive. Combined federal taxes are mildly progressive moving up the income scale. State and local taxes, under both sets of assumptions, are regressive throughout the income scale. The lowest-income classes pay effective rates of 20-30 percent while the highest-income classes pay around 6-11 percent.[14] In terms of who pays, the burden of taxes is borne proportionately by the poor as well as middle- and upper-income groups.

**Figure 10-2   Effective Rates of Federal, State, and
Local Taxes Under the Most and Least Progressive
Incidence Variants, by Population Percentile, 1966**

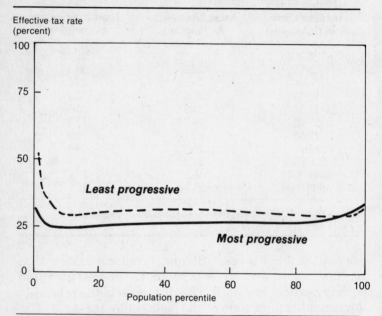

Source: Joseph Pechman and Benjamin Okner, *Who Bears the Tax Burden*, p. 5, © 1974 by
The Brookings Institution, Washington, D.C.

The Redistributional Impact of Taxes

Since the tax system is proportional for most American
families, the tax system has little impact on the
distribution of income.[15] Figure 10-3 shows the negligible
redistributive effect of taxes by means of the Lorenz curve.
The straight line represents the point of equality, where 50
percent of the families receive 50 percent of the income.
The curves represent the actual distribution of income —
the greater the inequality, the farther the curve is from the
line. In Figure 10-3 along the curve, the bottom 50 percent
of families receive only 20 percent of the income. The
combined effect of taxes, even under the most progressive
assumptions, has a redistributive impact of about 5
percent. Under the regressive assumptions the difference
before and after taxes is about 1 percent.[16]

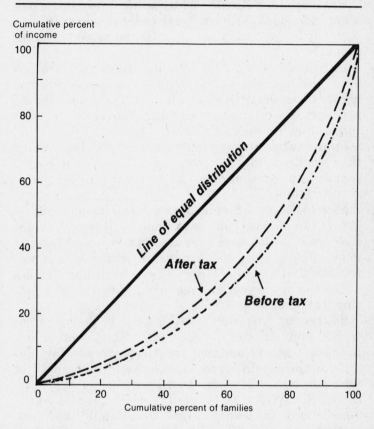

Figure 10-3 Lorenz Curves of the Distributions of Adjusted Family Income Before and After Federal, State, and Local Taxes, under the Most Progressive Incidence Variant, 1966

Cumulative percent of income

Line of equal distribution

After tax

Before tax

Cumulative percent of families

Source: Joseph Pechman and Benjamin Okner, *Who Bears the Tax Burden*, p. 7, © 1974 by The Brookings Institution, Washington, D.C.

Tax Burdens Among Groups in Society

The U.S. tax system affects different kinds of incomes and spending differently. The result is that the tax laws may impose higher burdens on some groups than others. Pechman and Okner concluded that the different impacts were as follows.[17]

Aged In general, families headed by a person over 65

pay slightly lower taxes than other families. Most states and the federal government provide special exemptions for the aged. The exception is the wealthiest families, where the aged pay higher income and property taxes.

Homeowners Persons who own their own home pay lower individual income taxes than those who rent. This is chiefly because mortgage interest and property tax are deductible.

Urban dwellers Although the differences are not large, persons who live in urban areas pay somewhat higher taxes than those who live in rural areas. Urban residents pay higher income taxes, but relatively lower corporation income and property taxes.

Family size Larger families tend to pay lower taxes than smaller families or couples with no children. This is primarily a function of fewer personal exemptions for smaller families.

Marital status Single persons tend to pay higher taxes than married couples or families. However, recent changes in the tax laws have made it more advantageous to be single in some of the higher-income classes. It was reported that a number of couples were obtaining divorces at the end of the year and remarrying soon after to gain single tax status.[18]

Source of income[19] Most income is derived from wages and salaries (70 percent); other sources are business, property, and cash-transfer payments. Families differ in their main source of income and, resultingly, in their tax burden. Income based on transfer payments (Social Security, ADC) is taxed at the lowest rate. At the other end of the scale, income from capital (business, property) is taxed at the highest effective rate, with wages in the middle.

Subgroups in the population are affected differentially by the tax system. Those with the lowest rates tend to be homeowners living in rural areas, with large families, and income derived from transfer payments. Groups with the highest rates tend to be renters living in urban areas, unmarried, with income derived from capital.[20] Overall, the tax system in the U.S. is not as progressive as many assume. While the Pechman and Okner study was done for 1966, the methodological sophistication of the analysis makes a long time lag inevitable. If the shifts in revenue patterns in the last decade are considered, particularly the growth in Social Security payroll taxes, the overall impact is undoubtedly more regressive now than it was in 1966. The tax structure has undergone no major overhaul in 40 years. While tax rates have been periodically reduced, over the past 20 years the burden has gradually been shifted from upper-income to middle-income groups.

Tax Expenditures

A tax expenditure is the loss of revenue resulting from special tax provisions. Such well-intentioned provisions may attempt to encourage certain kinds of behavior or aid a certain group of citizens. But regardless of whether one feels a particular tax provision is good or bad, it constitutes as indirect expenditure. In other words, tax expenditures are the equivalent of collecting revenue and then making a direct payment of equal amount to the taxpayer.[21] Accounting for tax expenditures makes it possible to put a precise price tag on tax loopholes.

The Budget Reform Act required that both the Congress and the executive branch make explicit accounting of tax expenditures. While a tax loophole is basically the same as a tax expenditure, the term "loophole" has taken on the connotation of a "rip-off" in our political rhetoric. The point is that loopholes or tax expenditures can be either desirable or undesirable, depending on one's perspective.

Tax expenditures may take a variety of forms:[22]
— exclusions, exemptions, deductions which reduce taxable income
— preferential tax rates
— tax credits, deducted directly from taxes
— tax deferrals

Tax expenditures have grown rapidly in the past 15 years. In FY 1967, they amounted to $36 billion. Ten years later, they had grown to over $100 billion, or 35 percent more than direct spending. By 1984, tax expenditures are projected to reach $269 billion, growing at an annual rate of 12.5 percent, while spending is projected to grow at an 8 percent annual rate.[23] At this rate tax expenditures will have tripled between 1975 and 1984. Of the total tax expenditures of $169 billion in 1980, $126 billion went to individuals, and $43 billion went to corporations.

Tax expenditures have a variety of policy objectives, and can be seen as alternatives to other kinds of government actions.[24] They either encourage certain kinds of economic activities or benefit taxpayers in special circumstances. Tax expenditures encourage investment, petroleum exploration, housing and home ownership, borrowing by state and local government, and gifts to charities. Exemptions for the aged and the blind and deductions for medical expenses and casualty losses benefit taxpayers with special problems.

There are now over 100 tax expenditures in the federal tax code, too numerous to examine individually. Table 10-3 lists some of the largest tax expenditures and their relative benefits to individuals and corporations. In recent years, tax reformers have succeeded in removing some of the special-interest tax provisions. These include a reduction in the oil depletion allowance, expansion of the minimum tax, enactment of a carry-over rule on assets transferred at death, and limitation on some tax shelters. At the same time, however, many more new provisions have been added, including corporate surtax exemption, employment tax credit, exemption for domestic international sales corporations, rapid-depreciation allowance, earned-income credit, individual retirement accounts, tax credit for the elderly, child-care credit, and employee stock ownership.[25]

Evaluation of special tax provisions varies, depending on who benefits. Murray Weidenbaum's analysis of the impact of tax expenditures revealed that 19 percent benefit low-income groups, 40 percent benefit middle-income groups, 17 percent benefit upper-income groups, and 24 percent benefit corporations.[26] Tax expenditures are not simply tax dodges for the rich. Exclusion of Social Security benefits primarily benefits lower-income individuals, although middle- and upper-income individuals benefit as well. Exclusions of pension contributions and earnings and the deduction of mortgage interest rates primarily benefits the middle-income groups. Capital gains, the investment credit, tax-free municipal bonds, and several other provisions primarily benefit upper-income groups and corporations.

Special tax provisions are not equally costly, nor are they equally controversial. But each needs to be reviewed

Table 10-3 Major Tax Expenditures — Fiscal Year 1977

(in millions of dollars)

Description	Corporations	Benefits to Individuals	Total
•corporate surtax exemption	$6,185		$6,185
•investment credit	7,585	$1,530	9,115
•deferral of income from domestic international sales corporations (DISC)	1,420		1,420
•deduction of state gasoline tax		600	600
•capital gains treatment	900	6,225	7,125
•exclusion of capital gains at death		7,280	7,280
•deduction of mortgage interest and property taxes		8,535	8,535
•exclusion of fellowships/ scholarships		220	220
•deduction of charitable contributions	805	4,445	5,260
•deduction of child-care services		420	420
•exclusion of employers contribution to medical insurance		4,225	4,225
•deduction of medical expenses		2,095	2,095
•exclusion of social security		4,460	4,460
•exclusion of unemployment benefits		2,855	2,855
•exclusion of pension contributions		6,475	6,475
•exemption for persons over 65		1,220	1,220
•exclusion of interest from state and local bonds	3,150	1,390	4,540
•exclusion of income earned abroad		160	160

Source: Senate Budget Committee, *Tax Expenditures*, March 17, 1976.

and scrutinized to determine if the costs are worth the benefit, or if the same end might be accomplished by some other more efficient means. Some tax expenditures are more justifiable than others, and more secure. Others are under attack and may be subjected to review in the coming years.

Income earned by Americans overseas Enacted during the Marshall Plan after World War II to encourage

Americans with technical knowledge to work abroad, this exemption costs the Treasury $160,000,000 a year in lost revenues. Many of these residents pay no taxes to the country of residence, and those who do may credit it to their U.S. tax liability on any income above $15,000.[27] A persistent advocate of tax reform, Representative Henry Reuss (D-Wisconsin) concludes, "Insofar as these provisions do anything more than cost the government money, they encourage the export of valuable U.S. capital and know-how."[28]

Interest-free Municipal Bonds This advantage helps persons mainly in the highest income bracket (50 percent and up) as well as financial institutions. The provision was part of the original income tax law based on the view that such interest could not constitutionally be taxed by the federal government. This constitutional interpretation is not widely held today.[29] The tax-free status of interest from these bonds is continued to help state and local government borrow money more cheaply, since such bonds can be sold at a lower interest rate than bonds with taxable interest. Opponents of this provision claim that it loses $8 billion a year for the federal government, far more than the interest saved by the states and municipalities, and serves primarily as a tax shelter for the rich.

The federal government could offer a credit to states and localities making their actual costs *less* than the current tax-free bonds.[30] The interest on the bonds would be taxed, and the revenues gained would exceed the cost of the interest subsidy. President Carter offered a proposal for a taxable bond option with a federal interest credit, but Congress has taken no action on this request.

Domestic international sales corporations (DISCs). The tax code allows exporters to establish a separate corporation to handle their transactions, and partially exempts the profits from taxes.[31] The goal of this provision is to encourage exports, but the Treasury Department concludes that this is an expensive, inefficient way to achieve this objective. It costs the government $1.3 billion for this "loophole." Carter also proposed the elimination of this provision, but Congress has not acted.

Social Security benefits Unlike other pension income, Social Security benefits are not taxable, regardless of the income of the individual. This exclusion cost the Treasury $6.4 billion in 1980. The Brookings Institution suggests that this tax expenditure violates common notions of tax equity.[32] The exclusion is most troublesome for taxpayers in the highest tax brackets, with income from other sources. Although this exemption seems secure because of political pressures, it is an example of how well-intentioned tax benefits for some become a shelter for others.

Deduction of interest on consumer credit Not only is home mortgage interest deductible, but interest on other consumer purchases is also deductible. This cost the Treasury just under $3 billion in 1980. The provisions favor consumption over savings, and mean that the general taxpayer is subsidizing others willing to go into debt to buy a new boat or a Mercedes.

Exclusion of military benefits The housing, clothing, medical, dental, and other benefits provided to members of the armed services are not taxable. This costs the Treasury $1.5 billion annually, and it is going up. Like other tax expenditures, there are arguments on both sides. Proponents suggest that it is necessary to attract quality personnel into the volunteer army. Others claim that it assists military personnel beyond what civilian employees receive and is a more costly means of attracting people than increasing salaries and taxing benefits.

Tax expenditures, examined individually, provide many worthy benefits to certain groups. But on the whole, they have some serious drawbacks. Many provisions, especially deductions, are regressive; the tax savings increase for persons with higher incomes. Tax expenditures tend to mask the flow of federal benefits. Direct expenditures are clearer and are subject to periodic review in the budget process. As the number of tax expenditures increases, the goal of simplicity and certainty continues to diminish. The tax structure becomes so complicated, attempting to achieve scores of desirable objectives, that the more fundamental goals of taxation become obscured.

Assessing the U.S. Tax System

Compared to that of Canada, Western Europe, and other developed nations, the total tax burden in the U.S. is still somewhat less than average. In 1972, taxes constituted 28 percent of GNP in the U.S. but over 30 percent for 11 developed nations, and over 40 percent in Norway, Sweden, Denmark, and the Netherlands.[33] In addition, the U.S. relies more heavily on income and property taxes than other countries, with less than average utilization of sales taxes. The increases in Social Security taxes in the 1970s have brought the U.S. more in line with the developed countries in the utilization of payroll taxes.

Another characteristic of the U.S. tax system is its federal structure, which makes it more difficult to examine the combined impact of all the various forms of taxes and tends to make the system relatively complex. Compared to the tax systems in most other countries, the federal part of the U.S. tax system is rated highly.[34] But as we have seen, there are a number of inequities at all levels.

One result of our tax structure is that revenues in the U.S. are volatile and vary widely with economic shifts.[35] Changes in taxes in the coming decades may attempt to stabilize revenues, to bring U.S. practice closer to that of other countries (particularly the European community), and to tap unused sources.

Such new taxes could take the form of a consumer tax like a national sales tax. At the present time, only state and local governments make use of these taxes in this country. Automobiles in Canada and Sweden cost thousands more than in the U.S. because of national sales taxes. The advantage of such taxes, as demonstrated by their popularity at the subfederal level, is they are relatively painless (once everybody gets used to them). They are paid at the time of consumption and are seen as being the same for everyone. The disadvantage is they are the most regressive of all taxes and impose a greater burden on lower-income groups.

New taxes may also take the form of a GNP tax for business. Unlike corporate profit taxes, such a tax would be based on the value of wages, materials, inventories, and products. A variant is the "value-added" tax where each producer pays tax on the portion of GNP he adds in the stages of production. Such consumer and business taxes may be a long way off but might look more attractive in future years, if revenues lag behind the costs of new services. In reforming and changing the tax structure, the most important consideration should be the impact on different income groups in society. In practice tax decisions are more frequently based on expediency.

FOOTNOTES

*Overheard on Capitol Hill.

[1]Joseph A. Ruskay and Richard A. Osserman, *Halfway to Tax Reform* (Bloomington: Indiana University Press, 1970), p. 3.

[2]*Ibid.,* p. 4.

[3]Russell B. Long, "Tax Reforms and Economic Growth," as quoted by Ruskay and Osserman, p. 209.

[4]The oil depletion allowance, originally passed in the 1920s, became the object of tax reformers in the 1950s. The 93rd Congress (1973-1974) finally agreed on a partial and gradual phase-out of this provision.

[5]George F. Break and Joseph Pechman, *Federal Tax Reform* (Washington, D.C.: Brookings Institution, 1975), p. 4.

[6]*Ibid.,* p. 5.

[7]*Ibid.,* p. 7.

[8]Joseph Pechman, ed., *Setting National Priorities: The 1980 Budget* (Washington, D.C.: Brookings Institution, 1979), p. 53.

[9]Using IRS 1972 Tax Model projected to 1977 levels with personal income tax laws as of January 1, 1976, Social Security rate of 5.85 percent on first $16,500 of taxable earnings. Source: Congressional Budget Office, "Overview of the 1977 Budget," January 23, 1976.

[10]Joseph Pechman and Benjamin Okner, *Who Bears the Tax Burden?* (Washington, D.C.: Brookings Institution, 1974), p. 3.

[11]These are variants 1c and 3b as defined by Pechman and Okner, p. 38.

[12]There are numerous reasons for the differences besides the year and the inclusion of state and local taxes. The computation of the income base is different as well as the more complex assumptions concerning the incidence of federal taxes.

[13]Pechman and Okner, pp. 5-6.

[14]*Ibid.,* p. 10.

[15]*Ibid.,* p. 6.

[16]*Ibid.,* p. 6.

[17]*Ibid.,* pp. 71-83 (summary).

[18]CBS, "Sixty Minutes," June 27, 1976.

[19]Pechman and Okner, pp. 77-83.

[20]*Ibid.,* p. 82.

[21]Committee on the Budget, U.S. Senate, *Tax Expenditures: Compendium of Background Material on Individual Provisions,* 94th

Congress, 2nd session, March 17, 1976 (hereafter cited as *Tax Expenditures*).

[22]*Tax Expenditures,* pp. 2-3.

[23]Congressional Budget Office, *Five Year Budget Projections and Alternative Budgetary Strategies for FY 1980-1984.* 96th Congress, 1st session, June 1979.

[24]Office of Management and Budget, *Special Analysis Budget of the United States Government FY 1980,* p. 183.

[25]U.S. Senate, *Report to Accompany First Concurrent Resolution on the Budget FY 1979,* 95th Congress, 2nd session, no. 95-739, p. 38.

[26]Murray Weidenbaum, "The Case for Tax Loopholes," reprinted in *A New Tax Structure for the United States,* ed. Donald H. Skadden (Indianapolis: Bobbs-Merrill, 1978).

[27]*Tax Expenditures,* p. 14.

[28]Committee on the Budget, U.S. Senate, *Concurrent Resolutions on the FY 1976 Budget: Compendium of Materials Leading to Passage,* 94th Congress, 1st session, October 1975, p. 863.

[29]*Tax Expenditures,* p. 152.

[30]Pechman, p. 158.

[31]*Ibid.,* p. 156.

[32]*Ibid.,* p. 157.

[33]Break and Pechman, p. 1.

[34]*Ibid.,* p. 11.

[35]Committee on Ways and Means, U.S. House of Representatives, *New Tax Directions for the U.S.,* by Richard W. Lindholm, December 15, 1975.

Spending:
Who Benefits?

*Given a chance to go forward with the policies of
the last eight years, we shall soon with the help of
God be within sight of the day when poverty will
be banished from this nation.*
—Herbert Hoover, 1928
*This administration today, here and now, declares an
unconditional war on poverty in America. . . . We
shall not rest until that war is won.*
—Lyndon B. Johnson, 1964

Decisions on priorities, programs, and operations
assess costs on society and confer a variety of benefits as
well. In understanding the relationship between benefits
provided and the larger arena of budgetary decision
making, it is useful to differentiate between different
kinds of goods and services provided. Public goods (or
collective goods) are available to all members of society

equally (certain groups cannot be excluded), and the consumption of that good does not reduce the amount available to others (this is called jointness of supply).[1] Private goods lack these two characteristics; in other words, they may be limited to specific groups and individuals, and the supply is finite — consumption by one reduces the amount available to others. In budgeting, money itself is scarce, but it may be spent to provide both public and private goods. Income maintenance through cash transfers is an example of a private good, because it is not equally available to all members of society, but it is also a public good in helping to eliminate poverty and promote domestic peace. Defense spending for national security and deterrence is a public good (although the members of the military and defense contractors gain private goods). Most budget outlays provide both public and private goods to the society. In many cases, public goods are intangible in nature.[2] Theories have been proposed linking the nature of goods to the behavior of groups in the political process, and the concept of public and private goods is useful in understanding the benefits of federal spending.

The Federal Rat Hole?

It is popular in some quarters to emphasize the amount of waste and duplication inherent in government spending. Those who would have us believe that most of our tax dollars go down a federal "rat hole" attempt to prove their case with examples.[3] Admittedly, one usually does not have to look too far to find some questionable expenditures.

For example, there are over 1,200 federal advisory committees, annually costing a total of $75 million. While many of them provide useful policy guidance and expertise, others are questionable, such as $180,000 per year to fund the Board of Tea Tasters. Support for the arts is another example. The National Foundation of the Arts and Humanities, in providing assistance to artists in many fields, inevitably funds some rather abstract and unusual projects. One instance was a grant of $750 to a poet who produced the seven-letter masterpiece "lighght." Noting that the poem cost the taxpayers $107 per letter, Representative William Scherle (R-Iowa) queried, "Can anyone even pronounce this poem?" National Science Foundation research grants also attract their share of criticism, especially in the social science programs. The granting of $55,000 to study "Newari Social Processes" and $135,000 to study "Language Behavior in the Chimpanzee" was questioned by some. A study of the effect of marijuana on sexual arousal at Southern Illinois University caused such a stir that the funding was canceled.

Over 15 federal agencies are involved with film making that costs $150 million a year. The result of this duplication is 14 different films on how to brush your teeth, 15 films on venereal disease, and military films on essentials of etiquette such as "How to Succeed with Brunettes" and "Blonds Prefer Gentlemen." Substantial sums (over $5 million) are spend on servants for generals and admirals. Enlisted men serve as valets, social secretaries, cooks, errand boys, waiters, cabin boys, baby-sitters, housemaids, chauffeurs, bartenders, and grocery shoppers. The Senate in 1973 voted to cut military servants from over 1,700 to 200, but the House felt that at least 675 servants were necessary. The Pentagon also runs "top brass" dining rooms where admirals, generals, and top civilian defense officials enjoy filet mignon and lobster for two to three dollars.

Senator William Proxmire (D-Wisconsin) is the leading congressional "rat holer." He regularly bestows a "golden fleece" award on the spender of federal monies who, in Proxmire's opinion, has done the best job of fleecing the taxpayer. Fortunately, Proxmire has a sense of humor. But a recent recipient of the aware was not amused and sued. A court ruled that Proxmire's congressional privilege did not protect him from slander or libel suits. The Senator announced his intention to continue, however.

Without question, inefficient programs and unnecessary and duplicative activities should be eliminated as much as possible. The "rat holers" serve some useful function in that regard. But more than anything, they divert attention from the real issues of the budget and often succeed in convincing some citizens that all federal spending is wasted. Scientific research and support of the arts are particularly difficult areas to evaluate benefits, and they are often easy targets for cheap shots from "rat holers." In actuality, support for scientific research and the arts is skimpy, already a low priority in the budget. The beneficial uses of these funds outweigh the more questionable projects.

The more critical questions of assessing the results of federal spending surround the three major expenditure categories in the budget: national defense, social welfare programs, and grants to state and local governments. In seeking some limited answers to the question "Who benefits," we shall focus our attention on these items.

National Defense

Money allocated to national defense in the budget confers a variety of private and public goods. Public goods that are enjoyed equally by all citizens include deterrence and international power and presence.

One of the major objectives of national defense is to provide a deterrent to nuclear attack and political coercion. This is accomplished primarily through strategic forces. The arsenal of nuclear weapons is not intended to be used in an all-out war but to provide sufficient destructive capability to deter an attack. Strategic forces include land- and submarine-based intercontinental ballistic missiles, long-range bombers capable of carrying nuclear weapons, and air-launched cruise missiles. With the rapid buildup of Soviet strategic weapons in the 1970s, the U.S. felt pressure to escalate their programs. The MX mobile ICBM was approved by President Carter in 1979, while the Senate was debating the Strategic Arms Limitation Treaty (SALT II). At the same time that the President was pushing for the SALT treaty to put a limit on the arms race, he was acting to mollify conservative critics and insure the balance in strategic power.

Deterrence is also provided through conventional forces and tactical nuclear weapons and is related to a second

Table 11-1   Outlays for National Defense
(in billions of dollars)

	1976	1980	1984
Strategic nuclear forces	$19.0	$ 25.8	$ 33.8
General purpose forces	66.2	93.2	122.0
Other	10.6	16.5	21.9
Total	$95.8	$135.5	$177.7

Source: Joseph Pechman, ed., *Setting National Priorities: The 1980 Budget* (Washington, D.C.: Brookings Institution, 1979), p. 164.

public good provided by defense expenditures, international power, and presence. Conventional forces — army, navy, air force, ships, planes, tanks, etc. — provide a deterrent to Soviet (or another nation's) intervention or aggression in another part of the world. It also provides the U.S. with the capability to intervene militarily in a non-nuclear engagement. Our main commitment is to NATO and the defense of Western Europe from the Soviet Union and the Warsaw Pact countries. The navy is both a symbol of U.S. strength and a means of responding to potential conflicts throughout the world. Likewise, the standing army demonstrates the readiness of the U.S. to respond to various challenges and situations.

Most of the defense budget goes to supporting conventional forces. Table 11-1 compares outlays for strategic nuclear forces and general-purpose forces for 1976, 1980, and 1984. After relative stability in the 1970s, national defense was projected to undergo real increases through the early 1980s. The Soviet invasion of Afghanistan only reinforced the pro-military spending sentiments. Deterrence and international power and presence are intangible benefits but are strongly supported by a vast majority of the citizens. The real issues involve questions of priorities and cost. How can the military provide the greatest deterrence and capability for the least amount of money?

Defense spending also confers private benefits in significant amounts, and those considerations often cloud the issues concerning defense as a public good. Of the $125 billion spent on national defense in 1980, about 60 percent went to personnel costs. The military employs almost one million civilian personnel in addition to the armed forces. These jobs are a substantial component of the domestic economy. Defense contracts, research and development, and procurement of weapons systems also have considerable economic impact, and the location of domestic defense installations has significant regional impacts.

The billions paid to large private contractors who produce weapons and military hardware for the Pentagon provide lucrative business for the corporation, jobs for its employees, and income for the state where the plant is located. Much has been written about the "military-industrial complex" and the symbiotic relationship between defense contractors, anxious to receive lucrative military orders, and military leaders, anxious to push new systems. The majority of large Defense Department contractors did more than 60 percent of their business with the federal government.[4] Senator Proxmire reported that the 100 largest defense contractors employed over 2,000 retired military officers of the rank of colonel or higher. While theories of a conspiracy are rather fanciful, the fact remains that military spending provides tangible rewards to Pentagon officials anxious to further their careers, defense contractors, union leaders who fear layoffs, and congressmen and senators who see it as a source of prosperity to their state and district.

The regional impact of defense spending is uneven. Defense contracts are let to certain states, such as Connecticut, California, Missouri, and Texas, more than others. The already wealthy regions, particularly the far West, receive the largest shares. Many of the nation's largest cities are losing in the defense bargain. A study by the Employment Research Associates found that most cities paid out considerably more in taxes for defense than they gained.[5] Only 15 of the 40 largest cities realized a net gain; half of the "winners" were in the far West, six in California alone. Washington, D.C., had the largest gain, receiving $3.1 billion more than residents paid in military taxes. On a per-family basis, cities like San Diego and San Jose did as well. Ten of 11 cities in the Midwest were net losers. The St. Louis area got back $1.5 billion more than residents paid, amounting to $2,600 per family. In contrast, the net loss was $1,900 per family in Chicago.

Miami was the biggest overall loser in the battle for defense benefits.

Issues in national defense do not rest only on questions of strategic capability and the Soviet threat. They also involve jobs, bases, contracts, and billions of dollars. Issues in the coming decade will require major choices on both conventional and strategic forces. Decisions on construction of missile systems like the MX or nuclear aircraft carriers commit funds for many years. Decisions on fleet size in 1980 will have implications for well over a decade. The high costs of the volunteer army may lead to a debate over reinstituting the draft. The amount of defense spending does not translate into a certain level of capability. But as long as defense spending also provides substantial private benefits, there will be strong pressures to continue to increase expenditures.

Social Welfare Programs

American Presidents have long sought solutions to the enduring dilemma of poverty amidst the relative affluence of the country. In 1964, President Johnson launched the War on Poverty, and in the decade that followed, expenditures for social welfare programs expanded fourfold. By 1980, the U.S. government spent $260 billion annually for income security, health, and social services. Who benefits from these outlays? How successful have these expenditures been in reducing the incidence of poverty in the United States?

Some public goods are associated with social welfare programs. Reduction in human suffering through improvements in nutrition, health, housing, and the quality of life of poor persons benefits the society at large. Programs designed to reduce poverty increase the safety and welfare of all citizens, and to the extent that they serve to break the cycle of poverty may reduce burdens on future generations. However, social welfare programs, cash transfer, and in-kind assistance most obviously provide tangible private goods to the recipients.

Many difficult methodological problems are involved in measuring poverty. Increasingly, agency officials and

**Table 11-2   Percentage of Social Welfare
Expenditures Going to the Poor***

Program	Percentage
Public Assistance	87%
Food stamps	85
Medicaid	75
Employment and Manpower Programs	72
Welfare and OEO Services	72
Social Security and Railroad Retirement	58
Housing Programs	55
Medicare	48
Veteran's Benefits	43
Workman's Compensation	33
Unemployment Compensation	21
Education Programs	19
TOTAL Social Welfare Expenditures	42.5%

*Pre-transfer poor, 1972 poverty level as defined by Social Security Administration.
Source: Robert D. Plotnick and Felicity Skidmore, *Progress Against Poverty* (New York: Academic Press, 1975), pp. 56-57.

researchers are expanding efforts and employing more sophisticated methods to provide better answers to questions. "Absolute" poverty is determined by setting a level of income necessary to sustain a minimum standard of living. "Relative" poverty, on the other hand, defines poverty by the distribution of income and the distance of low-income groups from the prevailing standard of living.[6] Both definitions of poverty are useful in indicating the extent and nature of changes in poverty.

How much of the money spent on social welfare programs actually goes to the poor? This can be determined by looking at income levels before any government transfer payments are made. Table 11-2 shows the percentage of expenditures that go to the poor; the remainder goes to individuals who are above the poverty level before any transfer payments. Less than half of federal spending goes to persons below the poverty line as defined by the government. This percentage has remained around 40 percent since 1964.[7] Many of these programs, such as Social Security, unemployment, and education, are not designed exclusively for the poor. Others, like public assistance and food stamps, are oriented specifically to the poor. Overall, it is important to

Table 11-3 Cumulative Impact of Social Welfare Programs
(reduction in numbers of families below the poverty level FY 1976)

	Families in Poverty (all figures pre-tax)	
	percent	number
(1) Without any transfer income from programs	27%	21,436,000
(2) After Social Security payments	15.7%	12,454,000
(3) After (2) plus other cash assistance (ADC, SSI)	13.5%	10,716,000
(4) After (2) and (3) plus in-kind transfers (Food stamps, housing assistance)	11.3%	8,978,000
(5) After (2), (3), (4) plus Medicare & Medicaid	8.1%	6,441,000

*All figures pre-tax.
Source: Congressional Budget Office, *Poverty Status of Families Under Alternative Definitions of Income*, June 1977.

recognize that most federal social welfare expenditures do not go to the poor. This may be upsetting to those who feel the federal government is not doing enough to help the poor. On the other hand, these figures might remind many middle-income families who bear a large share of the tax burden that social welfare spending benefits their income groups as well as the poor.

Has this share of federal expenditures eradicated poverty? A brief encounter with inner-city slums or rural pockets of deprivation makes a negative response obvious. But progress in reducing poverty has been made.

The cumulative impact of social welfare programs has a significant effect in reducing the number of families living below the level of absolute poverty.[8] Table 11-3 shows the effect of the various programs. Before any transfer payments, 27 percent of families in the U.S. would fall below the poverty line. Social Security, the largest expenditure category in the budget, reduces the percentage to 15.7, helping nine million families rise above the poverty level. The addition of cash-assistance programs such as welfare (ADC) and supplemental security income (SSI) lowers the percentage to 13.5. In-

kind transfers such as housing assistance and food
stamps help another two million families rise above the
poverty line, reducing the incidence of poverty to 11.3
percent. Finally, federal assistance for health care in the
form of medicare and medicaid lower the percentage to
8.1, or 6.4 million families.

Despite the relatively large outlays, a substantial
number of persons still live in conditions of poverty.
Although substantial progress has been made, the system
is fragmented and erratic. Some poor families receive
enough assistance to rise substantially above the poverty
level, while others receive little or no assistance.[9] The
effectiveness of social welfare programs varies according
to family size, age, race, and region.[10]

Families of two or more persons receive more assistance
than single persons. Social welfare programs benefit
whites more than nonwhites despite the fact that the
incidence of poverty is greater for nonwhites. Poverty
among families headed by a person 65 years or older is
reduced more than for families with a younger head of
household. Finally, social welfare expenditures are more
effective in reducing family poverty in the northeastern
and central regions of the country than in the South and
West.

Table 11-4 looks at the probability of poverty among 15
demographic groups. While the probability of poverty for
each group was reduced between 1965 and 1972, the
difference between groups has remained relatively stable.
Poverty is still more prevalent among black and other
minorities, among the elderly, and among the poorly
educated.

Poverty is affected not only by government programs
but by the state of the economy. As economic conditions
deteriorate, certain groups are more severely affected.
Inflation has its harshest impact on the poor. The
Consumer Price Index generally measures consumption
patterns of middle-income persons; a "poor person's price
index" (PPI) based on consumption by poverty families
reveals that prices rose more rapidly for poor people in the
1970s than for the rest of the country.[11] Unemployment
hits minorities and the young more severely than others.
The rate of unemployment for blacks is usually double the
national rate; the rate for young blacks is four to six times
greater than for the rest of the work force.

**Table 11-4   Probability of Being Poor for
Representative Groups***

	1965	1972
1. Black, female head with children	.77	.70
2. Southern, poorly educated black family	.64	.55
3. Black, urban elderly woman	.55	.40
4. White, urban elderly woman	.37	.25
5. Young, well-educated white male	.38	.30
6. Young black male	.36	.29
7. Middle-aged female head	.29	.25
8. Black, male head	.13	.11
9. Poorly educated, white male head	.14	.11
10. Elderly couple I — metropolitan white	.06	.04
11. Elderly couple II — nonmetropolitan black	.65	.51
12. Middle-aged nonmetropolitan family	.08	.07
13. Well-educated young family	.03	.02
14. Single, middle-aged man	.10	.09
15. Single, middle-aged woman	.14	.12

*Predicted probability of poverty computed from multivariate analysis, absolute poverty
definition.
Source: Plotnick and Skidmore, p. 103.

The impact of government expenditures for income
maintenance and social welfare programs is mixed. While
many families escape poverty, others remain below a
minimum standard. Many social welfare dollars go to the
nonpoor. More complete answers to the question of who
benefits will affect future decisions on income
maintenance and social welfare programs.

Social welfare issues in the coming decades will focus
both on the amount of budget resources allocated to this
function and to the structure of government programs.
Some questions still surround Social Security, the largest
assistance program. Faced with a declining cash reserve
and dire predictions of bankruptcy, Congress
substantially increased employer and employee
contributions and modestly increased benefits in 1977.
Many public misconceptions exist about Social Security.
Unlike private pension funds, Social Security is on a
current financing basis.[12] The most radical suggestions
for the program suggest that it be financed out of general
revenues, like other social welfare programs. Although
there is not majority support for altering the self-financing
nature of Social Security, Congress and the President will

have to take a hard look at benefit levels and the regressive impact of payroll taxes in the future.

The welfare system in the U.S. is a patchwork of programs that provides cash benefits and in-kind assistance to help people buy food, housing, energy, and medical care. The fact that the system is erratic and duplicative in providing benefits has led to calls for comprehensive reform of the various welfare programs into a new overall program of cash assistance. Whether called a negative income tax or guaranteed annual income, reform proposals have some support in both political parties. While spending for the major programs has expanded over the last decade, significant gaps in coverage still exist. Reform could be partial, integrating but maintaining the individual programs. Reform could be comprehensive, completely replacing the various programs with a single integrated assistance program. The costs of such a system are not automatically astronomical. Policy decisions on eligibility, level of benefits, and the amount that benefits would be reduced in response to a recipient's earnings will determine the cost. It is unlikely, however, that any comprehensive reform could be achieved without raising costs above the current levels.[13]

Proposals for a comprehensive program of national health care have been around for many years. The budgetary implications of a policy decision to implement such a program will be far-reaching.[14] Many choices are involved both in terms of how to finance the program and in terms of eligibility and benefit levels. The history of medicare and medicaid portends one of the most serious problems policy makers face: the skyrocketing costs of health care.

The rapid increase in federal health outlays has not been a function of increasing coverage. Between 1974 and 1976 the eligible population increased by only 5 percent while the costs of services jumped almost 50 percent.[15] The cost and success of any national health care program will depend on careful consideration of financing, incentives to keep costs down, quality controls for services, and careful assessment of the benefits in terms of medical care that will result.

Grants to State
and Local Governments

The third largest category of federal expenditures is grants to state and local governments. They have grown rapidly in the last decade, from $20.9 billion in FY 1969 to $82.1 billion in 1979. This total is made up of a number of federal programs, including general revenue sharing, community development block grants, public service employment, anti-recession fiscal assistance, and other categorical grants. Many of the programs were developed during the 1973-1975 recession when the cities were facing a major fiscal crisis. This countercyclical assistance by the federal government has continued through the economic recovery, but by 1980 both the President and Congress indicated that reductions in revenue sharing and countercyclical assistance were under consideration.

Who benefits from federal grants in aid to state and local government? Virtually every level of government enjoys some tangible benefits from federal assistance. The main beneficiaries have been the cities, where the need for additional funds is the greatest. In the past decades, large cities in the Northeast and the industrial Midwest have suffered serious erosion in their economic base. Even though tax efforts have increased, own-source revenues decline as people and industry leave the cities.

Table 11-5 shows the impact of federal grants on the financial condition of large cities. In 1957, federal aid constituted only 1 percent of cities' revenues. By 1978, this had grown to 47.5 percent, with many cities dependent on the federal government for over half of their revenues.[16] Despite this rapid increase in aid, many older cities face service cutbacks and layoffs. Without question, federal aid to cities in the 1970s prevented more serious fiscal crises and near bankruptcy like that in New York City.

State governments are in better financial shape, as are many of the newer cities in the Sunbelt. State and local governments ran an aggregate surplus in 1978, leading many in national government to question the need for such high levels of aid.[17] Relationships were strained by the number of state legislatures that passed resolutions calling for a constitutional amendment to balance the

Table 11-5   Direct Federal Aid as a Percentage of Own-Source General Revenue, Selected Cities, and Fiscal Years, 1957-78

City	Fiscal Years, Percentage				Per Capita Federal Aid‡	
	1957	1967	1976	1978 Est.	1976	1978 Est.
St. Louis	0.6	1.0	23.6	56.1	$ 86	$228
Newark	0.2	1.7	11.4	64.2	47	291
Buffalo	1.3	2.1	55.6	75.9	163	239
Cleveland	2.0	8.3	22.8	60.3	65	190
Boston	*	10.0	31.5	30.2	204	219
Baltimore	1.7	3.8	38.9	46.4	167	225
Philadelphia	0.4	8.8	37.7	53.8	129	204
Detroit	1.3	13.1	50.2	76.8	161	274
Chicago	1.4	10.9	19.2†	42.1	47	117
Atlanta	4.3	2.0	15.1	40.0	52	167
Denver	0.6	1.2	21.2	25.9	90	150
Los Angeles	0.7	0.7	19.3	39.8	54	134
Dallas	0.0	*	20.0	17.8	51	54
Houston	0.2	3.1	19.4	23.8	44	71
Phoenix	1.1	10.6	35.0	58.7	57	117
Unweighted Average of 15 Cities	1.1	5.2	28.1	47.5	95	179

*Less than 0.5%.
†Percentage based on federal aid excluding general revenue sharing; funds withheld pending judicial determination.
‡Based on 1975 population.
Reprinted in Roy Bahl (ed.), *The Fiscal Outlook for Cities* (Syracuse: Syracuse University Press, 1978), p. 32.
Sources: ACIR staff computations based on U.S. Bureau of the Census, *City Government Finances in 1957, 1967, and 1976.* Estimated city own-source general revenue for 1978 based on annual average increase between 1971 and 1976. Direct federal grants to each city for fiscal 1978 based on ACIR staff estimates of the federal stimulus programs for 1978 and Richard Nathan's estimates for all other federal aid in fiscal 1978 as set forth in his testimony before the Joint Economic Committee on July 28, 1977 (as reported in *Intergovernmental Perspective*, Winter 1976).

budget. Some irate congressmen threatened to balance the budget by cutting aid to state governments.

One of the problems of federal aid programs to state and local governments is that funds do not always go where they are needed most. One of the trends since the passage of general revenue sharing is known as *spreading,* the allocation of funds to thousands of local governments that had not previously received them. In the 1970s, the share of federal aid going to the largest cities (population over 500,000) declined from 62 percent to 44 percent.[18] In addition, economically healthier cities in the South and West have received greater increases than the older cities of the Northeast and Midwest.

Congress is largely responsible for spreading;

representatives from affluent areas want to receive their share of federal monies. Representatives from distressed areas must make concessions to insure the continuation of funds to their areas. Attempting to reverse the spreading trend, greater emphasis has been placed on *targeting,* concentrating funds on the most distressed areas. The Carter Administration has attempted to devise formulas that target funds to the neediest areas. These efforts must continue if federal monies are to provide the greatest benefit to the most depressed areas.

The question of who benefits from federal spending is a most difficult one to answer. There are virtually thousands of programs and activities of the federal government that confer benefits. The three largest categories of federal expenditures — defense, social welfare programs, and grants to state and local governments — provide a combination of public and private goods. It is difficult to measure the collective security of the nation and the general welfare of citizens. Private benefits, such as jobs, contracts, cash assistance, and grants-in-aid, are more readily observable. But budgetary politics encompasses all these considerations and more. The choices made in budgeting affect the lives of all citizens. The ultimate evaluation of the process must depend on how well the costs and benefits respond to the needs of society as a whole.

FOOTNOTES

*Sidney Lens, *Poverty: America's Enduring Paradox* (New York: Apollo, 1971), pp. 4, 312.

[1]Mancur Olsen, Jr., *The Logic of Collective Action* (New York: Schocken Books, 1968); and Bruce M. Russett, *What Price Vigilance?* (New Haven: Yale University Press, 1970), p. 94.

[2]Murray Edelman, *The Symbolic Uses of Politics* (Urbana: University of Illinois Press, 1964).

[3]Donald Lambro, *The Federal Rathole* (New Rochelle, N.Y.: Arlington House, 1975). The examples are taken from this source.

[4]Russett, pp. 18-20.

[5]Jonathan Wolman, "Many Cities Losing in Defense Bargain," *St. Louis Globe Democrat,* March 12, 1979, p. 4A.

[6]Robert D. Plotnick and Felicity Skidmore, *Progress Against Poverty* (New York: Academic Press, 1975), pp. 37-39.

[7]*Ibid.,* pp. 56-57.

[8]Congressional Budget Office, *Poverty Status of Families Under Alternative Definitions of Income,* June 1977.

[9]Plotnick and Skidmore, pp. 59-61.

[10]Congressional Budget Office, pp. XIV, XV.

[11]Plotnick and Skidmore, p. 127.

[12]Barry H. Blechman, Edward M. Gramlich, and Robert M. Hartman, *Setting National Priorities: The 1976 Budget* (Washington, D.C.: Brookings Institution, 1975), p. 175-184.

[13]Congressional Budget Office, *Budget Options for Fiscal Year 1977*, March 15, 1976, pp. 134-146.

[14]Karen Davis, *National Health Insurance — Benefits, Costs, and Consequences* (Washington, D.C.: Brookings Institution, 1975).

[15]Blechman, Gramlich, and Hartman, p. 55.

[16]Roy Bahl, Bernard Junip, Jr., and Larry Schroeder, "The Outlook for City Fiscal Performance in Declining Regions," in *The Fiscal Outlook for Cities,* ed. Roy Bahl (Syracuse: Syracuse University Press, 1978), p. 32.

[17]*Ibid.,* p. 3.

[18]Richard P. Nathan, "The Outlook for Federal Grants to Cities," in Bahl, p. 80.

Reforms

*In real life, budget decisions are undoubtedly
influenced to a greater or lesser extent by such
noneconomic and nonrational factors as pride and
prejudice, provincialism, and politics.**

Forty years ago, political scientist V.O. Key wrote that
we lacked a budgetary theory that could help us decide
how much money to allocate to various priorities.[1]
Concluding our examination of budgetary politics, it
should be apparent that there can be no single normative
theory of budgeting; choices are the result of a series of
fragmented and sequential processes. The budget process
has always been the subject of a great deal of criticism
and proposals to make it better. Critics have complained
about the lack of coordination, the lack of centralization,
the fragmentation itself. In the last 15 years a number of
reforms have been implemented, attempting to make
budgeting more rational and more comprehensive.

Planning Programming Budgeting

Developed by the Rand Corporation, PPB made its debut in Washington in the Department of Defense in 1961.[2] Secretary Robert McNamara used PPB to improve the quality of decision making and budget planning for national security policy. Four years later, in 1965, President Johnson instructed the Bureau of the Budget to institute PPB for all departments and agencies. PPB was a system designed to budget on the basis of program goals, not on line-items of activities, and to make decisions on the basis of quantitative comparisons of costs and benefits. It was an ambitious attempt to make budgetary decisions on a rational basis and had four main characteristics.[3]

Specification of Objectives PPB focused on goals to be achieved rather than on dollar amounts to be spent. Each agency was required to develop a program budget based on its particular goals and objectives.

Specification of Alternative Means of Achieving Objectives Having identified goals, each agency specified alternative methods for achieving those goals, different ways the desired ends might be achieved.

Analysis of Costs and Benefits of Alternate Means For each policy alternative, quantitative measures of costs and benefits were assigned based on analysis. The policy alternative producing the greatest benefit at the least cost was then selected.

Systematic Use of Analysis To engage in planning programming budgeting, analysis must be used throughout the process and extend into future years — hence an emphasis on future planning.

PPB was not only attractive, it appeared logical. Should not the government plan what to do rather than blindly meander along? Why, then, did PPB fail and slip quietly out of existence in 1971? The answer to this question is difficult to specify with precision. The Bureau of the Budget was given the task in 1965 of revolutionizing agency budget procedures on short notice. The first step in implementation was to reorganize agency budget structures so their activities could be grouped in a relatively small number of program packages (five to 10 major activities). The BOB required each agency to submit a program memorandum (PM), an explicit statement of goals and objectives. Second, the BOB required a program and financial plan (PFP) which mapped out the future implications of current decisions. Third, agencies were required to submit special analytical studies (SAS), analyses that formed the basis for agency budgetary choices.

One problem at the start was confusion. Many people involved in the process did not know what they were doing. Most agency budget officials did not have a thorough understanding of PPB and were used to doing things the old way. While the theory behind PPB was logical and simple, the system itself was complicated. The process of specifying goals, a necessary first step, proved to be very difficult and controversial. Even more difficult were attempts to *quantify* benefits of various programs. While it is possible to measure certain benefits, how can one assign a numerical benefit to cancer research or foreign policy? Even if benefits could be quantified, how are decision makers to choose between competing benefits from different types of programs? Budget priorities are established on the basis of values, not just analysis.

PPB failed for a number of reasons:[4]

It failed to penetrate the routine of budgeting. PPB reformers tried to impose a very formal structure over the existing budgetary process and it was not accepted. The BOB was partially responsible because of their many formal requirements. The result was that, while agencies complied by submitting the required PMs, PFPs, and SASs, they were often just meaningless exercises used to justify budgetary decisions made in the usual way, not through "authentic" analysis.

PPB was not suited to individual agency needs. Many observers felt PPB worked well in the Defense Department and, therefore, would work well everywhere else. (Actually, the success of PPB in Defense itself is questionable.)[5] However, the particular problems of policy analysis are very different from agency to agency; what worked in HEW might be irrelevant to the Justice Department. Comparison of alternative weapons systems in Defense bore little resemblance to the policy choices in the State Department. PPB did not recognize the need for individual agency variation.

The Bureau of the Budget lacked commitment to PPB. The new budgeting system was imposed on the bureau from the top. Many veteran officials were as resistant to the new system as many agencies were. As a result, the bureau often failed to encourage the agencies to make an honest effort at implementation.

Agencies were resistant to PPB, particularly in middle-level management. PPB tended to centralize budgeting at the top. To the extent that budgeting had previously consisted of aggregation from the bottom to the top, there was resistance. Many agencies felt PPB was an attempt to wrest control of their programs from them.

PPB took no account of Congress.[6] Some reformers forgot that budget requests ultimately leave the executive branch and go to Congress. The House and Senate Appropriations Committees were not prepared for the PPB material that was submitted and ignored it. They were used to working with line-item budgeting and demanded that it be continued. To the extent that PPB was used as an advocacy device to snow Congress into approving an agency's favorite project, the system developed a bad reputation on Capitol Hill.

The variation in PPB was tremendous. Some agencies made honest attempts to use analysis in their budgetary decision making while many only went through the motions. In the final analysis, while the formal system of PPB failed, many of the basic ideas reappeared in the subsequent budget management systems that were initiated in the 1970s.

Management by Objective

Like PPB, Management by Objective (MBO) was developed in the private sector and transferred to the public sector. Peter Drucker is credited with developing MBO in the 1950s, as a management technique for business.[7] MBO was implemented in the executive branch by OMB in the early 1970s, during the Nixon Administration. Like PPB, it was an attempt to make budgetary decisions on a more rational basis but, learning from the problems of PPB, it did not attempt as comprehensive an approach. Under the MBO system, agencies were required to specify goals and alternative means of achieving the goals, but there was less emphasis on long-range planning and more emphasis on monitoring and program evaluation.

The formal requirements for MBO were less rigid than those for PPB. OMB did not require that all agencies and programs be included in the MBO process. Agencies were instructed to be selective in determining objectives included in their budget and to concentrate on broad national priorities and large dollar outlays.[8] MBO was intended to be more decentralized than PPB, rather than centralizing power at the highest levels of decision making.

Despite the changes in MBO from PPB, it too was short-lived in government at the national level. By the start of the Carter Administration, it had disappeared. Many of the same problems remained. It was difficult to specify and agree on objectives, and to quantify benefits. MBO was not supported at middle and lower levels of agency management because it was still perceived as a system that increased control at the upper levels. The decision by OMB to remain imprecise in their instructions to agencies caused confusion for administrators who were unsure what was expected. OMB soon lost interest in the new system, and frequently cancelled meetings with agency heads to discuss progress towards their objectives.[9]

Both PPB and MBO, as formal systems, did not remain on the scene very long. But Richard Rose suggests that both systems evaporated rather than disappeared; parts of the processes and activities were absorbed elsewhere in the system.[10] Program analysis and the planning and evaluation units did not end abruptly. As one former budget official said, "The formal structure of PPB is dead; the analytical concept is still very much alive."[11]

Zero Base Budgeting

The latest budget reform implemented in the executive branch of the national government is Zero Base Budgeting (ZBB). While MBO was losing steam, ZBB was being applied at the state level, and became Jimmy Carter's promise of effective management and control. Like PPB and MBO, ZBB was developed in the private sector and applied to government. Peter Phyrr developed ZBB for Texas Instruments and later for the state of Georgia.[12] In 1977, several months after his inauguration, Carter instructed OMB to implement ZBB in the bureaucracy as he had promised in the campaign.

Zero Base Budgeting involves several steps. First, agencies must establish "decision units": the level at which meaningful decisions are made. They may be oriented towards a program structure (as PPB was), or may follow traditional lines of agency responsibility. Second, managers must formulate decision packages: a listing of objectives and levels of services and resources needed to provide those services. Decision packages can suggest alternative means to accomplish objectives, but more commonly, they suggest how much would be provided at different levels of funding. Some ZBB systems require that managers specify three levels of services: reduced, current, and enhanced. The intention is to provide reviewers with the ability to see how much they would lose if the agency budget is cut, and how much they would gain if they receive an increase.

Considering the different decision packages specifying different levels of services, the third stage of ZBB is ranking of decision packages. At various steps in the organization, managers must "prioritize" by ranking the decision packages in order of preference. These rankings may be revised by higher-level reviewers. At the highest level, choices are finally made in preparing the budget requests to submit.

An earlier version of ZBB was attempted in the Department of Agriculture in the early 1960s.[13] This was more of a forerunner to PPB than to the current ZBB system. As the preceding discussion suggests, Zero Base Budgeting is a misnomer; it does not begin from a base of zero and review all programs from the ground up. In most cases, agencies are asked to submit a figure for the minimum level of services that would be feasible. This may be 75 to 85 percent of current funding. The ranking process allows the use of various strategies in an attempt to protect the most-favored programs and sneak through some of the more marginal ones. The confusion surrounding the title tends to mislead the public. Budgeters do not sit down and ask each year, "Should we have a navy?" As Allen Schick observed, even a teenager does not have an identity crisis every year. ZBB is a limited system intended to focus on costs and changes at the margin.

What impact has ZBB had on the budget? In the first few years, the results were hard to find. Most of the budget items were funded at or slightly above current services levels.[14] Unlike PPB and MBO, ZBB was rapidly adopted by the bureaucracy and became part of the routines of budgeting. No separate offices were developed and ZBB used the same data used in regular budget preparation. But this ease of implementation can be explained by the fact that ZBB did not change the way budgets were made. The result is that ZBB has not had much of an impact on the budget, and has not made it more comprehensive.

Can ZBB, like its forerunners, be easily dismissed as just another fad? Have the efforts at reform been worth it, and have any meaningful changes resulted? Despite the failures, there *have* been changes in the way budgets are made. The process is clearly based on more careful analysis and evaluation than it was two decades ago. The changes have been gradual and have transcended the individual systems. ZBB appears to be mostly technique, but it is conceivable that it could have a limited impact in the future. And despite the failures, efforts at change have helped demonstrate weaknesses in the old system, even if they have not been able to remedy them. The directions of change are clear. The parade of reforms and new systems over the past years is gradually leading to a budget process that attempts to specify some objectives, analyzes some alternatives, and looks more explicitly at the long-term consequences of spending actions.

Multiyear Budgeting

The most significant budget reform in the past quarter-century was the Budget and Impoundment Control Act of 1974. It has significantly changed the way in which Congress deals with the national budget. PPB, MBO, and ZBB were primarily executive-branch reforms. But a number of reforms have been proposed that would affect both Congress and the bureaucracy.

National budgeting still operates on an annual cycle, despite the fact that the majority of budget decisions commit funds for periods of longer than one year. Neither budget reform in Congress nor ZBB altered the annual focus, but some preliminary steps have been taken towards multiyear budgeting. The CBO five-year budget projections now provide members with a view of the future. CBO estimates on the total cost of bills help clarify the total impact of legislation. It should be clear that decisions made today impinge on decisions that will be made tomorrow, and that many budget goals cannot be achieved in a single year. In the executive branch, the OMB included a statement in the 1979 budget that it intended to move towards more of a multiyear framework in the President's budget. The next major push in budget reform is likely to be towards some form of multiyear budgeting.

Advance Targeting

One form of multiyear budgeting is advance targeting. Instead of adopting targets just for the next fiscal year, Congress would approve targets for the next two to five years. Advocates of this approach claim it would be easier to see where current decisions are leading and what trade-offs will be necessary in the future. It would help clarify choices between increased defense spending, a balanced budget, or tax cuts. There are several difficulties with advance targeting. Given the controversy in the House over the budget resolutions, targets would need to be approved in separate resolutions if they were not to threaten the process. Of course, uncertainty and imprecision increase geometrically as one moves farther into the future.

Advance targeting would have to be taken in conjunction with the OMB if it were to have any effectiveness. The Humphrey-Hawkins Act requires the President to submit five-year plans, and both Ford and Carter have shown some indications of moving toward multiyear projections and planning. Overall, advance targeting would be a constructive step. Even if the original targets were altered substantially, advance targeting fosters the idea that budget choices have multiyear implications and trade-offs. At worst, advance targeting could be ignored. At best, it could mark an increased sophistication and a more explicit concern for future planning.

Biennial Budgeting

Some members of Congress feel that the annual budget process is too rushed, allowing too little time for adequate scrutiny of agency requests. The new time pressures on both the authorization and appropriations processes have given rise to proposals for a two-year budget cycle. Some have suggested dividing the sessions: the first session would consider authorizations, the second session would consider appropriations. Several bills were introduced during the 95th Congress to make this change.[15] Opponents claim that it would reduce the power of the Appropriations Committees and would reduce the quality of congressional oversight. Critics doubt the ability of agencies in the executive branch to project their spending needs accurately, giving rise to an abundance of supplemental requests.

Sunset Legislation

Concerned about the apparent immortality of bureaucratic agencies, and convinced that many programs outlive their usefulness and effectiveness, Congress has considered the "sunset" approach. Sunset legislation mandates termination of agencies and programs (i.e., letting the sun set on them) unless they are reauthorized after a thorough review. Proponents of sunset would trade a presumption of continued existence for a presumption of termination.

The growing popularity of sunset bills reflects a continuing dissatisfaction with the authorization process and congressional oversight and review. The predominance of indefinite authorization shields many programs from review, and the quality of review in annual authorizations is suspect. In general, sunset bills would:

— inventory all federal programs by function
— establish a timetable (five to 10 years) for mandatory review
— prohibit the creation of new budget authority unless programs were reestablished

Opponents have so far prevented sunset bills from reaching the floor of Congress for a vote. The sunset concept has been more successful at the state level; over half the states have adopted some form of sunset law. Opponents fear another increase in congressional workload. The separation of sunset from authorization review raises the possibility of duplication of effort. There is also the problem of assessing the value of small, inexpensive programs against the major programs.

Sunset would certainly provide some interesting political battles, such as the consideration of the effectiveness of the Occupational Health and Safety Administration (OSHA) or the Environmental Protection Agency (EPA). An alternative to sunset is to place all authorizations on a multiyear basis without mandating termination. Such a proposal would work within the current committee system and would have a better chance of passage.

Conclusion

Reformers should be smarter now. The shining star of rational-comprehensive budgeting has faded somewhat, but still beckons. Incrementalists concerned with political feasibility have been overly harsh in assessing the possibilities of changing the process of budgeting, but hopefully they have taught reformers something. Previous "failures" have actually resulted in gradual changes, increasing use of analysis and policy evaluation. Future changes might be more successful if it is recognized that reforms can only partially alter the nature of budgetary politics.

What is the final assessment of budgeting? Perhaps we can best conclude with what it is not, but might be. Budgeting has not served as a device for major reallocation. Outcomes reflect existing divisions in resources and influence in American society. "Have-nots" are not ignored, but neither are they the main beneficiary of allocations in the public sector. Budgeting has not served as a device for national planning. To plan, a government must understand the consequences of its actions. Until policy makers have a better understanding of consequences, it is unlikely that budgeting will truly be an exercise in national planning. Finally, budgeting is not a separate and divisible process imposed on our government; budgeting is simply an extension of our basic political system.

FOOTNOTES

*Verne B. Lewis, *"Toward a Theory of Budgeting,"* Public Administration Review, 12 (Winter 1952): 54.

[1]V.O. Key, "The Lack of a Budgetary Theory," *American Political Science Review,* 34 (December 1940): 1137-1144.

[2]David Novick, ed., *Program Budgeting* (Cambridge: Harvard University Press, 1965); and Fremont J. Lyden and Ernest G. Miller, *Planning Programming Budgeting* (Chicago: Markham, 1972).

[3]David J. Ott and Ottiat F. Ott, "The Budget Process," in *Planning Programming Budgeting,* ed. F.J. Lyden and E.G. Miller (Chicago: Markham, 1972), pp. 43-45; Charles Schultz, *The Politics and Economics of Public Spending* (Washington, D.C.: Brookings Institution, 1968); Virginia Held, "PPBS Comes to Washington," in *Politics, Programs, and Budgets,* ed. James Davis (Englewood Cliffs, N.J.: Prentice-Hall, 1969), pp. 138-148; Novick, *Program Budgeting.*

[4]Allen Schick, "A Death in the Bureaucracy: The Demise of Federal PPB," *Public Administration Review,* 33 (March-April 1973): 146-156.

[5]Aaron Wildavsky, *The Politics of the Budgetary Process* (Boston: Little, Brown, 1964), p. 199.

[6]James E. Jernberg, "Information Change and Congressional Behavior: A Caveat for PPB Reformers," in Lyden and Miller.

[7]Peter Drucker, *The Practice of Management* (New York: Harper & Row, 1954).

[8]Office of Management and Budget, *Preparation and Submission of Budget Estimates,* circular no. A-11, rev., June 17, 1975.

[9]Richard Rose, "Implementation and Evaporation: The Record of MBO," in *Contemporary Approaches to Public Budgeting,* ed. Fred A. Kramer (Cambridge, Mass.: Winthrop, 1979), p. 216.

[10]*Ibid.,* p. 217.

[11]Harry Havens, as quoted in Rose, p. 217.

[12]Peter Phyrr, *Zero Base Budgeting* (New York: Wiley & Sons, 1973).

[13]Aaron Wildavsky and Arthur Hammond, "Comprehensive Versus Incremental Budgeting in the Department of Agriculture," *Administrative Science Quarterly,* 10 (December 1965): 321-346.

[14]Allen Schick, "The Road from ZBB," in Kramer, p. 223.

[15]95th Congress, 1st session, HR 9077, for example.

A Glossary of
Budgetary Definitions

Advance Appropriation: An appropriation provided by the Congress for use in a fiscal year or more beyond the fiscal year for which the appropriation act is passed. Advance appropriations allow state and local governments and others sufficient time to develop plans with assurance of future Federal funding.

Appropriation: An act of Congress that permits Federal agencies to incur obligations and to make payments out of the Treasury for specified purposes. An appropriation usually follows enactment of authorizing legislation. An appropriation act is the most common form of budget authority, but in some cases the authorizing legislation provides the budget authority. Appropriations are categorized in a variety of ways, such as by their period of availability (one-year, multiple-year, no-year), the timing of Congressional action (current, permanent), and the manner of determining the amount of the appropriation (definite, indefinite).

Authorization (Authorizing Legislation): Basic substantive legislation enacted by Congress which sets up or continues the legal operation of a Federal program or agency either indefinitely or for a specific period of time or sanctions a particular type of obligation or expenditure within a program. Such legislation is normally a prerequisite for subsequent appropriations, or other kinds of budget authority to be contained in appropriation acts. It may limit the amount of budget authority to be provided subsequently or may authorize the appropriation of "such sums as may be necessary"; in a few instances budget authority may be provided in the authorization. (See *"Backdoor Authority."*)

Backdoor Authority *(Backdoor Spending):* A term generally used to denote legislation enacted outside the normal appropriation process that permits the obligation of funds. The most common forms of backdoor authority are borrowing authority (authority to spend receipts) and contract authority.

Borrowing Authority: Statutory authority (substantive or appropriation) that permits a Federal agency to incur obligations and to make payments for specified purposes out of borrowed moneys.

Budget Amendment: A proposal, submitted to the Congress by the President after his formal budget transmittal but prior to completion of appropriation action by the Congress, that revises previous requests, such as the amount of the budget authority.

Budget Deficit: The amount by which the Government's budget outlays exceed its budget receipts for any given period. Deficits are financed primarily by borrowing from the public.

Budget Receipts: Moneys received by the Federal Government from the public that arise primarily from tax revenues, but also including receipts from premiums on compulsory social insurance programs, court fines, certain license fees, and premiums from voluntary participants in Federal social insurance programs.

Budget Surplus: The amount by which the Government's budget receipts exceed its budget outlays for any given period.

Budget Update: A statement summarizing amendments to or revisions in budget authority requested, estimated outlays and estimated receipts for a fiscal year that has not been completed. The President may submit updates at any time but is required to transmit such statements to the Congress by April 10 and July 15 of each year.

Budgetary Reserves: Portions of budget authority set aside for contingencies or to effect savings whenever savings are made possible by or through changes in requirements or greater efficiency of operations. (See *"Deferral of Budget Authority."*)

Concurrent Resolution on the Budget: A resolution passed by both Houses of Congress, but not requiring the signature of the President, setting forth, reaffirming, or revising the Congressional Budget for the United States Government for a fiscal year. There are two such resolutions required preceding each fiscal year. The first required concurrent resolution, due by May 15, establishes the Congressional Budget. The second required concurrent resolution, due by September 15, reaffirms or revises it. Other concurrent resolutions may be adopted at any time following the first required concurrent resolution.

Congressional Budget: The budget as set forth by Congress in a concurrent resolution on the budget. These resolutions shall include: (1) The appropriate level of total outlays and of total new budget authority; (2) An estimate of budget outlays and new budget authorities for each major functional category; (3) The amount, if any, of the surplus or deficit in the budget; (4) The recommended level of Federal revenues; and (5) The appropriate level of the public debt.

Continuing Resolution: Legislation enacted by the Congress to provide budget authority for specific ongoing activities in cases where the regular fiscal year appropriation for such activities has not been enacted by the beginning of the fiscal year. The continuing resolution usually specifies a maximum rate at which the agency may incur obligations, based on the rate of the prior year, the President's Budget request, or an appropriation bill passed by either or both Houses of the Congress.

Contract Authority: A form of budget authority under which contracts of other obligations may be entered into prior to an appropriation. Contract authority does not provide funds to pay the obligations and thus requires a subsequent appropriation.

Controllability: The ability under existing law to control outlays during a given fiscal year. "Relatively uncontrollable" usually refers to spending that cannot be increased or decreased without changes in existing substantive law. Such spending is usually the result of open-ended programs and fixed costs, such as Social Security and veterans' benefits, but also includes payments due under obligations incurred during prior years.

Current Services Budget (OMB)

282 BUDGETARY POLITICS

Current Policy Budget (CBO): A budget that projects estimated budget authority and outlays for the upcoming fiscal year at the same program level and without policy changes as the fiscal year in progress. To the extent mandated by existing law, estimates take into account for budget impact of anticipated changes in economic conditions (such as unemployment or inflation), beneficiary levels, pay increases, and benefit changes.

Deferral of Budget Authority: Any action or inaction by any officer or employee of the United States which temporarily withholds, delays, or effectively precludes the obligation or expenditure of budget authority. The President is required to report each proposed deferral to the Congress in a special message. Deferrals may not extend beyond the end of the current fiscal year and may be overturned by the passage of an impoundment resolution by either House of Congress. (See also *"Impoundment"* and *"Rescission."*)

Entitlement Legislation: Legislation that requires the payment of benefits to any person or government meeting the requirements established by such law, e.g., Social Security benefits and veterans' pensions.

Expenditures: A term generally used interchangeably with outlays. (See *"Outlays."*)

Federal Debt: Federal debt consists of public debt and agency debt. **Public Debt** — That portion of the Federal debt representing borrowing by the Treasury Department and the Federal Financing Bank (except its borrowing from the Treasury). **Agency Debt** — That portion of the Federal debt arising when a Federal agency authorized by law, other than Treasury on the Federal Financing Bank (FFB), borrows funds directly from the public.

Federal Fiscal Policy: Federal Government policies with respect to taxes, spending, and debt management intended to promote the nation's economic goals particularly with respect to employment, gross national product, price stability, and equilibrium in balance of payments. The budget process is a major vehicle for determining and implementing Federal fiscal policy.

Federal Funds: Funds collected, owned, and used by

the Federal Government for the general purposes of the Government. There are four types of Federal fund accounts: General funds, special funds, public enterprise (revolving) funds, and intragovernmental funds. (See also *"Trust Funds."*)

Fiscal Year: Any yearly accounting period without regard to a calendar year. The fiscal year for the Federal Government begins on October 1 and ends on September 30. The fiscal year is designated by the calendar year in which it ends, e.g., fiscal year 1977 is the fiscal year ending September 30, 1977.

Forward Funding: The practice of obligating funds in one fiscal year for programs that are to operate in a subsequent year.

Full-Employment Budget: The estimated receipts, outlays, and surplus or deficit that would occur if the economy were continually operating at a rate defined as being at full capacity (traditionally defined as a certain percentage unemployment rate for the civilian labor force).

Function (Functional Classification): The functional classification is a means of presenting budget authority, outlay, and tax expenditure data in terms of the principal purposes which Federal programs are intended to serve. Each account is generally placed in the single function (e.g., national defense, health) that best represents its major purpose, regardless of the agency administering the program. Functions are generally subdivided into narrower categories called subfunctions.

General Fund: The fund credited with all receipts not earmarked by law for a specific purpose and from general borrowing. It is used for the general purposes of the Government through various general fund accounts.

Impoundment: Any action or inaction by an officer or employee of the United States that precludes the obligation or expenditure of budget authority provided by the Congress.

Impoundment Resolution: A resolution of the House of Representatives or the Senate disapproving a deferral of budget authority set forth in a special message ordinarily transmitted by the president. Passage of an impoundment resolution by either House of Congress has the effect of overturning the deferral and requires that such budget authority be made available for obligation.

Lapsed Funds: Unobligated budget authority that by law has ceased to be available for obligation because of the expiration of the period for which it was available.

Obligations: Amounts of orders placed, contracts awarded, services rendered, or other commitments made by Federal agencies during a given period which will require outlays during the same or some future period.

Off-Budget Federal Agencies: Agencies, federally owned in whole or in part, whose transactions have been excluded from the budget totals under provisions of law, e.g., the Federal Financing Bank. The fiscal activities of these agencies are included in either budget authority or outlay totals, but are presented in the Budget Appendix as "Annexed Budgets."

Offsetting Receipts: All collections and deposits into receipt accounts which are offset against budget authority and outlays rather than reflected as budget receipts in computing budget totals.

Open-Ended Programs: Entitlement programs for which eligibility requirements are determined by law, e.g., Medicaid. Actual obligations and resultant outlays are limited only by the number of eligible persons who apply for benefits and the actual benefits received.

Outlays: Checks issued, interest accrued on the public debt, or other payments, net of refunds and reimbursements. Total budget outlays consist of the sum of the outlays from appropriations and funds included in the unified budget, less offsetting receipts.

President's Budget: The budget for a particular fiscal year transmitted to the Congress by the President in accordance with the Budget and Accounting Act of 1921, as amended. Some elements of the budget, such as the estimates for the legislative branch and the judiciary, are required to be included without review by the Office Management and Budget or approval by the President.

Program: An organized set of activities directed toward a common purpose, objective, or goal undertaken or proposed by an agency in order to carry out responsibilities assigned to it.

Reappropriation: Congressional action to restore or extend the obligational availability, whether for the same or different purposes, of all or part of the unobligated portion of budget authority which otherwise would lapse.

Reimbursements: Sums received by the Government for commodities sold or services furnished that are authorized by law to be credited directly to specific appropriation and fund accounts.

Rescission: A legislative action which cancels budget authority previously provided by Congress prior to the time when the authority would otherwise have lapsed.

Rescission Bill: A bill or joint resolution which provides for cancellation, in whole or in part, of budget authority previously granted by the Congress. Rescissions proposed by the President must be transmitted in a special message to the Congress. If Congress approved a rescission bill within forty-five days of continuous session, the budget authority must be made available for obligation.

Revolving Fund: A fund established to finance a cycle of operations through amounts received by the fund. There are three types of revolving funds: public enterprise, intragovernmental, and trust revolving funds.

Supplemental Appropriation: An appropriation enacted as an addition to a regular annual appropriation act. Supplemental appropriations provide additional budget authority beyond original estimates for programs or activities (including new programs authorized after the date of the original appropriation act) for which the need for funds is too urgent to be postponed until the next regular appropriation.

Tax Expenditures: Losses of tax revenue attributable to provisions of the Federal tax laws which allow a special exclusion, exemption, or deduction from gross income or which provide a special credit, preferential rate of tax, or a deferral of tax liability.

Total Obligational Authority: The sum of: All Budget authority granted (or requested) from the Congress in a given year, plus amounts authorized to be credited to a specific fund, and the balances of unused budget authority from previous years which remain available for obligation.

Transition Quarter: The 3-month period (July 1 to September 30, 1976) between fiscal year 1976 and fiscal year 1977 resulting from the change from a July 1 through June 30 fiscal year beginning with fiscal year 1977.

Trust Funds: Funds collected and used by the Federal Government for carrying out specific purposes and programs according to terms of a trust agreement or statute, such as the Social Security and unemployment trust funds.

Unified Budget: The present form of the budget of the Federal Government, in which receipts and outlays from Federal funds and trust funds are consolidated. When these fund groups are consolidated to display budget totals, transactions which are outlays of one fund group to the other fund group (interfund transactions) are deducted to avoid double counting.

Adapted from: U.S. General Accounting Office, **Budgetary Definition,** *OPA-76-8, November 1975.*

Appendices

Appendix A Formulation of Executive Budget

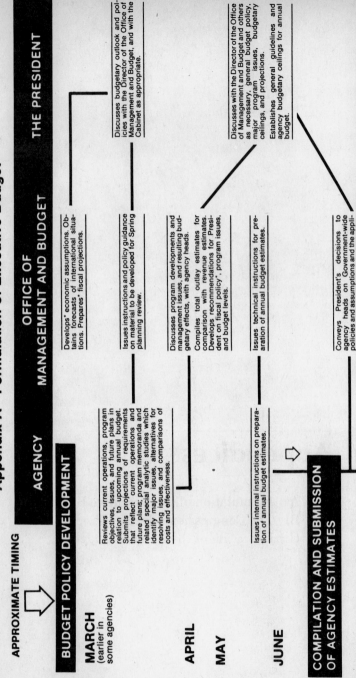

APPROXIMATE TIMING	AGENCY	OFFICE OF MANAGEMENT AND BUDGET	THE PRESIDENT

BUDGET POLICY DEVELOPMENT

MARCH
(earlier in some agencies)

Agency: Reviews current operations, program objectives, issues, and future plans in relation to upcoming annual budget. Submits projections of requirements that reflect current operations and future plans; program memoranda and related special analytic studies which identify major issues, alternatives for resolving issues, and comparisons of costs and effectiveness.

Office of Management and Budget: Develops* economic assumptions. Obtains forecasts of international situations. Prepares fiscal projections.

The President: Discusses budgetary outlook and policies with the Director of the Office of Management and Budget, and with the Cabinet as appropriate.

APRIL

Office of Management and Budget: Issues instructions and policy guidance on material to be developed for Spring planning review.

MAY

Office of Management and Budget: Discusses program developments and management issues, and resulting budgetary effects, with agency heads. Compiles total outlay estimates for comparison with revenue estimates. Develops recommendations for President on fiscal policy, program issues, and budget levels.

The President: Discusses with the Director of the Office of Management and Budget and others as necessary, general budget policy, major program issues, budgetary ceilings, and projections.

Establishes general guidelines and agency budgetary ceilings for annual budget.

JUNE

Agency: Issues internal instructions on preparation of annual budget estimates.

Office of Management and Budget: Issues technical instructions for preparation of annual budget estimates.

COMPILATION AND SUBMISSION OF AGENCY ESTIMATES

Office of Management and Budget: Conveys President's decisions to agency heads on Government-wide policies and assumptions and the application of policies and budgetary

JULY—
SEPT. 30

Allocates budgetary ceiling to programs. Develops and compiles detailed estimates.

Advises and assists agencies of form, language, and structure of appropriations, and on preparation of budget submissions.

OFFICE OF MANAGEMENT AND BUDGET REVIEW AND PRESIDENTIAL DECISION

SEPTEMBER

OCTOBER

Submits formal estimates for annual budget including projections of requirements for future years, and completed program memoranda and special analytic studies.

Analyzes budget submissions. Holds hearings with agency representatives on program, budget, and management issues in preparation for Director's review.

Reexamines* economic assumptions and fiscal policies. Discusses program developments with agencies. In light of outlook and policy discussion with President, prepares budget recommendations for the President.

NOVEMBER

Reviews budgetary situation and decides on budget allowances for each agency.

Notifies agency heads of President's allowance.

Revises estimates to conform to President's decisions.

DECEMBER

Again reviews* economic outlook and fiscal policy for discussion with President of tax and economic policies.

Drafts President's budget message; prepares budget with summary tables and appendix, special analyses, and budget-in-brief; arranges printing of budget documents.

Revises and approves budget message. Transmits recommended budget to Congress.

JANUARY

TRANSMISSION OF BUDGET TO CONGRESS
MID-JANUARY

*In cooperation with the Treasury Department and Council of Economic Advisers.

Source: Executive Office of the President/Office of Management and Budget.

Appendix B The Congressional Budget Process

INFORMATION GATHERING, ANALYSIS, AND PREPARATION OF 1ST BUDGET RESOLUTION

OCTOBER Previous Fiscal Year Begins

CBO 5-Year Projection Report
(As soon as possible after Oct. 1)

NOVEMBER President Submits Current Services Budget

DECEMBER Jt. Economic Committee Reports Analysis of Current Services to Budget Committees

JANUARY President Submits Budget (15 days after Congress convenes)

FEBRUARY

MARCH All Committees and Jt. Committees Submit Estimates and Views to Budget Committees.

BUDGET COMMITTEES HOLD HEARINGS —
BEGIN WORK ON 1ST BUDGET RESOLUTION

Legislation Providing Contract or Borrowing Authority Must Be Made Subject to Amounts Provided in Appropriation Acts.

ADOPTION OF 1ST BUDGET RESOLUTION

CBO Report to Budget Committees.

APRIL BUDGET COMMITTEES REPORT 1ST BUDGET RESOLUTION (ON OR BEFORE APR. 15)

HOUSE AND SENATE
CONSIDER 1ST BUDGET
RESOLUTION

MAY CONGRESS COMPLETES ACTION ON 1ST BUDGET RESOLUTION (MAY 15)

CONFERENCE ACTION AND
ADOPTION OF CONFERENCE
REPORT

Deadline for Committees to Report
Authorization Bills (some exceptions, and
waiver procedure).

Conference Report Joint
Explanatory Statement Allo-

CONGRESSIONAL ACTION ON SPENDING BILLS

MAY

Before Adoption of 1st Budget Resolution, Neither House May Consider New Budget Authority or Spending Authority Bills, Revenue Changes, or Debt Limit Changes (some exceptions, and waiver procedure).

Before Reporting 1st Regular Appropriation Bill, House Appropriations Committee to Extent Practicable, Marks up all Regular Appropriations Bills and Submits Summary Report to House, Comparing Proposed Outlays and Budget Authority Levels With 1st Budget Resolution.

After Adoption of 1st Budget Resolution, Each Committee Subdivides Its Allocation Among Its Subcommittees, and Promptly Reports such Subdivisions to Its House.

JUNE

CONGRESS ENACTS APPROPRIATIONS AND SPENDING BILLS

JULY

CBO Issues Periodic Scorekeeping Reports Comparing Congressional Action with 1st Budget Resolution.

As Possible, CBO Cost Analyses and 5-Year Projections Will Accompany All Reported Public Bills, Except Appropriations Bills.

Reports on New Budget Authority and Tax Expenditure Bills Must Contain Comparisons With 1st Budget Resolution, and 5-Year Budget Projections.

If a Committee Reports New Entitlement Legislation that Exceeds Appropriate Allocation in Latest Budget Resolution, it Shall be Referred to the Appropriations Committee with Instructions to Report Its Recommendations Within 15 Days.

AUGUST

BUDGET COMMITTEES PREPARE 2ND BUDGET RESOLUTION AND REPORT

ADOPTION OF 2ND BUDGET RES. AND RECONCILIATION

SEPTEMBER

Congress Completes Action on All Budget and Spending Authority Bills. 7th Day After Labor Day.

CONGRESS COMPLETES ACTION ON 2ND BUDGET RESOLUTION SEPT. 15

Thereafter, Neither House May Consider Any Bill or Amendment, or Conference Report, That Results in An Increase Over Budget Outlay or Authority Figures, or a Reduction in Revenue Level, Adopted in 2nd Resolution.

CONGRESS COMPLETES ACTION ON RECONCILIATION BILL OR RESOLUTION — SEPT. 25

OCTOBER

FISCAL YEAR BEGINS

Congress May Not Adjourn Until It Completes Action on 2nd Budget Resolution and Reconciliation Measure, If Any.

Source: Congressional Budget Office.

Appendix C Execution of Enacted Budget

TREASURY— GEN. ACCOUNTING OFFICE	AGENCY	OFFICE OF MANAGEMENT AND BUDGET
On approval of appropriation bill, appropriation warrant, drawn by Treasury and countersigned by General Accounting Office, is forwarded to agency.	Revenues are assessed, collected, and deposited by the agencies concerned as prescribed by law.	
	Revises operating budget in view of approved appropriations and program developments.	
	Prepares requests for apportionment by May 21 or within 15 days after approval of appropriations.	
		Makes apportionment by June 10 or within 30 days after approval of appropriations. May "reserve" funds for contingencies, savings, or developments subsequent to enactment. (May reapportion at any time, on own initiative or on agency request.)
	Allots apportioned funds to various programs or activities.	
	Administrative controls restrict obligations and outlays to apportioned and allotted amounts.	

APPROXIMATE TIMING

FUNDS MADE AVAILABLE

October

CONTROL OVER FUNDS

Continuous

Obligates money. Receives and uses goods and services. Makes monthly or quarterly reports to Office of Management and Budget on status of funds and use of resources in relation to program plans.

Reports periodically to Office of Management and Budget on management improvements and actions reducing manpower requirements and costs.

Examines reports on status of funds in relation to apportionments. Analyzes reports on use of resources and relationship of accomplishments and costs. Reports to the President from time to time on budget and program status, manpower, management improvements, and cost reductions.

Prepares and certifies vouchers and invoices for payment.

EXPENDITURE OF FUNDS

As bills become payable

Treasury issues check (except for certain agencies which issue their own) and reports on financial transactions in Monthly Treasury Statement and Treasury Bulletin.

PROGRAM EVALUATION, MANAGEMENT APPRAISAL, AND INDEPENDENT AUDIT

Periodic

General Accounting Office performs independent audit of financial records, transactions, and financial management, generally. Settles' accounts of certifying and disbursing officers. Makes reports to Congress.

Reviews compliance with established policies, procedures, and requirements. Evaluates accomplishment of program plans and effectiveness of management and operations.

Reviews agency operations and evaluates programs and performance. Conducts or guides agencies in organization and management studies. Assists President in improving management and organization of the executive branch.

Source: Executive Office of the President/Office of Management and Budget.

Index